Screenwriting

FOR

DUMMIES®

2ND EDITION

by Laura Schellhardt
Adjunct Professor, Northwestern University

Foreword by John Logan

WILEY

Wiley Publishing, Inc.

Screenwriting For Dummies®, 2nd Edition

Published by
Wiley Publishing, Inc.
111 River St.
Hoboken, NJ 07030-5774
www.wiley.com

About the Author

Laura Schellhardt holds an MFA in Literary Arts from Brown University and degrees in Theatre and Creative Writing from Northwestern University in Chicago. Her scripts have been produced in New York (SPF, The Hangar, The Exchange Theatre), Seattle (Seattle Repertory Theatre, ACT), Chicago (Northlight Theatre, Serendipity Theatre, New Leaf Theatre, Citadel Theatre), Washington DC (The Kennedy Center, Woolly Mammoth), Providence (Trinity Repertory Company, Brown University), Minneapolis (Theatre Limina), North Carolina (Center for Performing Arts), and Provincetown, Massachusetts (Provincetown Repertory Theatre, Provincetown Theatre Company).

Original works include *The K of D, The Chair, Courting Vampires, Shapeshifter, The Apothecary's Girl, Inheritance,* and *Je Ne Sais Quoi.* Adaptations include *The Phantom Tollbooth, The Mysteries of Harris Burdick, The Outfit* (Jeff Award Nominee), and *Creole Folktales.*

Laura is a recipient of the Theatre Communications Group 2007–8 Playwriting Residency, The Jerome Fellowship, the New Play Award from ACT in Seattle, and a Dramatist Guild Playwriting Fellowship. She has participated in the SoHo Rep. Writer/Director Lab and the O'Neill National Playwright's Festival. Laura has assisted in the development of new work at The Goodman, Steppenwolf Theatre, Northlight Theatre, and Trinity Repertory Company. She has studied writing with the likes of Paula Vogel, Maria Irene Fornes, Erin Cressida Wilson and has taught alongside Oscar-nominated John Logan of *Aviator* and *Sweeney Todd* fame.

Laura currently heads the playwriting program at Northwestern University in Evanston, Illinois and teaches workshops across the country.

Dedication

To John Logan — for a beginning

Author's Acknowledgments

The fearless Schellhardt crew: Mary Kate, Eliza, and Stephen — for your love, your example, and your laughter.

Mom — for your much exploited editorial services and for your support, postmarked and otherwise.

Dad — for your much exploited advice and for your support, post-marked and otherwise.

Laura Bancroft Powell — for your stories and your name.

Natasha Graf — for the original opportunity.

Reed Finlay — for the encouragement, literary and otherwise.

The extended support committee for the inspiration and the will: John Logan, Paula Vogel, Mary Poole, Rosie Forrest, Joseph Epstein, Mr. Meyer, Anna Marie Baskin, Uncle Mark, and Andy Grotelueschen.

Publisher's Acknowledgments

We're proud of this book; please send us your comments through our Dummies online registration form located at www.dummies.com/register/.

Some of the people who helped bring this book to market include the following:

Acquisitions, Editorial, and Media Development

Project Editor: Kelly Ewing

(Previous Edition: Tim Gallan)

Acquisitions Editor: Michael Lewis

Copy Editor: Kelly Ewing

(Previous Edition: Chrissy Guthrie)

Editorial Program Coordinator: Erin Calligan Mooney

General Reviewer: Bryan Michael Stoller

Senior Editorial Manager: Jennifer Ehrlich

Editorial Supervisor and Reprint Editor: Carmen Krikorian

Editorial Assistants: Joe Niesen, David Lutton

Cover Photos: Grant Faint

Cartoons: Rich Tennant (www.the5thwave.com)

Composition Services

Project Coordinator: Katie Key

Layout and Graphics: Reuben W. Davis, Alissa D. Ellet, Melissa K. Jester, Laura Pence, Tobin Wilkerson, Christine Williams

Proofreaders: Caitie Kelly, Toni Settle

Indexer: Potomac Indexing, LLC

Publishing and Editorial for Consumer Dummies

    Diane Graves Steele, Vice President and Publisher, Consumer Dummies

    Joyce Pepple, Acquisitions Director, Consumer Dummies

    Kristin A. Cocks, Product Development Director, Consumer Dummies

    Michael Spring, Vice President and Publisher, Travel

    Kelly Regan, Editorial Director, Travel

Publishing for Technology Dummies

    Andy Cummings, Vice President and Publisher, Dummies Technology/General User

Composition Services

    Gerry Fahey, Vice President of Production Services

    Debbie Stailey, Director of Composition Services

Contents at a Glance

Table of Contents

Foreword

So, you want to write a movie. Where do you start?

My personal advice to aspiring screenwriters is always the same: If you want to write, read. Start with Shakespeare. He will teach you everything you need to know about drama. Read everything. Read slowly and carefully. Read aloud and open yourself to emotion. Hamlet and Falstaff and Iago and Cleopatra and Rosalind will teach you about dramatizing character and conflict. Shakespeare's glorious combination of prose and verse will teach you about language. *King Lear* teaches you tragedy. *As You Like It* teaches you comedy. *Antony and Cleopatra* and the *Henry IV* plays teach you both.

Then go back and read Aristotle's *Poetics*. Then you might treat yourself to Ibsen and Chekhov. If you're feeling really madcap you might then move on to Sophocles, Euripides, Shaw, Pinter, Beckett, and O'Neill.

And then read *Hamlet* again.

My point is you must be a *dramatist*, a theatrical storyteller, first and foremost. The structural concerns of the ideal three act movie structure or perfectly timed "inciting incident" must be entirely secondary to your passionate desire to tell the story honestly. Be an artist first, then a technician.

My dear friend Laura Schellhardt, the author of the book you are holding, offers some valuable advice on ways to approach writing a movie. She presents any number of provocative and clever ways to understand the screenwriting process. Used wisely, this book can help you hew your way through the very dark forest of screenplay construction.

I leave a final bit of advice from my frequent colleague, director Ridley Scott. After I delivered a particularly mammoth draft of **Gladiator,** Ridley turned to me with a wry smile and said, "John, write less words."

So, I guess that covers it. Read lots of words, and write less of them.

—John Logan

John Logan's film works includes **Gladiator, Any Given Sunday, Star Trek: Nemesis, The Time Machine, RKO 281,** and **The Last Samurai.**

Introduction

. . . .

Screenwriting For Dummies? If this book wasn't part of the For Dummies series, I might've thought twice about writing it. After all, the last thing the world needs is another dumb screenplay. But rest assured that by "Dummies," I don't mean you. This book isn't for dummies — quite the opposite, in fact. Writing is challenging work. First of all, you have to decide who and what to write about. Second, you have to figure out how to expand your chosen characters and subject into a story — a 110-page story at that. To do that, you need some basic information and a newly organized daily routine. Finally, when you finish your script, you have to come up with a way to introduce it to Hollywood. To do that, you need some industry tips and marketing strategies. That's a lot of information.

So I repeat, this book isn't for dummies. This book is for writers — beginners, advanced, and anyone in between. This book is for both teachers and students — of cinema, of theater, of life. This book is for film-lovers and filmgoers and for dreamers of all sorts. If you have an active imagination, curiosity, and a sense of adventure, welcome. This book just may be for you.

About This Book

To say that I enjoy writing would be an understatement. I *love* writing, and I *love* films, and I fervently believe that screenwriting is a craft worth pursuing. I also believe that it's a demanding craft with many facets to consider. Most screenwriting books cover one of those facets in detail — how to write a first draft, how to find an agent, how to sell your script to the industry, to name a few popular topics. There's nothing wrong with focusing on one portion of this complicated art form, but if you have the space, why not tackle it all? This book has the space. From finding an idea to spacing it on the page to marketing it in Hollywood — in this book, you can find out about the screenwriting process from A to Z (or Action to Zoom in film lingo.)

Conventions Used in This Book

This book isn't heavy on special conventions. But it does have a few, and here they are:

✔ I reference a lot of films, plays, and television shows in this book, and to help you locate them in the text, the titles are in bold italics. For example, ***Lord of the Rings*** would look like this in the text.

✔ In this book, I also reference several novels because screenwriters often adapt novels for the screen. These titles appear in regular italics; for example, *The Cider House Rules*.

✔ Short stories and poems appear in quotes; for example, "The Lottery."

✔ Web sites and e-mail addresses appear in `monofont`.

✔ Important words to know also appear in *italics*.

Foolish Assumptions

You know what they say about assuming, but sometimes, it just has to be done. Although this book is for a wide variety of people, I did assume the following about you when writing it:

✔ You enjoy writing or think that you might.

✔ You've written a script or are looking to start one.

✔ You've been to at least one movie and enjoyed yourself.

✔ You believe that good stories can change the world.

How This Book Is Organized

Screenwriting is an art, a craft, and a business. Each aspect contains a lot of information. For your convenience and sanity, I've divided this book into five parts, each dedicated to one facet (there's that word again) of the process.

Part 1: So You Want to Write for Pictures

In this part, I introduce you to . . . well, to yourself — to your screenwriting self, that is. Artists sense the world in a slightly different way than people in other professions do, and screenwriters are no exception. These chapters focus on developing a writer's "eye" for detail, a knack for finding ideas, and the ability to organize a busy calendar around the expansion of that idea. If you've ever wondered how it "feels" to be a writer, turn to Part I and find out.

Part II: Breaking Down the Elements of a Story

This part tackles all the building blocks of a story — the sequence of events, the characters, the conflict, and how the whole thing sounds when you toss those elements together. It also touches upon the writer's responsibility to all those movie-goers who eventually journey through that story with you.

Part III: Turning Your Story into a Script

Part III involves the nuts and bolts of turning your story into something you can sell to Hollywood. From outlines to format to revisions, these chapters detail how your film should look both on the page and in the mind's eye of your reader. I also discuss how to adapt other mediums — poetry, fiction, theater — to the screen. And if you're writing with a partner? Flip to Chapter 18 for some tips on collaboration.

Part IV: Selling Your Script to Show Business

Part IV involves switching hats from artist/creator to businessperson. You have a product to sell — actually, you have two. You want to market your script, yes, but more importantly, you want to market yourself as a writer. This part helps you narrow your market and package your work accordingly. It then guides you through the crazy world known as show business — step by star-studded step.

Part V: The Part of Tens

I toss around a lot of examples in this final part. Want to know who's made a successful living as a screenwriter? Here are a few examples. Want to know who's "one-to-watch?" Here are a few examples. Want some scripts worth reading or a heads up on some screenwriting myths that you may want to avoid? That's right, here are a few examples.

Icons Used in This Book

In order to highlight some important and/or interesting information on the screenwriting profession, I've used the following icons throughout the book.

This icon does one of two things: It either suggests a theory or example worth bearing in mind as you read the ensuing text, or it reiterates advice from a previous passage that may be pertinent again.

Keep a lookout for this icon. It signals some time-saving suggestions and/or tricks of the trade.

This icon references a screenwriting term or some showbiz jargon and gives a plain-English definition. If you're really in a hurry, you can skip over these Jargon Alert paragraphs and still understand the chapter. But you may find the definitions to be helpful.

This icon alerts you to a theory or practice that may actually be detrimental to your writing routine or to your career. Don't skip these paragraphs; you'll regret it later!

Many chapters contain a sidebar, flagged with this icon, that presents an exercise for you. These exercises are totally optional, but you may find that they can help you develop your screenwriting skills.

Where to Go from Here

You can go anywhere you want in this book! Read it according to your personal needs as a writer or a writer-to-be. If you want to start at Chapter 1 and read the book cover to cover, great! (After all, I worked really hard on this book!) If not, that's fine, too — you won't hurt my feelings. The information in this book is accessible and relevant regardless of your path to it.

Also, no two writers are alike in what they're after, and this book is designed with just that thought in mind. Read it cover to cover or jump around. Worried about writer's block? See Chapter 14. Want to protect your work? Flip to Chapter 19. Not sure where to begin? This book has two, count'em *two,* tables of contents. The Contents at a Glance gives you a basic overall picture of what you can find in this book. Skim through it and see what ropes you in. Or simply close your eyes and point. When you find a topic that interests you, you can go straight to that chapter or use the detailed table of contents to get even more specifics of what to expect. Every chapter stands on its own, so take your pick and feel free to skip around at will.

Part I
So You Want to Write for Pictures

The 5th Wave   By Rich Tennant

"You know that kid that submitted a screenplay to us on the back of a restaurant menu? I'm passing on it. I like the screenplay, but I hate that restaurant."

In this part . . .

It all begins with an idea. You're driving through the city (or stuck in traffic as the case may be) when a childhood memory flashes before your eyes. This would make a great film. You're reading a newspaper, and a third-page crime scene sparks an array of chilling images. This would make a great film. You're minding your own business in some public forum when you overhear a startling conversation and — you guessed it — this would make a great film. This part of the book is about the all important idea — finding it, nurturing it, imagining it on the screen. Because you know what? It probably would make a great film, and if you don't write it, who will?

Chapter 1

Introducing the Art of Screenwriting

Screenwriting is a craft, and like any craft worth pursuing, you can never know too much about it. You wouldn't tell a doctor to stop scrutinizing advances in medicine, would you? Can a teacher ever learn enough about education? This chapter provides a glimpse of screenwriting and alerts you to where in the book you can go to find it. Consider it your preview of coming attractions.

Thinking Visually

Quick — in what children's book does a character require green glasses to enter a city gate? If you answered *The Wizard of Oz,* you're absolutely right. Dorothy needs green glasses to enter the Emerald City. And while they cut this detail in the film version, the question is nevertheless relevant to screenwriting. It's a question of vision — what do you need in order to see where you're going?

Screenwriting requires a unique vision, eyes trained to scan the world with particular acuity. It seems silly to say that screenwriters look at the world with a visual eye. Of course, they do. Doesn't everybody? After all, looking is a visual act.

And yet, there's a distinct difference between what screenwriters see and what people in other occupations see. Screenwriters break the world down into visual clips or scenes — in other words, into moving pictures. And screenwriters see with more than their eyes. Consider for a second that it's possible to see moving pictures while

- Observing the world around you
- Reading a novel, a play, or a poem
- Reading the newspaper
- Listening to music
- Listening to someone else's story

 Screenwriters look for moving pictures in everything, though some sources yield more than others. Want to know how your vision stacks up? Find a public place, sit down for a while with a pad and pen, and write down what you notice. Then, flip to Chapter 2 and find out how visual your eye really is.

Developing the Writer's Mind

Imagine a storage facility, with aisles and aisles of file cabinets, some overflowing and some empty but for one scrap of paper. Or imagine a playground full of children, yes, but other people as well, people you wouldn't expect to see. Maybe two construction workers are playing basketball, or a few CEOs are eating donuts on the lawn; students and couples and blue-collar employees are all in the same space. Or imagine a long hallway full of doors. Occasionally, people emerge, have an exchange of some sort, and return behind those doors. Now, imagine a blank canvas. Paints and brushes sit nearby, but they remain, as of yet, unused. Any one of these spaces may resemble the mind of a writer.

Writers collect and store tons of details. They amass images, pieces of conversation, intriguing characters, sounds, expressions, slang, and more. They also costume what they find, envisioning different outcomes. Add some boots, some dust, and a gun — *voilà*. You're in a western. Dim the lights, strip away the color, and give everyone a cigar — presto! You have the black-and-white, suspense-filled world of a film noir. Introduce a spaceship or a time machine, and suddenly, the world becomes science fiction. This is how writers spend much of their time — not exactly a dull profession. So, I suppose that the question here is, What does your mind look like? If you want to find out, turn to Chapter 3.

Approaching Screenwriting as a Craft

Writers take their vocation very seriously. They'll do almost anything to inspire that muse, and I do mean anything. Rumor has it that

- ✔ Alexander Dumas color coordinated his paper with the type of fiction that he was writing. Blue paper was for novels, yellow paper was for poetry, and rose-colored pages were reserved for nonfiction.
- ✔ Mark Twain and Truman Capote had to write lying down.
- ✔ Ernest Hemingway sharpened dozens of pencils before he wrote.
- ✔ Willa Cather read the Bible before writing each day.
- ✔ Poet John Donne liked to lie in an open coffin before picking up a pen. Now, there's a story for you.

I'm not implying that to take up the craft of writing you have to become an eccentric, but that may happen of its own accord. Writing is both fun and frustrating; it requires flights of whimsy as well as hard work. It's equal parts imagination and preparation. Striking a balance between the two worlds is a constant challenge. Catching the muse is one thing, but keeping her with you is another — that's where the tools of the trade come in handy. If you want a glimpse of some of those tools, turn to Chapter 4 where I discuss the craft of screenwriting. You find advice on how to flex your imagination, channel it onto the page, and maintain the writing schedule necessary to do both.

Finding Your Screenplay's Story

So how do writers find material? It depends on the writer, of course, but in their ongoing quests for stories, writers resemble any or all of the following:

- ✔ Archaeologists
- ✔ Detectives
- ✔ Gardeners (plant a seed, and it will grow)
- ✔ Reporters
- ✔ Research analysts
- ✔ Scavengers
- ✔ Secret agents
- ✔ Voyeurs

Great stories abound; you just have to know how to catch them, or hunt them down, as the case may be. You should also know what details attract you to a story. Are you a people person? Do locations draw you in? Are you compelled by certain kinds of events? You want to consider these questions before your story search begins. Chapter 5 helps you find the perfect story and discover which material you naturally gravitate toward.

Working through the Writing Process

As soon as you get an idea, you have to develop that idea. The development process isn't unlike chaperoning several restless children across the country in a small car. You're likely to hear the following questions over and over:

- How does the whole thing start?
- What happens next?
- Who are these people?
- What happens next?
- What's the problem?
- Does that make sense?
- What happens next?
- Can we go any faster?
- Are we there yet?
- Why, why, why, why, why?

The whole journey can drive you nuts without a good road map, and in screenwriting terms, that map is known as *plot*. I consider plot to be so important that I dedicate three chapters to it — Chapters 6, 7, and 8. After all, every story has a beginning, middle, and an ending, and the same questions apply to each part. There's a whole other set of questions for character building in Chapter 9 and yet another chapter (you guessed it — Chapter 10) dedicated to orchestrating vibrant language for those characters once you know who they are. As you may suspect, without a navigation panel, you're in for a long, bumpy ride. So if you want to pacify that back-seat yammering, turn to Part II and start reading. Otherwise, you're liable to pull the car over and walk home.

Formatting Your Screenplay

Here are a few things that I've figured out about the screenwriting trade:

- Always look before you leap.
- People do judge a book by its cover.
- Actions speak louder than words.
- Brevity is the soul of wit (and most films, I might add).
- Try to make a long story short.
- You never get another chance to make a first impression.

You don't have much control over most aspects of the screenwriting profession. Ideas often arrive unbidden, characters sometimes dictate what they want to say, the ending of your story may change several times, and you may even find yourself in a different genre. And when you're talking about Hollywood, forget it. The business is always in flux. One day, they're looking for war films, and the next day, they want candy and roses. They may be searching for a script with the word "wedding" in the title; you just never know.

One of the only things a writer has complete control over is the script's appearance, and in this industry, appearance is everything (at least at the beginning). So how wide should your margins be? How do you introduce a scene? Where do you insert special effects? And how long is too long? Getting readers to flip past the cover is half the battle, and correct formatting may ensure that they do so. (For more on formatting your script, flip to Chapter 14.)

Constructing Your First Draft

By the time you sit down to write your first draft, you'll be armed and dangerous. Among other things, your arsenal will include the following:

- Strong characters
- Equally strong conflicts
- Character goals and dreams
- Locations
- A series of events
- Remedies for writer's block
- Outlines of the action
- A solid writing routine

So, now that you're considering a first draft, how good are you at puzzles — or at weaving, matching, or redecorating? Screenwriting requires all these skills. Crafting a draft is really a matter of arranging your arsenal of information into some desired form and then linking those moments together.

In screenwriting terms, your *catalyst* or *inciting incident* propels the action into the big event, which then shuttles the story toward a *midpoint* after which it rises to a *climax* followed by a *resolution* of some sort. Make sense? If not, don't fear; just read Chapter 16.

Rewriting Your Script

So, what do you have in common with Plato, Ernest Hemingway, Katherine Anne Porter, and screenwriter John Logan? Before trying to answer, consider the following facts:

- Plato revised *The Republic* 50 times.

- Hemingway rewrote the last page of *A Farewell to Arms* 39 times.

- Katherine Anne Porter took 20 years to finish *Ship of Fools*.

- John Logan spent more than ten years rewriting his play *Never the Sinner,* during which time he removed a dozen characters.

So where do you fit in? All these anecdotes involve revision, and if you're serious about completing a script, you're going to encounter that process as well. Have you heard the phrase "If at first you don't succeed, try, try again"? Well, in screenwriting, success arrives in stages, and you almost always have to try, try again. After you outline the action and throw the story onto the page, you'll probably want to try, try again. First drafts are generally dynamic, but they're also unruly, which is why many writers believe that the real writing occurs in revisions. The phrase most often applied to this principle is "Writing is rewriting." Your first draft is written for the story and for you. Your internal editor isn't invited. But in the revision stage, the editor emerges in full form, sizing up each moment and weighing how it affects the whole. And will your revisions take you 20 years to complete? I hope not, but if you're worried that they might, flip to Chapter 17 for extensive advice on revisions.

Adapting Your Screenplay from an Outside Source

Have you ever read a story or watched a play and thought, "This would make a great film!"? If so, you've experienced the first step in the adaptation process: identifying a source. You can adapt all kinds of material for the screen. ***Memento*** began as a short story written by the director's brother, ***Chicago*** was originally a stage musical, ***A Beautiful Mind*** was first a biography. Strong primary source material abounds.

Adaptations are challenging for many of the same reasons that writers are drawn to them. They provide instant character recipes, events, and themes that seem perfect for the screen. Somehow, a writer must find a way to make an original piece out of what he or she is given. Separating from the primary source is a difficult but necessary endeavor. In a way, adapting is like getting two pieces of art for the price of one. So if you're interested in adapting a work into a screenplay, flip to Chapter 18 for a few tips on the process.

Just for fun

Are you a movie buff? Here's a little project to test your movie-trivia expertise. Know nothing about films but interested nonetheless? Consider this a project to launch your movie-trivia expertise. After all, you can never know too much about your craft of choice.

In the left-hand column, I list famous film quotations. In the right-hand column, I include the films that made them popular. How many lines can you trace to their source?

1. "I gave her my heart; she gave me a pen."

2. "Frankly my dear, I don't give a damn."

3. "If you build it, he will come."

4. "I see dead people."

5. "I do wish we could chat longer, but I'm having an old friend for dinner."

6. "When you realize you want to spend the rest of your life with someone, you want the rest of your life to start right now."

7. "My name is Inigo Montoya. You killed my father, prepare to die."

8. "Roads? Where we're going, we don't need roads."

9. "Life moves pretty fast. If you don't stop to look once in a while, you could miss it."

10. "It's not the years, honey, it's the mileage."

11. "You're gonna need a bigger boat."

12. "You can't handle the truth."

a. *Back To The Future*

b. *The Princess Bride*

c. *Raiders Of The Lost Ark*

d. *Say Anything*

e. *Ferris Bueller's Day Off*

f. *Jaws*

g. *A Few Good Men*

h. *Field of Dreams*

i. *Silence of the Lambs*

j. *When Harry Met Sally*

k. *Gone with the Wind*

l. *The Sixth Sense*

Answers: 1-d, 2-k, 3-h, 4-l, 5-i, 6-j, 7-b, 8-a, 9-e, 10-c, 11-f, 12-g

Selling Your Screenplay to Show Business

With all the creative work that you're doing, you can easily forget that film-making is a business as well as a craft. When you're through with revisions, you become the CEO of your own private company. That company is you. Selling your work is an entirely different part of the process; therefore, it requires a new arsenal: determination, confidence (even if it's feigned), a positive attitude, a marketing strategy, a creative network, and a knowledge of the business and its players.

Hollywood has so many paths that lead into it that you almost need a map to know where to begin. Should you approach an agent first, and if so, how? Should you send your script to producers, and if so, how? Should you be seeking out studios or independents, contests or festivals, television or film? And how, oh how, do you protect yourself and your work in the process? Part IV is dedicated to strategy, both personal and professional. Consider that part your map.

Chapter 2

Preparing to Think Visually

In This Chapter

▶ Distinguishing screenwriting from other art forms

▶ Using visual art to sharpen your screenwriting sensibility

▶ Looking at the world with a screenwriter's eye

▶ Organizing images to create the desired effect

So you want to write for pictures, huh? Are you sure? Of course, you're sure, you scoff. You love movies. You have ideas for movies all the time. You want to write one of your own. Yes, I say again, but are you sure that it's a movie you want to write? Is your idea best suited to the cinema, or would it be better served as a novel, as a stage play, or as a television drama? Perhaps you're envisioning several images that could well be grounds for a poem. For beginning writers, the line between those mediums may blur, but they're nevertheless different forms that require different sensibilities. Screenwriting, in particular, is a visual art. It demands that a writer look at the world with new eyes, swiftly condensing action and physical detail into moving pictures. Do you have those eyes?

This chapter dives in to various literary forms, noting their similarities and their differences, in an attempt to help you view the world with the eyes and mind of a screenwriter.

Exploring Other Mediums

When people talk about movies, they're generally referring to films that they've seen, rarely to films that they've read. When they want a good read, they pick up a novel, a short story, or a magazine. A select few pick up a collection of poetry, but rarely does anyone reach for a movie script, despite its availability. For this reason, the public (beginning writers included) is more comfortable with other forms of writing than it is with screenplays, so when a creative idea strikes, that idea is much more likely to lend itself to a medium other than film.

The jump to cinematic thinking isn't such a grand one, however, and the transfer from one mind-set to the other begins with a quick glance through those other literary forms. If you've struck upon a story already, you may want to peruse the following sections with that story in mind. Try to imagine it in each form. Doing so can help you clarify what aspects of the story lend themselves to cinema, and what aspects match other venues.

Fiction

Fiction makes up more than 80 percent of what people read these days, but it has little in common with screenwriting. Although the forms share an attention to detail and a tendency toward multiple characters and locales, fiction writers spend pages telling readers what screenwriters convey in a few well-chosen images.

In fiction, the mind of each character becomes a landscape. More time is spent exploring thoughts, emotions, and memories than is spent depicting action or crafting dialogue. In film, the opposite is true. A screenwriter can't just say a character mulls over his bad day. She has to show how he feels about it through images or action. Also, in fiction, the author tends to emerge in the form of a clear narrative voice, while screenwriters strive to fade into the background.

Basically, you know that your idea may be better served as a novel or short story if

- ✔ It has copious characters, plotlines, and locations.
- ✔ The action moves between the physical and psychological worlds of each character with ease.
- ✔ The characters' internal conflicts are as important as their physical actions.
- ✔ The story requires more than 200 pages to be explored fully.
- ✔ A clear narrative voice (or several clear narrative voices) guides the action.
- ✔ Many events are described in detail, but few are shown in action.
- ✔ Symbols and foreshadowing abound.

If you discover that your idea lends itself more readily to the page than the screen, never fear. Virtually every story has cinematic possibilities; the trick is to discover them before you start to write.

Stage plays

Though theater is growing more physical in nature, stage plays have traditionally relied on language to convey action, character, and theme. As a general rule, plays depict in dialogue what films depict in physical action, although, like everything, there are exceptions.

Unlike screenplays and novels, which bounce from locale to locale, introducing character after character, stage plays generally limit themselves in cast size and number of settings. Plays with large casts often ask actors to take on multiples roles, and plays with many locations tend to utilize lights, sound cues, and props to suggest leaps therein. Plays rarely try to re-create public locations as realistically as film does. (To do so wouldn't be financially or artistically wise.)

To break it down, your story idea may work better as a play if

- ✔ You can tell the story in 90 pages or fewer.
- ✔ The story concentrates on a handful of characters in a handful of places.
- ✔ Characters reveal themselves through dialogue or long speeches more often than through physical action.
- ✔ The story benefits from interaction with a live audience.
- ✔ The action suggests a heightened reality or is surreal/absurd in nature.

 The line between a theatrical idea and a cinematic one is often vague. If you're unsure whether you've dreamt up a play or a film, try to imagine your story as a series of pictures. If those pictures keep talking to you, you probably have a play. If your mind jumps from image to image, and if every image is full of physical action, you may be ready to write a film script.

Poetry and studio arts

These mediums share several elements in common with cinema. They rely on quick clips of words or images, often sensual in nature, which encapsulate an event or a tone. Film also relies on the organization of pictures to convey plot and emotion. Poetry employs metaphor, allegory, and rhyme, while visual art uses color, light, and the strategic manipulation of an image to communicate its central design. These forms generally aren't substantial enough to support a lengthy text; they instead hint at a larger story or provide a limited portion of it. Their subjects are better served in a few well-crafted stanzas or in one print altogether. In a way, a screenplay continues where the poem or visual piece leaves off. It tells the "before and after." It expands the subject into an idea that can sustain a dramatic through-line.

Your idea may work best as a poem, a song, or a visual art piece if

✔ The subject appears in a flash of color or light, or as a single image.

✔ The subject feels stationary in nature.

✔ The story lends itself to metaphor and rhyme.

✔ The story requires a verbal chorus to set it off.

✔ You imagine the image as a photograph or a portrait.

Poems and visual art pieces aren't often transformed into film, but they can easily become the inspiration for one. If you see your piece as a series of photographs, imagine them moving. Imagine all the photographs that go in between and then ask yourself how you might get from one image to the next. You may discover a film idea after all.

Screenplays

For clarity, certain elements are particular to screenwriting.

Your idea may be a screenplay if

✔ Events reveal themselves in action.

✔ The story contains a clear beginning, middle, and end.

✔ It suggests moments of intricate detail.

✔ It has a *hook,* an aspect of the idea that will grab attention immediately.

✔ It wants to be told in 100 to 120 pages.

✔ The story suggests the possibility of an equally compelling subplot.

✔ The story has the potential for wide commercial appeal.

Screenplays subsist on the visual details of every scene, and you may be surprised by how many details you find when you know how to look. Consider this example: Harold comes home from work early, hears a noise upstairs, creeps up to investigate, and discovers that he's being robbed.

Look at each portion of that scene closely. How would you break the action up? A novel would describe every nuance of the action, as well as Harold's heart beginning to race and the little voice inside his head screaming to run away. It may even flash to a memory from Harold's childhood of older brothers jumping out to scare him from behind closed doors. In a stage play, audiences may hear Harold's car in the driveway moments before keys jingle in the lock and Harold enters the room. After the sound effect, Harold slowly climbs the stairs. You may see what happens next or just hear the next bit as it unfolds offstage. Want to distill it even further? How about condensing the experience into one photograph or portrait? Perhaps a shot of a man ascending a staircase into a darkened hall, or a shot of his hand on the doorknob upstairs. All these forms are possible visual representations of the fear involved.

A screenwriter, however, breaks that scene into a handful of pivotal moments and then hunts for visual details in between. She envisions Harold's blue Chevy pulling into the drive, and then his feet crossing the front lawn. He stops to grab the mail; then, his keys jingle in the lock. The door opens to reveal his face when he hears the noise from upstairs. Perhaps his eyes narrow at the sound; perhaps he hesitates before one hand grips the banister and slides steadily up the rail. Remember, in film, your eye can go anywhere Individually, no one piece makes sense, but organized in a particular way, the pieces paint a vivid and generally silent story. Dialogue may be layered on as necessary, but in screenwriting, the situation exists first.

A novel approach to film

The fastest way to understand the differences in artistic mediums is to move between them yourself. The following selection is from *A Tale of Two Cities* by Charles Dickens, a novel that has been made into a film on several occasions. This particular scene takes place in court.

"It happened, that the action turned his face to that side of the court which was on his left. About on a level with his eyes, there sat, in that corner of the Judge's bench, two persons upon whom his look immediately rested; so immediately, and so much to the changing of his aspect, that all the eyes that were turned upon him, turned to them.

The spectators saw two figures, a young lady of little more than twenty, and a gentleman who was evidently her father, a man of very remarkable appearance in respect of the absolute whiteness of his hair, and a certain indescribable intensity of face. His daughter had one of her hands drawn through his arm, as she sat by him, and the other pressed upon it. She had drawn close to him, in her dread of the scene, and in her

pity of the prisoner. This had been so very noticeable, so very powerfully and naturally shown, that starers who had had no pity for him were touched by her; and the whisper went about, "Who are they?"

"Witnesses." "For which side?" "Against." "Against what side?"

"The prisoner's."

The Judge, whose eyes had gone in the general direction, recalled them, leaned back into his seat, and looked steadily at the man whose life was in his hand, as Mr. Attorney-General rose to spin the rope, grind the axe, and hammer the nails into the scaffold.

After you read through the selection several times, try to envision it as one image — a photograph or a painting perhaps. Will you portray the woman, the woman and her father, or the entire court? If you have a lyrical bent, try your hand at a poem or a scene from a stage play. Finally, distill the scene into five images, and try envisioning it as a film.

The Visual Life of a Screenplay

If your script becomes a film, a director and a cinematographer will eventually haggle over the composition of each shot and the overall look of your piece. Among other things, they discuss the following elements:

- **Color:** What colors pop out or highlight the shot, and what is the overall look? Is the moment realistic or surreal in nature? Compare the look of a Clint Eastwood western to a David Lynch film, and you see how important color choices can be.

- **Light:** What time of day is it? What season and weather conditions are at work? Is a specific lighting source suggested, and if so, what is it? The shots in *Ice Storm* are bleak and overcast, in stark contrast to overly bright films like Baz Luhrmann's *Moulin Rouge.*

- **Movement:** This element refers to the quality of movement both within each image and between shots. Do your pictures dart about in a dangerous fashion as in *Reservoir Dogs,* or are they languid and expansive as in *Gosford Park?*

- **Organization:** How an image unfolds is as important as the image itself. In other words, what portion of the moment do you reveal and when? *E.T.* has a shot in which the little alien hides himself among stuffed animals in the daughter's closet. That moment is successful because when the mother opens the door, the camera moves slowly from left to right, glancing past a stationary E.T. just as the mother does. The audience doesn't know where he is until that moment, either. For more on the importance of organization, see Chapter 3.

- **Sound:** Each moment of a screenplay exists in a three-dimensional world. What sounds fill out that location? Do any of them conflict with the emotional content of the image itself? If the shot is of a child lost in an amusement park, don't forget to imagine the music and the laughter of the park itself. Those sounds further isolate her.

- **Location:** In life, you can't always choose where important moments occur. In screenplays, you can. The location of each shot should be a specific choice on the part of the writer. It underscores the content of the scene. It's no accident that tragedy in *Dead Poets Society* takes place in a gorgeous New England landscape during a particularly beautiful winter's day.

- **Contrasting elements:** Some moments benefit from pitting opposing energies against each other. In many romantic comedies, one person walks the streets alone, surrounded by happy couples. In *The Untouchables,* one man is brutally murdered while another man enjoys an opera. The two moments are linked by the situation but also by the music. The intended emotion of a scene is often magnified by the addition of its opposite form.

From nothing to something

Following the guidelines listed in the section "From the outside in," try to create an image from the ground up. This project may help you detail a previously conceived story, or it may simply help strengthen your imagination.

Beside each visual element, I include the first decision. Use this detail as a launching point into eight grander images, layering on each element as you go. When you're done, circle any image that intrigues you and disregard the rest.

Color: Red and white

Light: Several flashlights clicking on in succession

Movement: Frantic and clipped

Organization: From the porch, to the yard, to the beach, to the boathouse, to the ocean

Sound: The chopping of wood

Location: An attic

Contrasting elements: Laughter and tears

Symbol and metaphor: Footprints on the sand

> ✔ **Symbol and/or metaphor:** Depending on how it's shot, an image can simply help establish a scene or provide a metaphor for the entire piece. In *Titanic,* the image of the necklace disappearing into the ocean takes on much greater significance after watching the ship go down and the protagonist's love interest disappear beneath the water as well.

Great, you say, so a director and a cinematographer will eventually discuss these elements. What does that have to do with me? At the beginning stages of the screenwriting process, it has everything to do with you. In your hunt for images, you become both director and cinematographer for the piece, and although all these visual details won't make it into your script, it won't be because you haven't thought them all through. Your images may also trigger ideas in the eventual director and cinematographer.

The key to understanding the visual world of a screenplay is the key to understanding any medium. You want to view the world as that kind of an artist. How do you do that? In this case, read screenplays, see movies, and practice looking at the world with an eye toward image. Eventually, the ability to break life into a series of pictures becomes second nature.

From the outside in

In this first method, you concentrate on one element off the list and create a visual moment with that element in mind. After you can picture that element clearly, choose another element and layer that choice in, and so on. Your goal is to imagine a moment or an image that satisfies all the senses. For example, say that you've chosen the element of light. You decide that the light in your image comes from a single candle. Next, you choose location and decide that the image takes place in an abandoned warehouse. You might choose sound next and layer in the dripping of water in the distance, or the scuttling of rats off in the corners of the room. You get the idea. By the time you're done, you have a complete image in your mind's eye. That image may or may not suggest a scene or a situation. In any case, you're training your imagination to create something from nothing.

From the inside out

In the second method, you begin with a preconceived image. This method is particularly helpful after you've settled on a story idea and have a few moments devised within it. Now, you begin what I call the "bolstering and breaking away" process.

First, go down the list and make sure that you've included each element in the image. Challenge yourself to make specific choices. You may know that it takes place at dusk, but do you know what color dusk is in your image? Dusk in the woods of Colorado is distinctly different from dusk in Manhattan. After you've gone down the list once, start stripping the elements away. One by one, those portions of the moment disappear until you're left with what? Which is the last element remaining? This process may help to suggest the most important aspects of each image as well as the movement within it.

From something to nothing

Now, I give you a full image and let you strip it down. Take away one sentence at a time.

Image: The sound of sirens. Red and yellow lights flash through the space, illuminating the scene of an accident. It is nighttime in the city and raining. Doors open up in a hall down the way, and teenagers flock outside. A school dance has just let out. Boisterous music filters through the streets. Some of the kids notice the accident and linger to watch. Others hurry home or take off hand in hand down the street. A hubcap spins off the car, rolls for a stretch, then clatters on the ground.

You decide how you want to eliminate details. And you do want to eliminate them. In film, description is brief, every word is important. If a detail wants to hang in for a while, take the others away and save it for last. Try reversing the order in which you eliminate them. Which order feels right? In this way, you find out how the image should organize itself and which portions of it you're particularly attached to.

Chapter 3

Diving In to the Screenwriter's Mind

*W*ith the incredible variety of movies that come out each year, you may think that the only thing screenwriters share in common is their profession. Like most artists, screenwriters have different methods of finding an idea and developing a story. Some ransack the local libraries, writing between ever-growing stacks of books. Some haunt coffeehouses, waiting for the next great conversation to pick up nearby. Some writers interview, and some adapt. Were you to question a small handful of writers, your head would soon whirl with differing opinions, approaches, advice, and techniques. So where does an aspiring writer begin?

For starters, take a closer look at writers. Literally. Look at them. You may notice a glazed or faraway glint in their eyes; their heads may tilt to one side as if listening for something behind them; their speech may clip along mechanically. Overall, you may feel that they're really somewhere else. And why not? After all, they're working. They're not sitting in front of a notepad or a computer, but they're still working.

A screenwriter's sensibility resembles that of a conscientious parent who has children romping upstairs. He or she never knows when something more important may call him or her out of the room. A screenwriter moves through the world with a heightened awareness — a writer's awareness. Can you develop this sensibility? Sure. It just takes practice and a few friends who are willing to put up with the new, perhaps improved, you.

Learning from Other Writers

The first step in approaching any artistic medium is to surround yourself with examples of the art form. If you want to paint, you go to a museum. If you want to compose, you buy scores of music or frequent concert halls. If you want to write movies, you do two things: First, you study the impact of films firsthand by going to the cinema and by supporting your local video store. Second, you discover much about writing movies by reading screenplays — lots of screenplays. The time you dedicate to reading can reap great rewards.

Here are just a few of the many things you'll garner from other writers:

- **Multiple points of view:** The most compelling stories are told again and again. They continue to be written because each writer has a unique approach. Reading other writers forces you to consider similar stories from not-so-similar angles.

- **Clarity of opinions and ethics:** The best screenplays ask difficult questions. Considering those questions as you read can help clarify your own set of beliefs.

- **A sense of language:** Strong writers possess a large vocabulary and an understanding of grammar. Different writers use different words in different ways. Learn from them.

- **An understanding of format:** Many new writers know what they want to say but are unsure of how to lay it out on the page. Reading other screenplays familiarizes you with the format.

- **An enjoyable way to spend a few hours:** Screenplays are fun, fast reads. Reading one is like traveling without standing in line or spending more than $10 on airfare.

Finding screenplays to read is now a fairly easy endeavor. You can find most popular scripts online for free. I encourage you to examine failure as well as success here. In addition to watching great movies and reading well-constructed scripts, study some box-office disappointments and scripts that failed to tell a compelling story. (The two are not always mutually exclusive.) If you can identify what components of the story caused it to fail, you may be able to avoid the same fate in the future.

All in all, reading screenplays provides a familiarity with the craft itself. You're learning through osmosis — the gradual, often unconscious absorption of details. Reading screenplays regularly can prepare you, and often encourage you, to sit down to write with confidence.

Reading for dramatic intent

After reading a screenplay once through for the general story, you may try scanning it again to concentrate on one portion of the development. Among the items to track are

- ✔ How the writer develops characters
- ✔ How the writer structures crucial events
- ✔ What images the writer repeats and why
- ✔ What techniques the writer employs to move from scene to scene
- ✔ The writer's dramatic intent

The first four items on the list tackle how and when the writer gives the audience relevant information. Detailing the people in the script, revealing key secrets, and manipulating images are all part of character and plot development, which I discuss further in Part II. For now, I just concentrate on the final item on the list — dramatic intent.

Dramatic intent, also known as the *premise,* refers to the screenplay's specific purpose or design. It alludes to the main question the screenplay asks or the thought a writer attempts to communicate through story.

What's the writer trying to say? What does the writer want to know? Keep these two questions in mind as you read for dramatic intent. The strongest, most complex scripts are written out of a great need: the need to understand life and human interaction or the need to test on the page something the writer has learned. This need determines the screenplay's subject. So when you're looking for dramatic intent, keep an eye out for three things:

- ✔ **Point of view:** Who or what does the writer want you to root for? To condemn? Does the writer have an opinion on the events you're watching, and how do you know? If you can answer these questions, you've probably located the writer's point of view.

- ✔ **Theory:** Does the script present a hypothesis that the action then tries to prove? Look at the movie *Crash,* an edgy look at the racial stereotypes alienating people from one another. Each scene proves that assumptions about race are not usually good ones.

- ✔ **Questions:** What questions keep you reading? Which ones crop up again and again? Every scene in the movie *When Harry Met Sally* asks the question, Can best friends sustain a romantic relationship? Generally, the characters' answers to the question may suggest the story's conclusion.

The most compelling screenplays engage the audience with the inquiries or opinions. If you answer the main question in the first few frames, people have no reason to continue watching your film. If you ask the question in a variety of ways, people can form their own answers. Present several arguments, and they may even change their opinions once or twice. In other words, you give them the ability to participate in your story rather than simply observe it.

Why read for dramatic intent? Screenwriters write in part because they have something to communicate. No doubt you have something to say and are, therefore, pursuing the craft. If you can locate another writer's intent, you may discover how to craft scenes that present your own. Look at scripts you admire. What questions do they pose? What about them keeps audiences guessing, or on the edge of their seats, or both? If you can locate the thematic questions of other films, you'll quickly discover what themes sustain an entire draft, and which fall short.

Recognizing a screenplay's genre

Take a walk through your local video store and jot down the categories videos are shelved under. These categories outline each movie's genre.

A film's *genre* refers to the artistic category it belongs to. The genre is generally determined by a distinctive style, form, or content. It sometimes alludes to the way writers approach their subject. Comedies and dramas, for instance, often approach the same subject in very different ways.

The most common genres include

- ✔ **Comedy:** Comedies approach subjects with humor (of course). *Dark comedies* and *romantic comedies* fall within this genre. Dark comedies, such as *Fargo,* tackle heartbreaking or frightening material in a comic way, and romantic comedies like *Sleepless In Seattle,* explore that crazy thing called love.

- ✔ **Drama:** Dramas tend to be true-to-life stories of a serious nature. They may contain humorous moments, but the overall effect is poignant and sometimes tragic. *There Will Be Blood* and *No Country for Old Men* are examples of this genre.

- ✔ **Sci-Fi and Fantasy:** These movies take audiences to a future time frame or an imaginary world. The characters may or may not be human beings, the rules of science may not apply, and the locations may or may not resemble ours. The *Matrix* films and the *Lord of the Rings* trilogy are successful examples of such a genre.

- ✔ **Action and Adventure:** These films portray characters tackling dangerous events in an atmosphere of excitement and suspense. The characters may be on a quest, as in the *Indiana Jones* series, or they may be in physical combat against a formidable enemy, as in **Rambo.** Generally, they encounter both — they're on a quest and must defeat the foe before they can complete it.

- ✔ **Family:** If you can take your children to see a film, it probably belongs in this genre. Family movies generally lack cursing, sexual content, and graphic violence. For this reason, they have the G or PG rating. This genre may include animation. **Monsters, Inc.** and **Ratatouille** are some successful examples of this genre.

- ✔ **Horror and Suspense:** These two different genres attack the same subject. *Horror films* tend to be more graphic in their violence, such as the **Saw** series or **Scream,** while *suspense films* generally depict a steadily unfolding mystery. Virtually every Alfred Hitchcock film falls within the suspense genre. When deftly executed, both genres make you want to lock all the doors and turn on the lights.

- ✔ **Art House and Independent:** These often low-budget films don't hail from large production companies. **The Blair Witch Project** and **Welcome to the Dollhouse** are some successful examples. These films often allow more creative freedom, which may account for their acute sense of style.

Many of the strongest scripts combine genres, thereby appealing to a broader audience. **Star Wars,** one of the most successful movies of all time, is both a sci-fi film and an action/adventure. **E.T.,** another blockbuster hit, is a sci-fi and a family film with elements of adventure. **3:10 to Yuma** is a suspenseful adventure film. If you can identify the genre (or genres) of any movie you see, you can quickly pick up the kinds of events associated with it. Although you can't follow a specific formula for writing a particular genre, an intimate knowledge of the categories can help you identify your own.

Art and Life: What's the Difference?

Well, for starters, yes, art and life are different, and acknowledging the difference is important, if only to give direction to your work. Much of what you write will stem from personal experience, events relayed to you, or stories you pull from primary sources like the news.

Just because it happened, doesn't mean that it's noteworthy, let alone screenworthy. An essay on what you did for your summer vacation may not be the best source material for a film — unless, of course, your summer vacation involved a torrid love affair, a deep-sea adventure, a family crisis, or a revelation on what it means to be human. If that's the case, it may have artistic potential. If that's not the case, abandon the premise and move on, because it's probably not art. You may, however, find yourself writing what you think should have happened in any given moment. Hindsight can be a great cinematic aid.

Art serves a purpose. Depending on your affiliations, you may believe life does as well, but art is generally striving to do at least one of the following things:

- ✔ **Clarify an experience.** Life moves so quickly, it's often difficult to know the significance of a moment while it's in progress. You may be distracted by family, friends, or career and miss potentially important events as they occur. Art places you in the spectator's chair so that you can view the larger picture and perhaps understand events more completely.

- ✔ **Interpret an experience.** It's not enough to live through a moment; human beings usually want to know why that moment occurred. This desire for understanding is the reason therapy has become such a lucrative profession. Art scrutinizes events and presents opinions on why they transpired, as well as offers thoughts on the consequences.

- ✔ **Intensify a sensation.** I don't go to movies simply to watch an interesting story unfold. I go to the movies to feel something — to be enraged, dismayed, horrified, elated, and so on. I go to the cinema in large part to encounter emotions on a grand scale. Art allows you to focus on and enhance the emotion surrounding human action.

What do these three goals have in common? They rely on an artist's selectivity. To clarify an event, you must break it into moments and place those moments into a comprehensible sequence. To interpret an event, you must have an opinion on it, and that opinion will dictate which portions of the event to script. To intensify a sensation, you must strategically arrange a scene to affect an audience.

Screenwriters aren't documentarians. They don't strive to recreate life exactly as it happened; they sift through life and choose which parts to show you, in what order, and for what purpose. Moreover, they do so in the most visually informative way. So while life may certainly inspire your art, and art may inspire your life, they're not the same thing. One you have control over; the other you do not.

Developing an Artistic Sensibility

You've probably heard the saying "Imitation is the oldest form of flattery." I'm not suggesting that you copy the stories, or even the style, of other writers, but you may want to try moving through the world as they do.

In the old stereotype, writers don all black and scowl at the world while scribbling furiously in a notebook, or they subsist on coffee and cigarettes while scribbling furiously in a notebook, or they drink heavily while scribbling furiously — well, you get the picture. Although you can certainly offset your creative anxiety in healthier ways, that stereotype does contain a small grain of truth: Writers are always scribbling, into a notebook or otherwise. Their senses are story-ready, carefully selecting details from their environment and sequestering them away somewhere for the next great script. Some writers are born with this awareness, but most hone their skills with each new project. To develop this sensibility in yourself, you need to take a closer look at the details writers collect and how they select among them.

What a writer sees

Imagine that you attend a school reunion. You see all the usual trappings: a welcoming committee equipped with name tags, tables piled with food, a beverage bar, party decorations, and perhaps a band. Most people find old friends, socialize a bit, and call it a night. Most people do, but not most writers.

People watching is a not just a hobby for screenwriters, it's part of their job. A screenwriter notices the tight smiles on everyone's faces, their quizzical look before they remember someone's name, the one-time school football star drinking too much in the corner, the former sweethearts who exchanged glances and then left arm in arm, and so much more. The writer can also recreate the scene in such a way that those images are evident to a casual observer. Under a writer's piercing gaze, these moments flourish and may quickly become the next scene in a script.

The writer's process is no different from any type of physical training. You're preparing your eyes to catch certain details — in particular, details that personalize the scene. Some of those details include

- ✔ **The scene's overall layout:** Screenwriting consists of visual images constructed in a telling way, by which I mean with choice details in mind. When you enter a space, test how quickly you can assess it, close your eyes, and then recreate it. How would you write it down so that someone else imagines the same space?

- ✔ **Anything out of the ordinary:** Scan the scene for unusual details. What seems out of place? Who seems ill at ease? The man in the suit wearing the lovely woman's wristwatch or the table of sports enthusiasts drinking hot cocoa? Many stories rise out of something curious.

- ✔ **Telling looks or exchanged glances:** If someone looks at another person for any length of time, usually something's going on. He may be recalling a past visit, trying to catch her eye, or checking up on her for someone else — any number of musings are possible. If two people exchange glances, a silent conversation's underway. Watch and see whether you can translate what's being said.

✔ **Loaded gestures:** Many conversations take place in a single gesture. A father puts his hand on his son's shoulder — this movement may be menacing, commanding, or supportive depending on how it's executed. The gestures of any given moment become a silent score of what's going on beneath the conversation. If you can track the gestures, you can recreate them later.

✔ **Personality quirks:** Someone's eccentricities, physical and emotional, immediately distinguish that person from others. Twin brothers may look, walk, and talk alike, but one of them may dress with care while the other seems to own a single sloppy outfit. If you watch the world long enough, you soon acquire a list of personality traits ready to enhance any character you create.

Looking at the world this way eventually becomes a habit. Your eyes automatically adjust to the process. When that occurs, you may be ready to retrain the next sense — your sense of sound.

What a writer hears

Imagine the school reunion. Interesting visual images crop up all over the place now, but what sets them off? Is it the loud dance music, the constant whispering behind you, the clinking of glasses in toast, or the flash and click of numerous cameras? Screenwriters pick up on all sorts of sounds that enhance a scene. Try locating the following in your own surroundings:

✔ **Noises that suggest the event:** Many scenarios come equipped with their own soundscapes. You'd be quick to distinguish a christening from an accident site, even with your eyes closed. Whether your scene takes place outside in a field or inside a prison cell, the surrounding noises immediately provide an atmosphere for your piece.

✔ **Noises that punctuate the scene:** Occasionally, you may notice a sound that enhances the moment. If you're watching a man cry softly to himself, the laughter of two lovers nearby may enhance the man's loneliness somehow. In the film *Little Children,* Kate Winslet is often surrounded by laughing children and young couples in love. The sounds that emerge as a result further enhance the despair she feels over her failing marriage and her guilt over an affair.

✔ **The rhythms of conversation:** Every conversation has its own unique tempo. The pace of the voices, the repetition of phrases, the moments of silence — a screenwriter listens to all these things. Silence, in particular, can be as effective as dialogue, if not more so, and it certainly contributes to the punctuation of conversation. Listening to the rhythms of conversation helps you compose your own dialogue.

> ✔ **Slang and jargon:** These terms refer to words and phrases that suggest a culture, a socio-economic background, or a profession. They suggest character immediately, sometimes even location. Filmmaker Spike Lee often utilizes street slang to differentiate between cultures, gangs, and prejudices. Television shows like **Grey's Anatomy** rely on hospital jargon to give them a believable edge.

You're not responsible for including all the sounds that you discover in the body of your script. However, if you can close your eyes and hear a scene, you'll be better able to write it. Sound is often a more intimate way of understanding your story. Because the noise represents the world of your characters, this process may also help you understand their internal dilemmas as well as the external ones.

What a writer remembers and what a writer forgets

Enhancing your perceptive skills can be a full-time job. When you consider the volume of compelling images around you, it's a wonder that most screenplays aren't four hours long. After your senses adapt to this new process of viewing the world, finding and recording those details are the easy parts. Like spring-cleaning, the difficulty comes in selecting which few you may keep and letting the rest go.

Of course, which exact details a writer cherishes and which he forgets will vary according to personality. However, if you're stumped as to what you may hold on to, consider the following information.

It may be important to remember

> ✔ **Details that create a compelling image:** By a compelling image, I mean one that is full — full of tension, full of emotion, full of movement, full of life. A screenwriter's job is to grab an audience's attention through such images. You should be able to see a character's emotional state on-screen. Remember what catches your eye in this way.

> ✔ **Details that raise a question:** Questions are the key to strong writing. Personal questions fuel the desire to write and find answers; the characters' questions determine the choices they make throughout your story. Any detail that forces a question is worth remembering.

> ✔ **Details that tug at your moral or ethical code:** Hopefully, every script you write will serve some purpose — to inspire, to spark debate, to inquire, to entertain, and so on. In order to communicate clearly, a writer needs to know what she stands for and why. Any details that refute or support your own views may come in handy later.

✔ **Details that establish a debate:** Many films rely on ongoing arguments to bolster the momentum. Whether the argument exists between characters or audience members, if your script sparks a debate, it successfully engaged someone. Watch for the moments in real life that elicit arguments of various kinds.

✔ **Details that help you understand the human condition:** Most art strives to understand life and its injustice, its irony, its savage nature, and its glory. Once in awhile, you encounter a moment that provides a piece of the human puzzle. Remember those moments above all.

If the detail in question doesn't fit into one of these categories, it may be worth abandoning. Remember that you're constructing every image with an aim in mind. If the details you include distract from or compete with that aim, getting rid of them isn't only a good idea — it's your job.

Consider this example: I'm constructing a scene from the school reunion, and I want the audience to focus on one girl hovering by the buffet table stuffing food into her purse. If her eyes dart over the crowd, if she has the hollow look of a woman who hasn't eaten in a while — these are details to preserve. They strengthen the tension of the moment. The fabric of her purse, the size of the table, the number of brownies she takes — these details are unimportant. They distract from the scene's primary focus — the action of a person quietly stealing food.

This process also becomes second nature as you orchestrate your own scenes. The screenwriter's job is to tilt the audience's head toward the most dynamic portion of each scene and let that portion jump into the next. Eventually, the story will become so clear that it demands the necessary information and refuses the rest for you.

TRY IT

Journaling your environment

This project may help jumpstart your newfound artistic sensibility.

Carry a notebook with you for the next few days, a small one not likely to attract attention. After you find a comfortable place to observe your surroundings, begin composing two lists. In the first list, include any visual details or images that you see. The list doesn't need to be in any particular order. Just record whatever your eye lands on as it moves across the space. In the second list, keep track of any and all sounds you hear around you. Depending on your location, you may be able to close your eyes. See how specific you can be, from the conversation behind you to the fans buzzing overhead. When you've done it in one location, try it in the next. Eventually, a pattern may emerge.

Want to take the project a step further? Select two details from each list and combine them in a new scenario. How may the images be connected? How can the sounds help set that relationship off? A small tape recorder can be useful for this project as well.

Recognizing a Story When You See One

If your curiosity's intact, many situations will command your attention. Sometimes, you may feel as though the more events you discover, the more ideas you have to investigate. By the time you're 15 years old, you probably have enough material to generate numerous screenplays. Yet only a few of those ideas will become stories that become scripts, and many will slip away.

Why is this the case? Often, just because a story interests you doesn't mean that it's film-worthy. It may only interest you for a few days, you may not have the experience to truly understand it, or it may generate an opening image and little else. Chasing every idea that comes your way is exhausting and often futile. Knowing how to recognize a story when it appears saves you time and ensures you a greater chance at cinematic success.

Identifying the call to write

Take a second and think about the stories you remember from your childhood. Recall the events that happened to you as well as those moments that someone else relayed. What is it about these moments that remains with you? Can you pinpoint why they may have lasted in your memory?

The call to write generally emerges after some stories have suggested themselves to you. If you've come to this book with an idea in mind — one that's been pestering you for a long time or one you'd feel ashamed to ignore — your idea probably has staying power. Simply phrased, that means that if you dedicate the time and energy to it, your story will get told.

If you've come to this book curious about the craft with a pocketful of ideas all equally compelling in some way, you may want to sit with them for a while until one calls to you louder than the rest. Take a second to look at the reasons you may be called to write:

- ✔ You write because you have something to say and only you can say it.
- ✔ You write to immortalize an event you've discovered or lived through.
- ✔ You write to immortalize an important human being.
- ✔ You write to better understand life or the human spirit.
- ✔ You write because an idea thrills you, and you want to share that thrill with other people.

The items on the list are purposefully grandiose in scale. You may also be called to write as an outlet, because it's a fun way to let off steam, so to speak. That kind of writing is important for your emotional well-being, but it won't necessarily elicit a palpable story. These reasons will.

You'll know that you've been called to write because the idea will plague you. Other stories may whisper to you and float away, but some will tug at your arm a while, growing stronger by the day. If you've been imagining people and locations for your tale, if scenes present themselves to you on a regular basis, the time's probably come to answer the call and start writing.

The four important P's of story

After you've selected one story to focus on (or after the story's selected you, as the case may be), you need to piece it together. A screenplay takes form as you begin envisioning the four basic components of storytelling:

- ✔ **People:** Who's in your story? Imagine everyone for now, from the waitress in the diner to the love interest; you can always trim the cast list down later.

- ✔ **Place:** Where does your story occur? Does it span a concentrated amount of time in one location, or do you envision jumping between numerous time frames and locales?

- ✔ **Picture:** What do you see when you think about the story? What images, colors, textures, movement, and so on? What does your story look like?

- ✔ **Plot:** What are your story's pivotal events? In its most basic sense, plot refers to what comes next. (I speak about plot in greater detail in Chapters 6, 7, and 8.)

If your idea is a strong one, envisioning these components won't be difficult. Sometimes, a story survives even if you only have one piece to the whole puzzle. But you need to see one piece fairly clearly for any type of script to evolve. Remember, you're just imagining the details now. You'll write them all out later, after lots of research and dream time.

Finding an opening image

The beginning of any story is magical. You may feel as if, after stumbling around in the dark, you come across one image from which anything is possible. If you've identified the four P's of your story, you'll have several sets of images to choose from:

- ✔ **Person:** If you start with a person, who is it, and what is he or she doing? *Monster's Ball* revolves around race relations and prejudice in the south. It begins by following a father and son who hate each other, but who hate black people more.

✔ **Place:** If you start with a location, where is it, and how does an audience discover it? Many movies that take place in a major city fly over the ocean before finally landing on the skyline in question. This technique keeps the audience guessing for a few moments before landing somewhere concrete.

✔ **Picture:** Perhaps another type of image begins your piece. The image of a smoking gun lying on the sidewalk certainly pulls an audience in and suggests a conflict that we've yet to discover.

✔ **Plot:** If your story centers around a few major events, beginning the story in the middle of one of them may be a good idea. The movie *Rookie* begins with a ball game in a run-down field decades earlier. That field later becomes an important baseball diamond for the entire town. The more active, the better with this technique. Tossing your audience into an action sequence is a great way to grab their attention.

If you know what you want to say, you'll know which image to begin with. After you've settled on one, you need to spur that image into action and, eventually, into a scene.

Crafting a scene from a single image

You've developed several clear images, and you'd like to construct something more. Here's a technique that I call the Great What If that may help you generate some more material, using what you already have.

The Great What If refers to a set of hypothetical situations that you layer on top of your chosen image that spur it into action. The What If could alter or enhance any portion of the image itself. The trick is to pay close attention to what happens *after* you pose the hypothetical.

For example, suppose that I settle on the image of a child playing jacks on his front porch. Here are some what-if scenarios that I may layer on:

✔ What if it's midnight, and he's been playing for days?

✔ What if the ball slips out of his hands and falls between the floorboards?

✔ What if someone interrupts the game by stepping on the jacks and kicking the ball off the porch?

✔ What if someone starts whispering in his ear?

✔ What if every bounce of the ball causes the earth to shake?

Each one of these hypothetical situations forces a change, thereby nudging the image into action. The possibilities for change are endless. You may come up with several opening moments for your script by utilizing this technique. Write them all down. Eventually, one moment will emerge victorious.

Chapter 4

Approaching Screenwriting as a Craft

1 begin writing workshops by posing the question, "Do you think that someone can teach you how to write?" Though most people attend workshops expecting to be taught something related to writing, the response to this question is nevertheless mixed. One theory, floating around for years, implies that artists are born, not made; and many people fear that they lack the natural abilities of a writer. This fear is often so great that it prevents them from putting pen to paper at all.

To this theory, I offer a resounding "Pshaw!" A skilled writer must possess three qualities: the desire to tell stories, the experience to round out those stories, and the stamina to see them through to completion. You may come into the world with these qualities or discover them later in life. Most new writers possess the desire and some experience, but few possess the endurance necessary to finish a work. They have a storyteller's imagination, but they lack a sense of craft. Without that sense, their stories remain ideas forever or meander around on the page until the writers give up. This chapter takes a closer look at natural talent and offers advice on how to further your own. It then outlines techniques designed to funnel that talent onto a page. In short, it's a chapter on screenwriting first as an art and then as a craft.

In a way, this chapter is about elusive words — words like *talent, imagination,* and *craft.* The essential ingredients for an artist all elude concrete definition. It seems only appropriate then that I begin with the most maddeningly intangible word of them all — *creativity.* In a way, the fact that creativity has no concrete definition is rather fitting. As soon as you concoct one, some creative individual will no doubt arrive to question its validity and suggest an alternative. So rather than try to define the indefinable, I just concentrate on what seems to be involved.

A Look at the Creative Process

At first glance, creativity involves problem solving — or, in other words, questioning validity and suggesting alternatives. I don't mean to imply, however, that creative people sit around waiting for problems to arise; they don't. Creative people are inherently curious. They pose questions that no one else has thought or dared to ask. In this way, creative people seek out problems *and* attempt solutions. Writers are no different. The most common problems that a writer faces are Which story do I tell? and How do I tell it?

In recent years, scientists and sociologists from all over the world have taken an interest in the process of creative problem solving. They believe that many people encounter the same five phenomena on the journey toward a solution. They have labeled these five stages as

- ✔ **First insight:** The stage in which an idea or a question suggests itself. This is the moment that a writer discovers a story or the seeds of one.

- ✔ **Saturation or the "input" stage:** The period of study or investigation that ensues. Any research a writer does — interviews, people-watching, reading, studying other films, daydreaming, and so on — falls under the category of saturation.

- ✔ **Incubation:** A period of reflection to process the new information. For a writer, this time generally involves working through the idea on a page, sharing the idea with friends, and good old-fashioned waiting for inspiration.

- ✔ **Illumination:** A moment of inspiration when a possible solution suggests itself. When writers talk about the muse, they really mean the moment of illumination.

- ✔ **The verification or evaluation stage:** The testing period, during which the individual, in this case the writer, determines whether his solution really works.

None of these stages has any set length of time, although most writers experience illumination as a brief, often unexpected flash. Some writers spend years researching a story; some only a few days. Some find inspiration right away, but for others, the incubation time is endless. In any case, though no two writers arrive at a story in the same way, they tend to share these five stages. So the next time you're tearing out your hair because a story eludes you, never fear. It's part of the process.

Imagination: Your Creative Arsenal

Aspiring and established artists alike often spend years fretting over the notion of talent. Chiefly, what is it, and do they possess it? My general reply to writers who inquire, "Do I have talent?" is, "I don't know. Tell me a story."

Without definition, the notion of talent is so grandiose that it seems to belong in a mystical realm of its own. Talent is something you're born with. Talent means that you're skilled in some area. Talent allows certain blessed individuals to channel words onto the page while others nearly go crazy waiting for inspiration. All these statements are true. They're also vague and of little help to writers struggling to better their dramatic abilities. Yet, substitute the word *imagination* for talent, and the question of whether you possess it may become clear. You probably do.

Writing talent is generally a mixture of life experience and the ability to imagine beyond it. You have, in however many years, constructed a creative arsenal comprised of the following:

- Anecdotes
- Beliefs
- Dreams
- Emotions
- Fears
- Images
- Legends
- Opinions
- Memories
- Questions

This arsenal is, in a sense, your talent pool. It informs your choices as a human being and a writer, and it can't be taught. Your ability to access that arsenal and convert it into stories, however, is an acquired skill that begins with the writer's strongest muscle: the imagination. When flexed on a regular basis — through artistic exercise and constant writing practice — the imagination will generate material for you. Your best bet is to prepare that muscle now.

Flexing the imagination

Separating talent from craft is important. Talent is something you have, and craft is something you garner. Each element is controlled by a different mode of thought. For a better explanation, take a look at Table 4-1. It illustrates how each mode looks at the world.

Table 4-1	Talent versus Craft
Talent Notices	*Craft Records*
Interesting conversations	Specific words and phrases that make the conversations unique
Dynamic stories	Potential beginnings, middles, and ends
Compelling people	Details of personality and appearance that make that person stand out
Inspirational environments	The color, scope, light, and textural components of those environments
Grand emotions	Situations leading to and away from those emotions; words and actions that reveal them
Eye-catching images	The physical construction of images, possible scenarios surrounding them, and metaphors associated with them

Notice a pattern? Talent, or imagination, selects the material while craft searches for ways to translate it onto the page. Your first job as a writer, then, is to surround the imagination with as many options as possible. The more you learn and the more you see and hear, the more ideas you have to choose from later on. Here are a few simple, inexpensive ways to begin flexing the imagination:

- Attempt a crossword puzzle.
- Cook a meal for at least four guests.
- Do something that scares you.
- Exercise (any physical activity will do).
- Frequent public spaces.
- Listen to music.
- Look through scrapbooks.
- Read and/or watch the news.
- Read, read, read.
- Rewrite an age-old story.

- Take up photography.
- Travel someplace new.
- Visit a museum.
- Write a letter to someone you know.
- Write a letter to someone you don't know.
- Write a letter you wish someone would send to you.

Your goals when flexing the imagination are simple: Stimulate the senses, learn as much as you can, and document what you find.

This part of the writing process should be fun. If nothing on this list interests you, find something equally stimulating that does.

Putting the imagination to work

The imagination's first official job is to hunt for a story. And because the imagination can only hunt in fields that the artist has explored, a writer should strive to be "multitentacled," as John Logan of *Gladiator* fame puts it. This means having a hand in as many pockets of knowledge as possible. You never know where a story resides.

First off, make a list — mental or actual — of areas you know little about. Try to record at least three people or events from any or all of the following categories that you want to investigate:

- Athletes and athletics
- Current events
- Economics
- Education and social reform
- Environmental and agricultural concerns
- Historical eras and/or events
- Legends and myths
- Other artists
- Other cultures
- Politics past and present
- Religion and faith
- Science and/or scientific discoveries

The list isn't meant to overwhelm you, though it may, or to make you feel ignorant in any one area. Its purpose is to challenge you to search beyond what you already know. Researching any one of these fields grants a writer unending possibilities, it broadens his talent pool, and it forces the imagination to question, What if? What if you wrote about the Berlin wall? What if you set your story in England after the plague? Which angle would you take? Which story would you choose? Remember that everything you learn informs your work.

If an idea still eludes you, consider the following four arenas. Most stories spring from one of these sources:

- ✔ **Current events:** Glance through the paper, listen to public radio, or watch the evening news. You find yourself besieged with story possibilities. Seek out unlikely sources as well. The obituaries and the classified ads suggest both quirky characters and lives worth celebrating. The controversial film *Munich* was clearly based on the Munich Massacre. *The Pursuit of Happyness* is based on the real life story of Chris Gardner, who went from being homeless to running his own brokerage firm.

- ✔ **Fiction:** These stories emerge almost entirely from the writer's imagination. They may materialize as original human adventures like *All About Eve* or *The Royal Tenenbaums,* or they may take on some new world altogether as in *Star Wars, Star Trek,* and *Lord of the Rings.* In this type of film, the characters and structures in place may be loosely based on the human experience, but details of location and culture remain unique.

- ✔ **Historical accounts:** History provides some of the most compelling stories. The events are generally documented in some form and may suggest characters and pivotal events right away. A quick glance through articles, criticism, personal letters, journal entries, literature, and art of the time may also suggest language and images that will be crucial to your piece. Such movies as *Gone with the Wind, Braveheart, Apollo 13, Gladiator,* and many others capitalize on historical sources.

- ✔ **Personal experience:** Here's where the old adage "Write what you know" comes in. Situations that you've lived through or that have been handed down to you are often easy to envision and already hold personal meaning. The characters, usually based on people you have an intimate knowledge of, tend to emerge quickly as well. The challenge is to extend the event's significance beyond your own experience and create characters that differ from the real people. *Erin Brockovich* is based on one woman's life, as are the *Bridget Jones* films. Neil Simon and Woody Allen are also notorious for writing comedies based on their lives.

Fictional stories require a writer to concoct the details from scratch and, therefore, require a slightly different approach. I refer to original plot development in Chapters 6, 7, and 8. The other three sources, though — historical accounts, current events, and personal experience — involve actual happenings, so your approach to those stories may be similar. Start by asking the following questions:

✔ **What exactly do I know about the account?** Record as many details as you can recall. Where did it take place, and during what period of time? How did it start and end? Who was directly involved and/or affected? What is your sense of the account — was it funny, tragic, foreboding, awe-inspiring, intimate, or epic? The more you can record now, the easier it will be to assess what kind of research or dream work you'll need to do later on.

✔ **How reliable are my sources?** Historical documentation is often recorded from a point of view. The plantation owner's account of slavery, for example, would be far different from that of a slave. Family stories are similar in this regard. Most people only remember events as they were personally affected by them. Finally, these days the media often choose sensation over strict fact when composing a report. Check your sources and check their particular bias. If you can only locate one side to the story, imagine another.

✔ **What don't I know?** Even after extensive research, your story will undoubtedly have holes. Consider this dilemma to your advantage as you can dream up some action to fill those gaps. The most compelling scripts often emerge from events you know little about. Why? Because unanswered questions are the heart of drama. They create mystery, and they demand that the writer dream up some answers.

✔ **What interests me most about the event?** The answer to this question will keep you writing long after the novelty of the idea has worn off. Often, the most intriguing portions of an idea are those that you know the least about or those that elicit some strong emotion — fear, confusion, anger, awe, and so on. This is your angle on the story, and it's what makes it unique.

✔ **What interests me least?** This question will help you edit or pare down your script. Taking on an entire event is difficult, and doing so often weakens the effect of any one storyline. *The Queen,* for example, follows Queen Elizabeth II's life at the time surrounding Princess Diana's death. It does not tackle her childhood, her early years or much after the funeral; that would be an impossible film to sit through. After you know what details interest you least, imagine how the story shifts without them.

Creating a script based on real events is a common but nonetheless challenging process. A precarious balance exists between preserving the essence of a situation and crafting an original version of the story. You want to maintain the integrity of a historical moment while raising it above the facts and into the heightened realm of drama. The artist's right to dramatize and shape real events around a specific purpose is known as *artistic license.* When employing artistic license, you're using real events as a blueprint for a largely fictional work.

When tackling real events, you should consider the following at all times:

✔ Your emotional distance from the event

✔ Your personal judgment of the proceedings

A strong, emotional involvement with a subject may enhance or destroy your script. It often impairs a writer's clarity and the clarity of the final product. Here's the test: Can you imagine changing key elements of these people — their opinions, their fates, their genders — if necessary? If you can't imagine changing them, don't write them yet. You should be able to see the people in your script as characters that you can alter to fit your ultimate design. Also, don't judge the characters in advance, or you unwittingly delegate an audience to the role of passive observer rather than active participant. In other words, don't create good or evil characters; create human beings that perform good or evil actions. Let audiences judge for themselves.

Identifying your writing voice

The term *writing voice* is often used interchangeably with the word *style,* yet they differ in one small regard. Your writing voice determines what catches your attention and what you want to communicate. Style refers to the techniques and language you choose to communicate with. Your voice stems from imagination; style stems from knowledge of craft.

You already possess an artistic voice. It's the result of your life experiences thus far, and it will alter as you experience more. Unsure of what that voice sounds like? Try answering the following questions. The answers may suggest your unique way of viewing the world.

✔ What subjects are you drawn to and why?

✔ What kind of stories do you pursue? Comic or tragic? Supernatural? Realistic or surreal? Romantic?

✔ What is the scope of the stories you're drawn to? Intimate, epic, familial?

✔ How do your stories reveal themselves? Through character, dialogue, image, or an equal mixture of the three?

✔ What kind of language do you use when expressing yourself? Poetic, terse, lengthy, mysterious?

✔ How do you move from one image to the next? Chronologically or out of sequence? Quickly or in slow motion? Do images blend together or cut back and forth?

✔ What patterns, if any, exist in your previous works? Consider works of any kind; don't limit yourself to writing works.

Every writer experiences and expresses a subject in a unique way. The result? Many different films about roughly the same subject. Consider this scenario: A woman is sitting at a window table in a coffee shop. She's reading a book and drinking espresso. She twirls a pen in her right hand between sips and occasionally glances up to scan the street before retreating back to her book.

Hand this image to three screenwriters, and you'll end up with three diverse scenes. One writer begins with the image of the hand twirling the pen and then slowly moves up the arm to the eyes staring out at the street. Another writer pays close attention to the book itself, zipping from the blue cover to the title to the first page, keeping the woman's face in shadow. The third writer reveals the whole scene at once, allowing the audience to guess the situation. All approaches stem from one image, yet they differ in several distinct ways:

- ✔ The order in which details are revealed
- ✔ Color
- ✔ Texture
- ✔ Light and shadow
- ✔ Pace between details
- ✔ The proximity to the subject

While I caution the writer against adding camera directions to your work, you should certainly think like a camera in scripting your images. Images are the initial components of style, and it doesn't hurt to begin tracing them through your own story ideas now. How would you have revealed this image? A note of caution, though: Voice and style are not something to lose sleep over. If you continue to test your imagination, if you continue to read and reflect and question, they'll take care of themselves.

TRY IT

The imagination project

I find newspaper headlines useful in many ways — from story suggestions, to plot twists, to revision work. They're also grand for strengthening the imagination.

I list five unrelated headlines below. Choose the one that catches your attention first. Don't think too hard in making your decision; the first choice is usually the instinctual favorite and the place to start. After you've settled on a headline, let your imagination twist it into one solid image. Who or what is in the image, where are they, and what might be going on?

- ✔ "A Pardon For Walter Burnett"
- ✔ "Dinosaurs Flock To The Field"

- ✔ "Ice Cream Social Gets the Cold Shoulder"
- ✔ "Ten Saved, Three Still Out There"
- ✔ "Diamonds Missing From Local Ballpark"

Created an image? Great. Now imagine an audience in a darkened theater. You're about to show them this image. How will you do it? Concoct at least three versions of this moment, bearing in mind the elements of style: color, texture, the order of details and the pace between them, light and shadows, and the proximity to the subject. Record each version and compare. Which one do you like best? Though predominantly a project for your imagination, you may also discover something about your writing voice in the process.

Craft: A Vehicle for Your Imagination

After you've defined talent and discovered how to access it, the more difficult work can now begin.

As I suggest in the "Imagination: Your Creative Arsenal" section, earlier in this chapter, there is a difference between a talented individual and a writer. That difference is known as *craft*. Craft acts as a shuttle between the idea and the finished screenplay; it's how you get from one part of the process to the other. I may harbor many imaginative ideas on how to build the perfect car, but I wouldn't try until I'd taken Automotives 101. The same is true of writing. Ideas do not a screenplay make. You need a sense of craft.

So what is craft exactly? Or rather, what does it involve? On a general level, it can be broken down into three elements: *form, technique,* and *discipline*.

Form

Form refers first to the dramatic structure of the work you're creating. Films generally require a clear beginning, middle, and end — though they're not always revealed in that order. ***Eternal Sunshine of the Spotless Mind,*** for example, bounces between past and present, as the characters' memories are slowly erased. The three parts of the story still exist in this film; they just exist in a different order.

Form also refers to the script's technical format. Novels exist in chapters or lengthy portions separated by jumps in time or narrator. Plays exist in scenes or vignettes arranged in a particular way on the page. Screenplays are generally divided into three acts with particular attention to font type, page layout, and length. Having a concrete knowledge of both dramatic structure and screenwriting format is important. While your formatting should remain consistent, you may eventually stray from traditional story structure. However, learn the basics first. They tend to work. I talk more about both parts of form in Part II.

Technique

Even without a definition for craft, you probably know a well-crafted film when you see one. In such scripts, the writer demonstrates an ease with any or all of the following elements:

- Action
- Character depiction and growth

✔ Choice of location

✔ Conflict

✔ Description

✔ Dialogue

✔ The manipulation of theme

✔ The use of time

Technique refers to the "how" of all these elements. There are as many ways to reveal any one of them as there are types of films. For example, if your story's main event involves a murder in high society, will you underplay its effects in favor of character development à la *Gosford Park?* Will you use it to generate the comic mockumentary style of a film like *Waiting for Guffman?* Or will you write another *Illusionist* and spend your time discovering how magic will help your protagonist and his love escape the Empire that entraps them?

How you tell your story is infinitely more important than what's being told. In the hands of a less skilled writer, the quiet family drama *You Can Count On Me* would hold little impact. As it stands, the characters' ordinary dreams are portrayed in such extraordinary ways that the story feels as important as any epic. It's all in how a writer conveys information. I detail each of the listed story elements individually in Chapters 6 through 10.

However, I should detail three elements of technique now. They are the foundations of clear writing — dramatic and otherwise — and they affect all elements of a story. They are

✔ Vocabulary

✔ Grammar

✔ Organization

Consider these items your assets, your big guns, so to speak. Strive to master each, if for no other reason than that they help you control your stories. Have a clear idea but no clear thought on how to express it? A knowledge of these three items can help.

Vocabulary

As a writer, a limited vocabulary thwarts your ability to travel. Think about it. Want to travel to Britain for your film about the bourgeoisie? How will you craft the characters without a sense of language? If a lord opens his mouth in the first scene and says, "Hey guys, like, what's going on?" you're sunk. Look at verbal masters like Spike Lee. He realistically conveys multiple ethnicities and educational backgrounds through the vocabularies of his main characters alone.

It never hurts to have a running list of writers and the words they brandish. I encourage you to sift through writers of all types when compiling your own collection. If you're looking for words with a poetic lilt and a Southern bent, Tennessee Williams is your man. Want your language terse and intense? Looking for socially minded vulgarity? Read David Mamet. And for one- and two-syllable words that resound together with ten times their individual worth, read Robert Frost. This list acts as a reference guide should you need a quick lesson in one vocabulary or another. That way, if you do write a film on the British bourgeois society, you'll know to read Charles Dickens.

Learn to love words — words like baggage, scrumptious, contrivance, wicked, daft, okey-doke, crackers, keen, wily, and winsome, to name a few of my favorites. Each one packs a different wallop (another great word). Respect their differences, respect what they do, and accrue as many as you can. You should always have a dictionary and a thesaurus nearby, either in book or Internet form. The more you know, the more places you can go.

Grammar

Ah, the dreaded grammar. For many people, it conjures up visions of high school, pop quizzes, and extended hours in front of a chalkboard. If this image is what you see, don't worry. Does it help to have a comprehensive understanding of our language and its structure? Yes. Should you bolster your grammatical skill? Probably. Can you write scripts even if you scraped through high school English? Yes. You just need to know the basics. Because books on grammar abound, I offer you a few beginning tips:

- **Differentiate between character voice and scenic description:** Few people speak in grammatically correct English, and it's a good thing. You'd be bored to tears if they did. Your characters will speak in different ways, with different grammatical structures. Write them as you hear them; don't get hung up on grammar. You are, however, also responsible for description — of location, of character, and of action. You want that portion of your script to be clear, efficient, and effective. Description is where the grammar lessons come in handy.

- **Be consistent with sentence structure:** Do you need to write in complete sentences? No. You should, however, at least know how to construct a complete sentence, which requires a knowledge of nouns and verbs, and you should be consistent with whatever sentence structure you choose. If your description begins in phrases, stick with phrases: "Enter Allen. Goes to door. Checks outside. Closes it again and hurries upstairs." If you prefer full sentences, "Allen enters the room. He goes to the door and checks outside. Satisfied, he hurries upstairs," and then maintain this choice throughout.

- **Avoid the royal "we":** Many writers use the royal "we" in description, alerting the reader to certain details in the scene. For example, "Sam enters. We see that he's concealing something under his jacket." I usually caution against relying on this technique too frequently. Drawing attention to the reader distances him or her from the story; your screenplay suddenly becomes a script with an audience and not a world of its own. Also, if you simply write what happens as it happens, the reader will see it. You might write "Sam enters. He is concealing something under his jacket." I see it, you needn't tell me that I do. Reserve the royal "we" for details in the scene meant only for the audience and the camera. If in the middle of a party, for example, the image of a car appears out the window, you might say, "In the window, we see a car approach." We see it; the characters don't.

✔ **Eliminate excessive adjectives and adverbs:** The resounding rule here is when in doubt, cut them out. You can't avoid all descriptive words, if the wallpaper is stained and peeling, you should tell me that. However, the addition of a few lines of dialogue often alleviates the need for adjectives. You don't need to tell me the mountains are beautiful if a character says, "They're more beautiful than I'd imagined." If the day is hot, let it affect the characters in scene. Discovering a detail is much more effective than being handed one. You can exchange most adverbs for a strategically chosen verb. Why not replace "She walks quietly upstairs" with "She tiptoes upstairs"? Or "The castle is heavily guarded" with "Hundreds of soldiers guard the castle"? Verbs are powerful words. Trust them. Let them work for you.

✔ **Avoid passive voice:** Your high school teacher and I may share one thing in common — our opinion of passive voice. It probably irritated her, and it irritates me. Active voice means that the subject of the sentence does something, as in "Molly washed the car," "Harold sweeps the floor," "Margaret plays the piano." Passive voice means that something is done to the subject of your sentence: "The car was washed by Molly," "The floor is swept by Harold," "The piano is played by Margaret." Feel the difference? The first sentences are accessible; they have energy and life. Passive voice tempers that energy, making the sentences safe. Screenplays are about action, so write them with active strokes.

As with all rules, after you've mastered the basics, you can branch past them should the need arise. The preceding rules are intended as guides toward more effective writing. What you do after you absorb them is up to you.

Organization

If art is in the details, the writer's voice is most often in the organization of details. Organization asks two questions:

✔ What do I want to reveal?

✔ How do I want to reveal it?"

It asks these questions of every portion of the screenplay, from the overall plot structure to the dialogue in-scene to every sentence of description. You're writing for an audience; you want to lead them somewhere. Strong organization clarifies what information that audience receives first, toward the middle, and what the writer's saving for last.

If a woman is reading in a cafe, do you want my eyes to travel from her hands to the book she's reading then to her face? If so, your first line of description may read: "Manicured fingers wrap around a book. It's a copy of *War and Peace*. The reader turns a page, and the book tilts for a second, revealing a brunette of startling beauty." If she turns her head to reveal a scar on her cheek, even better.

Now, there's a reason for organizing your sentence in this way. Want an example of organization at its best? The opening sequence of **The Big Chill** jumps between various people receiving bad news and clips of one man getting dressed. In the final shot, the man's sleeves are cuff-linked. Both his wrists have been cut and stitched over. In this way, the writer waits until the last moment to reveal that the man being dressed is dead. Your organization is important. It tells a reader, a director, the camera, and, therefore, an audience how to watch your film.

Discipline

Imagine that you're the high-powered CEO of company, or that you own and run a small business. Imagine, for that matter, that you're a butcher, a baker, or a candlestick maker. It wouldn't occur to you not to show up to work one day. People are counting on you, there's money to be made, and the job requires your presence. Now, imagine that you're a screenwriter. It shouldn't occur to you not to show up to work. The same principles apply.

Discipline is what separates a writer from someone who likes to write. It may be the most important element of craft. Why? You can find hundreds of reasons *not* to write: You have children to look after; you have meetings to attend; you travel constantly; you have phone calls to make or errands to run or letters to mail; basically, you just have no time. I'll tell you something: None of that is going to change. If you're a writer, you have to find time to write.

If you want to churn out a 120-page script, if you want to churn out more than one, you have to consider writing your job. I repeat: It's not a luxury, it's your job. Maybe it's your second or third job, but it's a job nonetheless. Procrastination is what separates would-be writers from actual writers. So first things first — you need a place to work, and you need a working schedule.

Creating your workspace

In theory, a writer requires only two things of a workspace: It should be yours, and it should have a door that closes. In order to concoct cinematic worlds on the page, you need to shut out the one outside. That said, you need a few other accoutrements as well. The following lists outline both necessities and possible additions to any writer's office.

You will need

- ✔ A computer and a working printer with easy Internet access
- ✔ Extra ink cartridges and printing paper
- ✔ Pads of paper
- ✔ A stash of pens and pencils
- ✔ 1½-inch to 2-inch brass brads for binding
- ✔ A three-hole puncher
- ✔ A quality dictionary and thesaurus (online or otherwise)
- ✔ A hard drive to back up your writing files

You may need

- ✔ A bulletin board for images and other research
- ✔ Index cards for arranging scenes
- ✔ A CD player nearby (some writers require music)
- ✔ A timer for timed writing projects

You also won't need certain items in a writing space. Televisions, telephones, and video games all hinder writers from completing a project in peace. If you must have a telephone in the space, make sure that you can turn it off or unplug it as necessary. Be cautious with e-mail. You may need e-mail for your work, but it may also prove a distraction. Seek privacy at all costs. After all, this is your job we're talking about.

Managing your time wisely

The most prolific writers write habitually. They punch in every day, and they get the job done. Or perhaps I should say, they get the job done *because* they punch in every day. Think about it. Of the numerous things you do with your life, which of them are routine? Brushing your teeth, walking the dog, going to business lunches, exercising, carpooling, making phone calls and, oh yes, writing. If you want to make it into that workspace every day, writing has to be part of that routine.

Think that's impossible? Think again. Try revising your schedule with the following rules in mind:

- ✔ **Prioritize the time.** Your writing time has to be as important, if not more important, than all the other things you have to do during the day. Alert your friends and family of your schedule to avoid unnecessary interruptions. Place it high on your list of priorities.

✔ **Plan ahead.** Don't wait to see how much time each day allows you; plan your work time in advance. Set up a weekly schedule, if not a monthly routine. A schedule is important. Chisel out the time.

✔ **Show up.** The muse is just another word for the imagination, which, if you remember, is a muscle. If you tell yourself that you're going to write, that muscle prepares to do so. If you don't show up, you confuse that muscle and therefore the process, and it will be that much harder to write the next time.

People often ask me, "Do I have to write at the same time every day?" Ideally, yes, because it makes the process easier. If you write at the same time every day, your mind eventually shifts into writing mode at that time. You find yourself prepared to write before you even sit down. However, schedules these days are fierce and often don't permit continuity. If this is the case, choose another scheduling goal. Do you have a few hours? Promise yourself that you'll write for two hours regardless of when they occur. Setting a page requirement is another option. Promise yourself five to ten pages a day and fill those pages when you can. It may take some doing, but with these tips in mind, you'll be off and running, or should I say, and *writing*. Of course, you should also write when the muse appears, whether she's on schedule or not!

Part II
Breaking Down the Elements of a Story

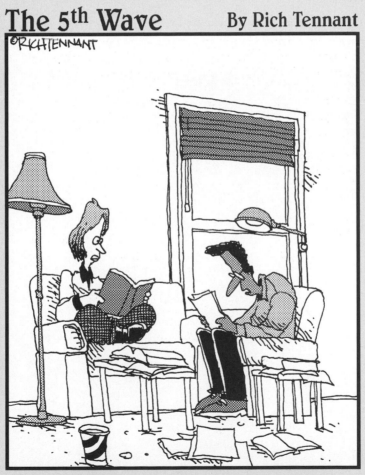

"I'd like to become a screenwriter.
I'm just not sure I have that much
dialogue in me."

In this part . . .

An idea does not a story make (not necessarily anyway). But a strong story might result in a solid first draft, so this part is dedicated to developing a story strong enough to transfer painlessly onto the page. Where does the story start? Who's involved? What's the conflict, and why do we care? These are a few of the questions facing every writer with a premise. The following chapters provide examples, techniques, and projects to guide you toward some answers.

Chapter 5

Unpacking Your Idea

So, you have an idea for a screenplay. It interests you; you've mentioned it to your friends, and it interests them. You're convinced that it may even interest people other than your coworkers and immediate family. Fantastic — now what?

An idea is just a glimpse at the whole story. Your imagination sparks, and for a moment, an entire chain of events presents itself. Unfortunately, unless you have a sense of how to pin those thoughts to a page, they may disappear again. Your next step involves fanning that initial spark into a flame and then into a fire. Thus, an idea becomes a story; a story becomes a script.

I Have This Great Idea. Now What?

Can you identify which part of your idea excites you most? Do you know why it may excite someone else? Any idea of what type of script you have and what keeps the action moving forward? These next few paragraphs highlight what steps the screenwriter must take before beginning the writing process.

Pinpointing your interest in the idea

Before you tackle writing an entire draft, think about why and how you discovered the idea in the first place.

Picture it: You're enjoying a night on the town with friends when suddenly, an attractive somebody catches your eye. Your heart skips a beat, and your mind begins to race; in other words, you're hooked. You must get to know this unique somebody new.

Freeze. Before pursuing this mysterious stranger, ask yourself two questions: Why this person, and why now?

What attracts us to another individual is generally clear: his blue eyes, her contagious laugh, the way he tilts his head when he smiles. The journey toward a story isn't so dissimilar from the scenario just depicted. You'll be excited by your first idea. Your heart may race; your breath may catch; you may want to run out and alert the media. Flirting with an idea is a wonderful feeling, but it's also temporary. Just like forging a relationship, completing an entire script takes effort and determination — not to mention hours of time spent at a computer or notepad. You're about to commit yourself to that effort, so pinpoint *why* your idea's great while it's still fresh in your mind.

While trying to locate your interest in the idea, ask yourself these questions: Was my idea sparked by

- ✔ **An event?** If an event sparked your idea, how did you discover it? Was it an article that you read in a newspaper, a story relayed to you by friends, or did you witness the incident firsthand? Recreating the scene helps keep your initial excitement alive. Also, be as specific as you can in what you remember. For example, you're at a football game when it starts to snow. The crowd begins to leave, but you notice one fan in the front row cheering the team on despite those walking past him. This incident alone may spark an idea for a story, but look carefully. Is it that general image you're intrigued by, or the fact that he cheers louder the harder it snows, or is it the way he refuses to take his eyes off the field? Isolating the details may provide information that you'll need later.

- ✔ **A person?** If a person caught your eye, your imagination may be creating a character. Try to recall the person in question. If you read about her in a book, you may be able to find out more through historical research. If it's someone you know, you may be able to watch her more closely, interview her perhaps. If it's someone you glimpsed in passing — a woman feeding pigeons on the Cathedral steps, for example — you'll need to think carefully about why that person grabbed your attention. Was it her physical appearance —how her hair matched the matted feathers of the birds? Her vocal tone in calling them to her? Or was it something that she did? Eventually, you'll be creating characters for your own script, so practice recreating the people you observe now.

- ✔ **A conversation?** Sometimes, you can grab an idea from something you overhear. Whether you're eavesdropping or debating a point with a friend, conversation sparks very vivid images. Why? Generally, the conversations that I remember are those told with great conviction. They're already interesting, which alleviates the need for me to make them so. Also, it's easy to get a sense of people by what they choose to say and how they say it. An overheard conversation may well become a scene in your script or suggest several characters, so try to remember what you heard and how it was said. (I detail more exact ways to document those pieces of information in the next section.)

✔ **An image or location?** You may find yourself inspired by an isolated image or an environment. Again, ask yourself what specifically draws your attention here. David Mamet's play (later a film) ***Glengarry Glen Ross*** was inspired by time spent in a real estate office. The details of that location — the fluorescent lights, the peeling wallpaper, the cigarette stains on the chairs — all informed the final product. Memorize the details of your image, from the placement of objects to the sounds and smells of a locale. They may color your eventual story.

✔ **Another art source?** Perhaps other artistic mediums provoke you: photographs, paintings, literature, other plays, or films. Scan each selection you find. What fascinates you about it? The use of shadow, the texture of paint, a fleeting moment with a character? Your work may begin where another artist's ends. The Oscar-winning script ***Shakespeare in Love*** was the result of a number of Shakespeare's plays and several imaginative writers.

Documenting your interest in the idea

After you've narrowed down the origins of your idea, document them in some way. You're not unlike a detective in this sense; you've found clues to your story, so you'll want to refer to them later on. Here are a few suggestions on how to document your idea:

✔ **Write it down.** The sooner you capture the moment, the more details you'll recall later. Write down everything that occurs to you — the time of day, where you were (or are, if you're that fast), what you noticed first, and so on. If you're an artist, sketch the image if you like. Memories tend to fade, so keep a notepad with you at all times (especially in the car and by your bed) and write quickly.

✔ **Record it.** If you're lucky enough to have a video camera or a tape recorder when an idea hits you, by all means, use it. Obviously, you don't want to invade another person's privacy, but if you're privy to an interesting conversation, it's always better to capture it firsthand. Some people carry a small tape recorder around with them so that, should something strike them as funny or appropriate to the piece they're writing, they simply record it and write it down later. It's also safer to take notes this way while driving.

✔ **Take a picture.** Having a camera ready is never a bad idea. Your cell phone (if it has a camera) works well for this activity, too. Like scribbling in your notebook, snapping photographs of what catches your attention may become second nature. Because photography is a visual medium, it may also help you to see the world as a filmmaker might.

✔ **Acquire the source.** Pocketing part of the moment may also help jog your memory. For example, if you're out walking and you notice a ring lying on the sidewalk, let your imagination go. Thousands of stories may come to mind: a lover's quarrel, a lost family heirloom, and an attempted proposal to name a few. You might keep the ring to remind you of those story ideas later on.

When you've become adept at pinpointing where your idea began and documenting the source, you may notice a pattern in the subjects you're drawn to. People may interest you; locations may not. Sounds may capture your attention. Perhaps you find yourself collecting paintings of children, workmen, or landscapes. That pattern may suggest where your strengths lie as a writer or what kind of stories you're drawn to right now. For the time being, be diligent and remember that knowing what drew you to your story in the first place will keep you writing long after the initial excitement over the idea wears off.

Getting to Know Your Audience

Screenwriters write for an audience. Sometimes, that audience is small and defined; sometimes, it's a general age group; sometimes, it's your Aunt Betty or people like her. Whoever it may be, that audience and your awareness of it keeps your writing clear, efficient, and honest. Writing is a form of communication, so it's important to determine who you're talking to and why they might want to listen.

TRY IT

Extending an idea into a story possibility

If you're interested, this project motivates your imagination and generates story options. Find something or someone to observe. When you notice a change in the behavior, in the environment, or in the image, come up with three possible reasons for the change to have occurred.

For example: You observe a girl on a park bench. Periodically, she pulls her hair in front of her face, as if hiding. Here are three possible reasons she does that:

✔ She's concealing a scar she received as a child.

✔ She's avoiding an old flame who just walked into the park.

✔ Her behavior is a secret sign between her and another person in the park.

Those are just three possible motivations that may lead to a story idea. Now, you try it.

Matching the story to the audience

Even if your goal is to write a script that delights audiences of all types and ages, you may want to consider who it will realistically reach. If your story involves violence, it probably isn't for children. Similarly, certain kinds of audiences are statistically proven to frequent certain films. It may be advantageous to know who you'll probably sell the most tickets to when it comes time for your movie to be released.

The following sections cover some questions to ask yourself when identifying your audience.

What do you like about your story?

Generally speaking, if you're excited about an event you've witnessed, someone else will share your enthusiasm. The more passionately you can recount that event, the larger your audience will be. I know very little about the stock market, but the whirlwind energy of the trading-room floor makes me wish that I did. The movie **Wall Street** transformed that energy into a box-office hit.

Using the information you've collected on your story so far, clearly define three things that you love about your idea. I call them "those three things." Those three things keep cropping up when you talk about your idea and never fail to re-ignite your enthusiasm. Does your story take place in Italy, a location that enchants you? Is your main character a brooding young man with a secret profession? It may be something as vast as the landscape or as minute as the image of children running across a beach — if it excites you, write it down. You will return to those three things later for inspiration, scene ideas, and tone. They will also help define your audience.

Who shares your taste?

The quickest way to discover your audience may be through a quick scan of your social circles. Who among them holds similar views on entertainment, politics, or personal relationships? Who might share your interest in those three exciting things that you've discovered in your idea? The people you identify and people like them will undoubtedly make up a large portion of your audience. If those people vary in age, gender, and social makeup, your story may have a universal or mass appeal. If they all resemble you in form as well as opinion, you may be writing for a target audience.

A *target audience* is a film industry's best guess as to who might spend money to see your film. This statistic is generally compiled through surveys and test audiences, and by comparing your script to others of similar subject or genre. Remember that films are marketed in a variety of ways. The audience you attract determines that marketing approach.

The pros and cons of focusing on audience

Locating your target audience may help clarify your story, but it may also hinder your creative freedom. The following two lists suggest possible arguments in each direction.

Pros:

Your target audience may help you market your script. Think of audiences as customers. If you know who your customers are, you may know how to reach them when it's time to sell your product. If children are your target audience, you may advertise during Saturday morning cartoons; if avid sports fans are your target audience, you'll advertise during the Super Bowl.

Your target audience may suggest research possibilities. Target audiences enjoy similar things. If you know what they like to see, you'll know where to look for existing inspiration. If children are your target audience, you'll have an assortment of literature, cartoons, films, video games, and reference books to research while gathering ideas for your own script.

Your target audience may help answer questions on tone, conversation, and subject matter. You're bound to find a handful of films out there that resemble yours in some way. Watching them may provide examples and inspiration on how to approach writing yours.

Cons:

Your target audience may distract you from your original story. Investigating stories similar to yours, cinematic or otherwise, may be detrimental to your storytelling. You may doubt the power of your story in comparison to others. You may also find other writers influencing what you come up with.

Your target audience may cause you to stereotype your characters. Discovering what types of people target audiences are drawn to isn't difficult. If you become too eager to please an audience, you may fall back on writing stereotypes and clichés instead of people.

Your target audience may affect the depth of your dialogue. Target audiences see similar films, and similar films often sound alike. In trying to please your audience, your choice of language may lose its unique edge by catering to what they're used to hearing.

Bear in mind that films with the same audience as yours may be radically different in story and not at all threatening to your process. You may see your story so clearly that researching someone else's film couldn't possibly alter it, or you may think it best to write this first draft without distraction. In any case, the main difference between your script and everyone else's is that *you* are writing it, and eventually, *you* will decide how much an audience will affect your writing choices.

Who might your target audience be?

Identifying your target audience is really a matter of understanding what kind of people like your kind of film. Take a look at this list for some ways that you might approach finding out:

- ✔ **Compare your idea to existing stories.** It's never a bad idea to know what films are similar to yours in subject and what kind of interest they generated. If you're writing a story about a man-eating crocodile, you may find it helpful to know who liked the movie *Jaws.*

> ✔ **Know which category of film your idea fits into.** Take a walk through your local video store and jot down the categories around you. Assuming that your story becomes a movie, which becomes a DVD, would it eventually be shelved under Comedy or Romantic Comedy? Drama or Suspense? Adventure or Sci-Fi? Those categories come equipped with their own audiences.

> ✔ **Pitch your idea to different types of people and record their response.** Mention your idea to people you don't know very well, and a pattern may emerge in their responses. If the same type of people — all women, all teenagers, all children — respond in a positive way, they may be your target audience.

A *pitch* is a brief summation of your movie concept that emphasizes its exciting and novel qualities. Pitching an idea isn't unlike selling a product; it requires a dynamic presentation and a solid knowledge of your story's strong points, such as its tone, genre, and what existing films it resembles. It may also include what actors you envision for the roles and who your audience will be. I discuss the pitch in greater detail in Chapter 20.

Connecting with your audience

Certain story elements are almost always appealing to large audiences, and many of them date back thousands of years. Here are some surefire ways to connect with an audience. See whether they exist in your own idea.

Passion

People go to the movies to see life painted in bold strokes. I don't go to a movie to see stories that are less interesting than my own; I go to lose myself in worlds of greater adventure, comedy, and truth than my own. In other words, I'm after passion. Look at the following list of universal passions and see whether they exist in your story idea:

> ✔ Love

> ✔ Hatred

> ✔ Joy

> ✔ Hope

> ✔ Greed

> ✔ Envy

> ✔ Awe

> ✔ Fear

> ✔ Betrayal

    ✔ Revenge

    ✔ Triumph

Other passions exist, but many of them fit into one of the preceding categories. Love, for example, may be broken down into infatuation, lust, and obsession. Fear may be divided into confusion, distrust, and panic.

Notice that I'm *not* choosing words with a vague or gray connotation but rather, strong words that suggest action. A crush isn't nearly as interesting as an obsession, nor is a spat as exciting as a battle. Choose words that suggest something is at risk in your story. Search for words that raise the stakes.

Raising the stakes is a term that alludes to those elements of your story that are at risk and worth fighting for. The people in your script must want something desperately, to the point at which they feel that they'll die if they don't get it. By raising the stakes, you're making it more important that they achieve their goals. In the movie *E.T.,* the children at first help E.T. get back home because that's where he belongs. The writer later raises the stakes by making it clear that he will, in fact, die if he doesn't reach the spaceship in time.

Mystery

Great stories ask great questions, or they present situations in which questions abound. Look at your idea. What questions do you have? Does your story's mystery lie in an event, a person, or both? If I witness two characters whispering to each other, I'll at least wait to see what was said. If a character behaves in a way that seems out of the ordinary, I'll want to know why. **The History Of Violence** revolves around the question of whether or not the protagonist was once a ruthless killer. Questions give you somewhere to go, which, in screenwriting terms, means another scene to write. The more questions your idea raises, the easier it will be to transform it into a full draft.

Creating scenes full of mystery keeps an audience leaning forward in their seats. Omitting information that may be necessary to understand your general story will confuse and frustrate your audience. Mystery occurs when you've set the scene but left out the reasoning behind an action or a conversation. Remember that mystery occurs when you know generally what is going on but want to know the details.

Spectacular events

Thousands of people in the United States flock to fireworks displays every Fourth of July. Why? In part, they attend to foster a sense of community, but they also go because they're drawn to the enormous demonstration of beauty that fireworks provide. Audiences like to be thrilled, shocked, and dazzled, and screenwriters are in a perfect spot to capitalize on that desire. From the helicopter chase in **Outbreak,** to the Quidditch tournaments in **Harry Potter,** films continually rope us in with their own version of visual fireworks. Your spectacular event may be as large as a volcano eruption or as small as a red balloon disappearing into the sky. Both scenes command an audience's attention, and an audience that gasps together, stays together (at least until the credits roll).

Knowing What Happened Before Your Story Began: Creating the Backstory

Most writers dream a little before they tackle writing their scripts. Actually, they dream a lot. Before you craft an environment, you want to know its history, its geographical location, and its condition. Before you write a scene between parents, you want to know what attracted them to each other, how long they've been together, how many children they have, and the like. Before your characters go to war, you have to know what moments in political history led them to that battlefield.

The ability to write complex events inhabited by complex people comes from knowing everything you can about why those events occurred and who those people are. The details you unearth may not all make it into your final draft, but they will add color and depth to the eventual script. Compiling your information now will also allow you to write with fewer interruptions later because you will have answered many questions in advance.

Backstory refers to everything that occurred in your story's past. A character's backstory may include family background, job history, psychological condition, and any memories that continue to haunt your protagonist. The backstory of a situation includes events that led up to it and a suggestion of why that situation's occurring now.

Elements of the backstory

You may find it helpful to invent your script's history one section at a time. Just as detectives follow a certain line of questioning, so will you subject your story to an inquisition of sorts. Here's a list of categories that you may want to consider in your search for a backstory.

- ✓ **Convictions and beliefs:** What are your character's political, social, and economic views? Does your character have any theories on life in general or in detail? How did he or she come to feel that way?

- ✓ **Education:** Consider both formal education and acquired education in this category. Where your character went to high school may be as important as the three months he spent on the streets playing the drums.

- **Family background:** Invent your character's family history, including the aunt she was named after but never sees. Friends are included in this category as well.

- **Geographic location:** Detail any environment that helped shape your character's present circumstances. Create everything from the climate to the socio-economic makeup of the community to the carefully manicured lawns.

- **Key past events:** Virtually every main event in your story will be possible because of something that's occurred in the past. What events led up to those in your story, and why did they occur?

- **Past successes and failures:** People are shaped in part by their best and worst memories. Knowing what your character's track record is may be helpful in certain situations that arise in the script itself.

- **Phobias:** Your characters' fears dictate what they avoid in life and, in some cases, what's pushing them to succeed. Think specific and general; a fear of rose thorns may be just as compelling as a fear of commitment. The film *Arachnophobia* was fueled by the main character's fear of spiders. Often, you can track a character's personal growth through her phobias and how close she is to overcoming them.

- **Profession:** How do your characters make a living? Do they enjoy working at the library, or are they biding their time? How did they get where they are?

- **Quirks:** What makes them unique, physically and psychologically? In *Forrest Gump,* the main character is compiled of odd characteristics, one of which is how fast he can run. The film *A Beautiful Mind* tackles one man's battle with schizophrenia. A character's quirks can propel your story forward.

- **System of values:** People differ in where they draw the line between right and wrong. What do your characters value most in themselves? In a lover? In a child? What types of behavior would make them ill?

- **Talents:** What has your character always been good at? Does he utilize that talent, or has it gone by the wayside? Perhaps your story starts on the day an opportunity arises for that talent to emerge.

- **Time period:** What part of history are you tackling? Whose history will you portray? Is yours a Civil War story or that of a future age? If you plan to flash between moments in your character's life, how many moments and what were they?

Each of these categories suggests its own series of questions that you might answer about your story. Jot those questions down as they occur to you; you'll undoubtedly return to them with each new person and environment you create. Although it's impossible to highlight everything you discover in a single script, much of your story may come from the information you invent now, and your characters will gain dimension.

Developing a screenplay through backstory

Imagine that you're a tourist in a foreign country — you don't speak the language, the people aren't familiar, and anything might happen to you next. This experience isn't unlike that of most movie-goers. They need someone to guide them through their journey and a guidebook to understand the importance of what they see along the way. You are their guide; the backstory is their guidebook.

A detailed backstory may be your greatest source of support as a screenwriter. It renders your characters unique and colorful, which will inform how they speak and behave throughout your story. It helps establish a clear world for your characters to explore and provides the fuel for most — if not all —of the future scenes in your script.

Consider the information that you have: You've created a time period, an environment, and some character biographies. You may also have envisioned several situations leading up to your story's main events. Your next step involves conveying those details to an audience that knows next to nothing about your story.

You can easily convey time periods and locations through costume, dialect, a lingering description of the landscape, or a caption alerting your audience that the story takes place in Paris, 1763. Past events and character traits are often more elusive. Although there's no single formula for using this type of backstory to generate scenes, you may want to consider the following process as a way to begin:

1. **Identify the detail that you want to develop.**

   It might be an event, a trait, a location, a family member, or a friendship. Choose one element. For example, I've decided that my main character moved around constantly as a child and is unable to settle down as an adult. That unsettled sensibility is the detail in question.

2. **Visualize three ways the detail manifested itself in the past.**

   In particular, concentrate on what moments might reveal the detail to a stranger. For example, I envision my character as a child. She's kept her bedroom decidedly blank, anticipating the next move. She fidgets constantly in school, often upsetting her classmates. She travels with an imaginary friend — the only constant in an ever-fluctuating environment.

3. **Visualize three ways the detail manifests itself in the present.**

   Every character exists in at least three roles during the course of a day. Your main character might be at once a mother, a neighbor, and a renowned biologist. Decide how the detail affects your character in several venues. For example, I imagine that my character is a marathon dater, unable to settle on any person for a length of time. She juggles three jobs at once, constantly dashing from one end of town to another. Although she's lived in an apartment for a year, she has yet to completely unpack.

4. **Decide which scenes might exist in your screenplay.**

   Flag any scenario you visualized that will help an audience understand the story you want to write. If more scenarios occur to you along the way, jot those down, too. You'll return to those notes later when you begin piecing your screenplay together.

Not every piece of information you come up with will find its way into your screenplay. If I'm telling a Civil War story, I may concentrate on my character's political history and ignore his family background. On the other hand, if my Civil War story centers on Abraham Lincoln, his upbringing might be important. The type of story you're telling will dictate which details you reveal from the past. But remember, whether you focus on it or not, everything you imagine will enhance and strengthen your script.

Identifying the Tone of Your Piece

Distinguishing a film's genre from its tone is important. In Chapter 4, I outline the most common movie genres. They include comedy, drama, action and adventure, family, sci-fi, fantasy, horror, and suspense. You can generally determine a movie's genre by the story's content and the audience that it might appeal to. So if the genre of a film refers to *what* a writer is depicting, the film's tone refers to *how* the writer depicts it.

A movie's *tone* indicates a certain quality, mood, or atmosphere that the writer establishes through the careful manipulation of the pace, texture, and selected images. Tone can often be understood as the way a movie makes you feel as you watch it. A comedy may feel dark and slightly twisted (***War of the Roses***) or frivolous and light (***Legally Blonde***) depending on its tone.

In creating a tone for your own screenplay, try exploring three pivotal story elements:

- ✔ **Pace:** The speed with which your story is told. The pace is determined by the length of your scenes, how fast your action moves, and how quickly you provide your audience with information. It's also sometimes determined by your film's genre. Comedies move faster than dramas. Action adventures move faster than suspense films. (For more on genres, see Chapter 3.)

- ✔ **Texture:** The colors, sounds, and other sensory details that you include throughout. How intimately you depict each scene determines the film's texture.

✔ **Tension:** The mental, emotional, or psychological thread between characters. Tension comes in all different forms — angry, uneasy, frightened, and sexual, to name a few. The thread becomes strained as the tension mounts.

You might regard the genre as a kind of spectrum housing various types of comedy, drama, suspense, and so on. You're trying to decipher where your film lies on that spectrum. For example, the comedy genre includes anything from the fast-paced chaotic nature of *Nacho Libre* to the slapstick humor of Laurel and Hardy. Still unsure? Ask yourself this question: What words would I use to describe the overall feel of my story? Is it secretive or raucous, whimsical or ominous? Any of these descriptions may be your tone.

Why do you need to know the tone of your script? Sometimes, you don't. Sometimes, a tone will suggest itself as you're writing, and you can enhance it then. Sometimes, you'll complete a draft and realize that you've unconsciously selected a tone. However, knowing the texture of your piece in advance may help you decide which details to highlight as you write.

Establishing Your Story's Time Clock

A script that spans several generations will unfold differently from a script that encompasses a few days. Most films handle time in one of two ways:

✔ **In one concentrated span of time.** Most great stories occur during one portion of someone's life or in one tight span of history, so most screenwriters restrict their use of time. Films of this nature generally suggest early on what event the action is moving toward and push the audience toward it chronologically, scene by scene. The writer may track several characters simultaneously, but they usually exist in the same time frame and are moving toward similar conclusions. *Juno* is an example of one such structure. *The Aviator* is another.

✔ **Mediating between time periods.** Scripts of this nature also tend to move chronologically toward one goal, but they provide details from the past and the present and, perhaps, offer glimpses of the future along the way. These films often employ memories, dream sequences, and/or flashbacks to advance the action. *Stand By Me* is a prime example of this structure. *Memento* is another.

Regardless of how much or how little time your story covers, it will eventually culminate in some final event. That event and how long it takes your characters to get there is known as a time clock.

A film's *time clock* refers to the amount of time a writer allots for the main characters to achieve their ultimate goal. The time clock gives the story shape — the action must be completed in a certain amount of time or else. The time clock may be a measurable amount of time, or it may be based on some impending event.

Time clocks vary in type and specificity. They may be

- **Literal:** Literal time clocks are actual clocks that are set from the beginning and mentioned throughout the film. The characters in *Speed* must keep the bus moving over 60 miles per hour to keep the bomb from going off. Their time clock is limited to one tank of fuel. In *Night Mother,* Sissy Spacek tells her mother that she's going to kill herself before the night is over. Her mother has roughly two hours to persuade her against it. Because the audience never forgets that time is running out, these films are packed with dramatic tension. You can almost hear the clock ticking away in each scene, which is why this element is often referred to as the "ticking clock."

- **Historical:** These films feel like slices of life. The writer makes it clear that she'll present a short period of time that's important for reasons yet to be disclosed. Those time frames may encompass portions of a true historical epoch as in *Age of Innocence* and *Braveheart,* or a stretch of time in someone's personal history à la *Stand By Me* and *The Green Mile.* Audiences remain in their seats because they want to see where the characters will go and because they think that they may learn something along the way.

- **Psychological:** These time clocks are character generated. They usually involve a personal revelation or psychological breakthrough. *When Harry Met Sally* is a prime example of a film that works this way. We're waiting for one or both of these characters to realize that they're meant for each other. In *Affliction,* Nick Nolte's character is plagued by personal demons he acquired from his father. We know the movie's coming to a conclusion when he has to face those demons head on.

- **Competitive:** Like glimpses of evolution, these films are fueled by a survival of the fittest regime. Here, opposing forces battle for final control, and the movie is over when one of them destroys the other one. It's always just a matter of time before something drastic occurs. Audiences don't know when that moment will be, but they know that it's coming. In *Lord of the Rings,* it's just a matter of time before the dark lord takes over Middle Earth. Frodo must destroy the ring before that happens. In *Jaws,* it's just a matter of time before the shark consumes (literally consumes) the town. The police chief must destroy it first.

- **Abstract:** These time clocks are few and far between and tend to be part of art films or independent shorts. An abstract time clock is one the audience may or may not be aware of until the end. It's like the phrase "My whole life flashed before my eyes. . . ." That can happen in the time it takes for someone to swim the length of a pool or to wake up from a dream. The lap of the pool and the length of the dream may become time clocks. The entirety of ***Jacob's Ladder*** takes place in one man's dying hallucination. You don't discover that until later, but the writer knows the story's over when the hallucination ends.

Time clocks organize your action, and all great stories have one, so it's best to consider yours now. Without one, there's no end to the event you might tackle, and therefore no clear end to your script.

Deciding When to Start Your Story

Why start your story now? is a two-part question. It really asks, Why should you personally start writing now, and Why does your story begin when it does? The first portion of the question can be answered in the following ways:

- ✔ You'll forget the story if you don't start writing now.
- ✔ You'll lose your momentum if you don't start writing now.
- ✔ You've taken time to enhance the idea; the story is becoming clear.
- ✔ You've set aside time in your schedule to concentrate on a script.
- ✔ This is a story that needs to be written now.
- ✔ If you don't write it now, someone else may.
- ✔ You've put off writing long enough.

Writing isn't unlike a sport. If you practice every day on a set schedule, your muscles will remain supple and ready to work for you. If called to race a marathon, you could do it. Your imagination is also a muscle that will tire without regular exercise. You've invested time in an idea, and though the initial euphoria may have worn off, you now have an arsenal of creative paths to explore. If the initial excitement remains, better yet. Start writing soon.

Why does your story begin when it does? is one of the most important questions you have to answer before sitting down to write. There are as many different answers as there are types of stories. However, one thing is clear: Your story begins when it does because something unusual is about to happen. Lives are about to change.

Consider successful movies you know. In ***Juno,*** the protagonist has just learned she's pregnant. ***Gone with the Wind*** begins on the brink of the Civil War. ***Lord of the Rings*** thrusts us into a mystical world at war. These stories also begin at the moment a change will occur for the main characters. Juno will need to decide who will raise her child. Scarlett O'Hara will suffer poverty and heartbreak for the first time. Frodo will have to leave home in search of a ring. All these movies begin on the verge of a grand shift, and that shift propels the ensuing action.

Try to identify the biggest change that might occur in your own story. Is it a shift within

- ✔ The family?
- ✔ The workspace?
- ✔ The environment?
- ✔ The political, social, or economic scene?
- ✔ A character's romantic life?
- ✔ A character's emotional or physical well-being?

Generally, if the story is about to change in one realm, the other realms will shift around it. Should someone close to your main character die, for example, that death might affect his work, his friendships, and perhaps his romantic attachments. Choose the grandest shift you can find and begin your story there.

Why start your story on the verge of something new? Because change is inherently dramatic. Change puts characters in a vulnerable state where they'll have to make choices for the first time. It forces them to rely on their basic instincts to succeed or, in some cases, survive. It allows the audience to learn along with the people they're watching.

Your beginning moment also suggests a time clock for your action. Even if your story is based on a famous person, you can't tackle his or her entire life; you simply don't have time. Nor would people find it interesting to see every moment dramatized. You'll want to concentrate on a small portion of that journey, and that portion will suggest its own conclusion. In **Star Wars,** Luke Skywalker begins his quest yearning to avenge his family's murder, and the audience will want to see if he's able to do so. Anything after that attempt is information for another film. Identify this shift in your own story, and you'll have your opening scene.

Getting to Know Aristotle: A Dramatist's Best Friend

Aristotle was a Greek philosopher who lived from 384 to 322 B.C. So what does he have to do with screenwriting? In some ways — everything. An author of many notable works, his doctrine titled *Poetics* may be the first text devoted entirely to literary criticism, and the terms he employs within it have become the cornerstones of dramatic arts today. For a writer, Aristotle's six poetics are the building blocks of any well-crafted script.

Aristotle's Poetics are

- **Plot:** A *plot* can be defined as a series of actions, and an action can be defined as an event that causes something else to occur. A boy borrowing his father's car isn't necessarily an action. A boy borrowing his father's car after being told not to do so *might* be an action, as it will undoubtedly spark an argument later on. If the events in your story don't cause other events to occur, you don't have a plot. You simply have a series of events.

- **Character:** A *character* is any person or presence in your screenplay that performs an action or causes another character to do so. I say "a presence" to allow for the possibility that something other than a human being may be a character in your script. Ghosts, for example, cause people to act in certain ways, and the cast of characters in many family movies might include animals or make-believe creatures.

- **Thought:** The thought of your screenplay can be broken down in several ways. It refers to the initial thought that sparked your interest in the idea as well as the thought you put into the construction of a story. It refers to the thoughts that your characters express throughout your script, which may differ widely from your own. It also refers to the points of view that you may want to convey to an audience. In this sense, the thought of your script may also be its theme.

- **Diction:** The *diction* of your script refers to the types of words you choose to depict your action. Like fashion trends, words suggest a personality or type. The words you choose quickly denote a character's education, profession, sexual persuasion, political bent, age, ethnicity, and emotional or mental state. I talk about diction at greater length in Chapter 9.

- **Music:** Like thought, *music* has several definitions. It can refer to the actual music that you employ in your screenplay, be it the live band you're writing about or any music you hear underscoring your piece. It can refer to the general *soundscape* — sound effects that you highlight or silences between characters. It also refers to the sounds of the words themselves. If you could mute the meaning of each word and concentrate on the consonants and the vowels, you'd have the script's music.

- **Spectacle:** *Spectacle* has recently taken on a negative connotation, referring to any expensive, grandiose technical effect that a movie employs to dazzle an audience. Yet, in fact, it originally meant any moment that visually impressed an audience, be it small or grand in scale. The blazing city in **Gone with the Wind** might amaze an observer, but so might the first moment that Scarlett O'Hara walks on-screen in her enormous dress. Spectacle moments are often what makes the story film-worthy and unlike everyday life. Without them, the movies may seem very dull.

The *Poetics* provide a clear roadmap for any writer. Before you sit down to the page, you may find it helpful to glance through them individually to clarify story choices that you've already made. How do the categories work together? Where do they overlap? Have you been thorough in your research? They will help you later when you've completed a first draft and face the daunting task of rewriting. I have them pasted above my computer screen for just that moment. They remind me that I need only tackle one component at a time as I go back through with my red pen. Also, if your writing falters, it usually means that you don't know enough about one of these elements, and it's time to return to your backstory. When the *Poetics* are fully realized, your screenplay will sing.

What's It All About? Writing a Nutshell Synopsis

The nutshell synopsis is one of the great ironies of screenwriting. You spend months, if not years, developing your idea, researching your backstory, embellishing your characters, and identifying a tone. Then, you're asked to condense all that information into five sentences or less. It sounds crazy, but it's an exercise that pinpoints the crucial moments in your story while preparing you for the demands of the Hollywood scene, which includes pitching your idea to executives in a few minutes or less.

A *synopsis* is a short description of your screenplay that highlights the main characters and the journey they go on, with particular attention to conflict and resolution. A *nutshell synopsis* is a shorter version of the same, generally running from three to five sentences in length. Neither form of synopsis includes dialogue, unless absolutely necessary.

A *treatment* is longer than a synopsis and narrative in nature. It's part synopsis and part short story. It runs anywhere from 4 to 20 pages in length, depending on the scope of your film, and it describes each act of your script in chronological order. It also does not include dialogue, unless that exchange is pivotal to the story.

The ability to tell a story effectively in a short amount of time is a skill that most successful screenwriters have turned into an art form. In Hollywood, time is money, so you won't be given enough time to say everything that you know about your script. If you've done your job, it would take hours to tell, and you're probably going to get 5 minutes. So start thinking now about what details you would keep.

It might help to break the idea down into five concrete sentences. I've included some examples of opening phrases to get you started. The element you're trying to emphasize is in boldface at the start of each phrase.

- ✔ **Character:** My story is about a (insert character type here) in (insert location here).

- ✔ **Goal:** S/he wants more than anything to find (insert hope/ dream/ passion here).

- ✔ **Journey:** Her/His journey begins when (initial event here) and s/he decides to (character action here).

- ✔ **Conflict:** S/he runs into trouble when/with (insert conflict or conflicts here), which s/he tackles by (character action here).

- ✔ **Resolution:** The story ends when (insert event here), and s/he discovers that (insert conclusion here).

You can alter and rearrange these sentences in many different ways to suit your particular screenplay. You may abandon the sentence structure altogether and come up with phrases of your own. However, the elements that I'm choosing to emphasize create the spine of most stories, and you'll probably want to include them in any synopsis you construct.

After you've devised a paragraph of five sentences, try telling your story in three. Now try one. It may seem impossible, but when you're through, you'll know exactly what your script is about.

Turning your synopsis into a movie trailer

Here's a quick and fun way to vamp up your nutshell synopsis. Movie trailers are a film company's best bet for drawing an audience into the theater. They generally employ a combination of vibrant music, quick flashes of action, and a dynamic announcer to rope people in. Imagine that your film is about to be released, and you're in charge of marketing it. Using your synopsis as a guide, construct a movie trailer that will dazzle the public and send them to the box office with money in hand. You might also consider the perfect tagline for your film's poster. What one phrase could draw audiences to your movie in droves?

Chapter 6

Plot Part I: Beginnings

· ·

In This Chapter

▶ Making your opening images great

▶ Planting your story's conflict

▶ Structuring your first moments

▶ Glancing through successful film openings

· ·

*P*lot and character are the pillars of all great stories. Without a solid plot, nothing happens in your screenplay; without compelling characters, things happen, but no one cares. So which pillar do you construct first?

Well, consider that most people approach stories by inquiring, "What's that story about?" Then consider the question that you'll be asked most often by friends, family, future agents, and producers when they discover that you're writing a script: "What's your story about?" Finally, consider the question that you'll ask yourself when you reach a stumbling point and can't seem to generate any pages: "What's my story about?"

Yes, it's the same question, but, more importantly, it's the *first* question you're likely to encounter at every stage of a new draft. Sure, people will inquire *who* you're writing about, but they'll probably do so *after* you've supplied a synopsis. And if you look toward the five minutes you get to convince the Hollywood heavyweights of your script's worth, you'd better have a dynamic plot ready to rope them in quickly. And how do you construct such a plot? It's a challenging process that begins . . . well, with your beginning. This chapter concentrates on crafting an opening for your story that will entice readers and audiences alike to remain in their seats.

Enhancing Your Opening Images

Close your eyes. You're sitting in a darkened theater, staring at the screen. At first, nothing happens. Perhaps some images dart past as the credits role. Finally, the screen flickers to life. You're about to watch the opening sequence of your film. What do you see?

The first ten minutes of every movie determine what an audience expects from the remaining two hours. A story's setup determines, in large part, how your story will unfold. And if it doesn't suggest the movie to come, it should. Here are a few things a strong opening should do:

✔ Introduce your main character(s)

✔ Establish a routine or pattern of life

✔ Suggest a conflict that may break that routine or pattern

✔ Introduce your subplots and suggest their conflicts

✔ Set the tone and style of the piece

✔ Suggest a villain or opposing force in the story

✔ Suggest something important at risk

✔ Raise a compelling question

These eight components comprise the rules of your screenplay. By rules, I mean that these components provide the boundaries or structure within which your action occurs. If the movie starts as a horror flick, it shouldn't switch to a light comedy halfway through; if I spend the first 20 minutes getting to know one young man, I'll watch for him throughout the remainder of the film. You may want to think of these rules as the game plan upon which your audience forms expectations about the ensuing action. You will fulfill or thwart those expectations as you go, and quite often, you'll do both. So you've got a lot riding on those first moments. How do you construct them to speak volumes in an efficient way? Much like a three-dimensional puzzle, you build it piece by moving piece.

Person, place, or thing: What do you want to present first?

You can't establish all eight components at once, it's too confusing. However, you can determine the primary element of your opening — in other words, where your audience should look first. You'll probably want to know who's on the screen, where they are, and how each scene looks when the film starts to roll, so consider the following elements in advance.

The people

Movies are always about people. Even if you focus on a historical event, you'll be tracking how that event affected a person or group of people. For example, the movie *Titanic,* though centered around a great historical tragedy, primarily depicts one couple's budding romance. The audience witnesses the fear, horror, and hope of the event through them.

Unless you're constructing a documentary, which relies more on facts than fiction, you'll know in advance from whose eyes your audience will experience the story. So decide whether your script revolves around

- One person
- A small group of people
- A community or nation
- Several communities or nations

Because your film probably consists of a plot and at least one subplot, you'll want to determine the subject(s) of each.

A *subplot* is a smaller storyline that supports the film's main plot. It generally comes equipped with its own set of characters, conflicts, and actions. The characters in a subplot may or may not be moving toward the same objective(s).

By determining your film's subject, you soon pinpoint its scope, be it an epic adventure of warring nations (*Lord of the Rings*), an intimate family affair (*You Can Count On Me*), or something in between (*Malcolm X*). You choose initial images that suggest that scope.

The location(s)

In a stage play, confining your story to a small number of locales is often beneficial. Movies, however, can lead audiences anywhere: from the office lobby to the city street to the cafe to the cafe's storeroom to a phone booth in the cafe's storeroom. A screenwriter has no limit to where he or she can go. So let me first distinguish between location and location. Sound crazy? It's not, I promise. You can define the word in two distinct ways:

- **Physical locations:** The site-specific locale of each scene, where every moment takes place
- **Esoteric locations:** The contrasting worlds your script unites — be it social/political spheres or the internal world of a character

The physical locations will take care of themselves as you write, and they may become overwhelming when considered in advance. Esoteric locations are more important and more manageable. They help both writer and audience understand the story's larger themes. They suggest locations that a writer might periodically return to, images that frame the action like posts in a fence. For example, the number of physical locations in Mel Gibson's *Braveheart* is staggering. The writer jumps from tavern to alley to glen to lake to dungeon to battlefield and back again. Yet the movie's core depicts two distinct worlds at war — the working-class Scotsmen and the controlling British aristocracy. More specifically, the film unites the main character's world with that of the English villain after he destroys Gibson's young wife in the opening sequence.

Eventually, you'll need to consider your budget when deciding upon elements like location. Small-budget films can't usually afford a surplus of location shifting, so if you're writing for a smaller production company, you'll want to limit your landscape a bit. However, when you're first creating a story, I suggest dreaming large. Go where the story seems to want to go; you can always scale back later.

Your use of time

It's crazy to suggest that you'll know exactly where your story's going at the start of a first draft. You probably won't. And you don't need to — not yet. But consider how much time your story intends to span because it will affect your opening sequences. You'll also want to know if your plot moves chronologically forward, or if you intend to jump between past, present, and future. I describe dramatic time clocks in Chapter 5, but suffice it to say that scripts spanning generations unfold differently than those spanning a few days or, in the case of films like *My Dinner With André,* those spanning a single evening.

You'll want to alert your audience early to the time choice you've made. How? If you're writing an epic historical drama, the first image may be of a city that's been destroyed in war. If you're writing an intimate family affair, you may begin with shots of various characters going about their morning routines. If your movie propels the audience ever forward, the audience will assume that you'll continue that trend. If you plan to jump around, you may follow a scene set today with a scene set in 1945. You may allow a character to reference time travel or muse about the future. You can employ a flashback right away. You can solve the problem in numerous ways, but remember, an audience will assume that your plot will be current and chronological unless you tell it otherwise.

How do you suggest alternate time periods? If you're writing a period piece, you might let the costumes, a description of the city, and the type of vehicles present or absent orient your audience, or you may precede the action with a caption reading, "Italy, 1886." If you're inventing a time period, as the *Star Wars* trilogy does, find a way to alert the audience that it's about to enter a strange place and a strange time. *Star Wars* launches each movie with an informative prologue that scrolls through space. Whatever technique you employ in the first 10 to 20 pages, you can use it again later because the audience will be prepared.

The atmosphere

Layer in the atmosphere or tone of your story. Some films do so immediately. Five minutes into the movie *Jaws,* the audience knows that it's watching a horror film. *Waiting for Guffman* introduces its mock-umentary tone right away with interviews of highly exaggerated character types. Some films do this gradually. *Rear Window* begins pleasantly enough, but it soon becomes clear that the protagonist is witnessing a murder. From that point on, the suspense is palpable.

The stakes

The *stakes* of a story refer to what's at risk in any situation. If your story's about a bus full of people, nothing in that scenario is immediately intriguing. If you tell me a bomb's on the bus, I'm interested. If you tell me that the bus is carrying someone's grandmother, several teenagers, as well as a main character I relate to, I'm suddenly invested in their safety. Now, something's at stake. That storyline became the box office hit *Speed.*

The stakes in a film can be anything the audience roots for or worries about. If the stakes prevent the audience from leaving until after the concluding scene, you've done your job.

Conflict: What's wrong with your story?

If your opening shots don't grab an audience's attention, you'll have an even harder time gaining their interest later. You don't have to shock or horrify the audience to do grab their attention; you can seduce, con, humor, or badger them into watching —but for heaven's sake, do something.

After the first five steps are in place (see the section "Person, place, or thing: What do you want to present first?" earlier in this chapter), *conflict* becomes the key ingredient. Conflict sparks action. Conflict raises questions, and the audience's desire to answer those questions creates tension. Keep two things in mind: You have limited time, and you're writing about the most compelling time in your characters' lives. If they've experienced these conflicts before, they'll know how to behave, and your story is over. The encounter you're dramatizing is different; it will change lives. So most screenwriters start as close to that struggle as possible. Generally, the opening sequence does one of two things:

- ✔ **It provides a brief look at the story's platform.** Your characters, like most human beings, have a routine — a "normal" way of life. And what's crazy for you and me might be this character's average day. Even if she never does the same thing twice, that ability to not repeat herself becomes her routine or her platform. Movies that begin with a clear routine provide a suggestion of how the characters may act when that sense of normalcy is disturbed. Harry Potter begins his journey as an orphan being raised by hideous relatives. This is his routine until he receives a letter informing him that he's a wizard. *American Beauty* spends a full half an hour detailing the main character's rough family life and mundane job, so that the audience feels a sense of relief when that platform shifts.

✔ **It starts the story mid-conflict.** These movies plunge the audience into the action at the point of attack. Everything is questionable — who the script's about, what's just gone wrong, how it will affect everything else. Although this method is a great way to jumpstart your film, you still need to convey how life looked prior to the conflict so that the audience knows what's been lost. You simply give viewers that information later. *Lord of the Rings* and *Star Wars* are examples of this method. Both films begin with a narration that launches the audience into a new world on the brink of war.

The *platform* of a story refers to a generally safe and stable way of life that exists prior to a life-altering event. The platform may be comprised of habits, job schedules, points of view, everyday routines, political or international stability, and anything a character might take for granted as secure. The *point of attack* then refers to the event or the moment in the script where the platform falls apart.

Possible ways to begin your story

There is no one way to start your script. The subject matter you've chosen to convey and the genre you're working within determine your opening. However, several trends are common in opening techniques, and one just may work for you. Many movies convey their choice of opening in one of five ways:

✔ **Action:** Start your movie with a chase scene, or a fight, or a feat of extreme risk. If you toss your audience immediately into action, they'll lean forward immediately, if only to follow what's going on. Virtually every James Bond film begins this way — *Casino Royale,* in particular.

✔ **A long first scene:** These openings firmly establish the initial event, detailing it from various angles and, sometimes, points of view. *The Untouchables* is an example of such a beginning.

✔ **Fleeting moments:** These openings move through an average day or the initial conflict quickly, often concentrating on the more intimate details of each scene. They may also bounce between locales and characters. *The Big Chill* opens this way.

✔ **A narrator:** Here, a main character talks the audience through the opening sequence, pointing out key details or secrets, perhaps introducing characters along the way. *American Beauty* and *Ferris Bueller's Day Off* begin this way.

✔ **A montage:** A *montage* is a series of shots strung together in rapid succession, generally underscored with music and often without dialogue. The opening sequence of *Juno* begins this way.

You'll discover other techniques as you watch and read screenplays, but most of them fall within one of these categories. Again, there is no one way to start a story, and I'd be the last person to suggest that you should follow a set formula. Sometimes, the best technique is to visualize a scene, write it down quickly, and return to polish it later. I address the opening components in this way to make the process manageable and to provide examples of proven opening techniques. The subject of your first sequence, the location, the atmosphere, and time frames — these are simply categories waiting to be embellished with your details. Together, they help you provide a lot of information in an efficient manner and raise at least one question compelling enough to keep audience members in their seats.

Tracking Success: Three Compelling (and Contrasting) Movie Beginnings

Everyone's tastes in movies differ, so, frequently, the best way to discover how you want your script to look is to study the movies that compel or repel you. After you're aware of what a great opening should do (see the preceding sections), look at the movies you love. How do they set up the action? What information do they immediately transfer to the audience? What images do they use to present that information? Any movie that fails to pull you in fails because the writer neglected one or more of those components. The successful beginnings pack as much as they can into a small amount of time.

With so many strong films to choose from, I had a hard time narrowing the focus down to three. However, three it is. I've chosen these scripts to give you a sense of different ways to launch equally enticing stories. You can obtain all these screenplays online or through the library, so you can track how the images look both on the screen and on the page.

I encourage you to read these scripts as well as see the films. Doing so will help you later when you envision the beginning you want but aren't sure how to lay it out on the page. I track some of these movies through Chapters 7 and 8 as well to give you a sense of how the writers keep the tension mounting and ultimately conclude each tale. For now, see what you can discover from their opening scenes.

The Untouchables

Brian DePalma's movie, written by David Mamet, is a perfect example of the mid-conflict beginning. The first three shots set up the villain, the conflict, and the unlikely hero in rapid succession. Here's how they look:

✔ **Scene 1:** Al Capone lounges in a barber's chair surrounded by the press and his staff who at once trim his nails, massage his neck, and shave his face. A short summary in the corner of the screen alerts the audience that the movie takes place in Chicago in the 1930s, mid-Prohibition. It further states that the city has been taken over by Capone and his ganglord friends. When a reporter inquires about Capone's brutal tactics, Capone vehemently denies involvement in any violence whatsoever.

✔ **Scene 2:** A little girl walks into a bar and holds her pail up to the counter to be filled. A man next to her leaves his briefcase on the stool, clicking the top of it before he hurries out. The little girl grabs it and runs after him, calling that he's forgotten his briefcase. The case explodes in her hands, killing her and demolishing the bar and street outside.

✔ **Scene 3:** Elliot Ness from the Treasury Department reads of the damage in the local paper. His obviously pregnant wife reminds him of the time and tells him to make a good first impression. It's his first day as Special Agent.

In three scenes, Mamet introduces the main forces and the main conflict — the battle to clean up Chicago. He gives you a realistic time clock — Elliot Ness and Al Capone must eventually meet. He also alludes to the stakes. A child is killed in the second scene. This tugs at our heartstrings and establishes Capone as a ruthless murderer. Ness's wife is pregnant; the audience will root for him to survive.

American Beauty

This 1999 Oscar-winning film begins with a narrator and palpable tension.

✔ **Scene 1:** A young girl, partially clothed, glares into a hand-held camera complaining about her father whom she considers to be a royal embarrassment. When the man holding the camera asks if she'd like him to kill her father, she coyly replies, "Yeah, would you?"

✔ **Scene 2:** The voice of the narrator, Lester Burnham, introduces himself, and, in the same breath, he cautions that he'll be dead in less than a year. He then casually guides the audience through his morning. Scenes follow of him waking up and masturbating in the shower, of his wife in the garden, of the homosexual neighbors both named Jim, and of his cynical teenage daughter. His commentary throughout suggests a pervading disgust at his life, at himself, and at something he feels he's lost along the way. He ends this sequence by saying, "It's never too late to get it back."

Here, the writer sets up the entire story in two scenes. The story is about the final portion of Lester's life. The time clock is a psychological one. His goal is to break the mundane routine he feels trapped in. The audience has met virtually every important character in ten minutes.

Jaws

Spielberg's breakaway hit offers one of the most satisfyingly horrific beginnings in film history. The scenes are shot realistically, without distracting technical effects, and capture the audience in less than five minutes.

✔ **Scene 1:** A group of teenagers are drinking and chatting around a campfire. One young man and one young woman exchange glances and hurry toward the ocean, tossing clothes off as they run. The woman plunges into the water, while the man struggles with his shoes, obviously quite drunk. The scene shifts below the water, as a shark watches the woman swim. Her feet and arms flail above the creature. Suddenly, she's tugged from below and then dragged, kicking and screaming, around in a circle. The man has fallen asleep on the beach and doesn't hear her continual screams for help. Eventually, she's pulled below. All is silent.

✔ **Scene 2:** The chief of police wakes up next to his wife and receives a call that someone has gone missing. He jumps into his truck and drives down a road past a billboard of a girl on a surfboard welcoming tourists to Amity Island.

✔ **Scene 3:** At the beach, the policeman and the boy from the previous night discover the girl's severed hand lying washed up on the sand.

As horrible as these opening moments are, I repeat that they're also highly satisfying. Although most filmmakers might have lunged immediately into the grotesque shots of her death, Spielberg waits a bit. He jumps between the woman's perspective at the surface, and the shark's view from below. The billboard suggests that the tourists will be coming soon — so the stakes and the time clock are set. And we've met the opposing parties — man and beast.

TRY IT

Construct two openings for the same story

You can approach this project in two ways. You may want to begin by jotting down a generic scenario to practice on, or you may want to revisit the synopsis of your own story and begin there. In either case, consider the opening moments with two methods in mind:

✔ **With a platform:** Construct three images that set up an average day for your main characters.

✔ **Mid-conflict:** Construct three images that suggest the first big change in your characters' everyday routines.

After you have those three images, put them in an order that raises the most questions in the audience. Do you think that this sequence could be a solid opening for a film? You can also try envisioning already released movies with different openings. Imagine how *Jaws* might look if the writers took the time to introduce the town prior to the first attack. One of these openings is bound to be a more compelling choice than the others.

Chapter 7

Plot Part II: Middles

The middle of a screenplay, otherwise known as the *second act,* is usually the most difficult and, therefore, the most daunting portion to write. It's the longest section, often three times the length of either the beginning or the end. Its aim is to test the main characters' fortitude, throwing obstacle after obstacle in their paths as they charge (and sometimes hobble) toward their destinations. Writers often feel emotionally drained after completing this section and/or wretched for having put people they care about through so much turmoil. The middle also demands a writer juggle many tasks: increasing tensions and threats, revealing character secrets, and keeping an audience guessing as the writer barrels toward a conclusion.

Most moviegoers visit the restroom during a lull in the action in the second act of a film. Don't let them! (Or at least make them worry that they'll miss something great while they're gone.) Writers anticipate every scene, ignoring what *might* come next for what the story dictates *must* come next. Then they convince the audience that it's too important to miss. Sound daunting? Read on. This chapter offers advice on how to answer the anxiety-ridden question, "How do I know what happens next?" If you know it's worth sticking around for, there's bound to be a way to alert someone else.

Deciding What Comes Next

Bravo, you have an opening sequence, and it's perfect! You've introduced your main characters and established the world they live in. You may even have suggested what's wrong with the world they live in. You're ready for the next step, and the next step is . . . ? In part, that answer depends on you and your writing habits.

There are three common approaches to structuring the remainder of your script, and the one you choose depends upon the level of organization you require to write. Here are the three methods:

- ✔ **Piecemeal:** This method is based on the theory that writers take a journey *with* the character and should sense what happens next. Writers who construct plots this way generally research their stories inside and out, making it possible to visualize the next event and the ensuing character responses. You may want to select this method if you fear that an outline will limit your creativity. However, this method offers little comfort if you encounter writer's block.

- ✔ **Dot to dot:** In this method, a writer pre-selects three to five pivotal events and then constructs scenes that carry an audience from point to point. This technique works well for writers who both crave and fear the structure of an outline. The targets are chosen in advance, but the path to them remains unclear.

- ✔ **Full roadmap:** A writer who uses this approach spends more time planning his script than he does writing it. After constructing a thorough scene-by-scene outline, the writer tracks everything from character changes to secrets revealed to the growing threat (whatever or whomever it may be). Though the thought of extensive outlining may seem daunting, it keeps a writer focused and on track. It remains the preferred method of plot construction among screenwriters.

Again, the method you choose depends on your writing habits. I say your *writing* habits and not your personal habits because unorganized people are sometimes meticulously prepared writers and vice versa.

So how much research have you done? How well do you know your characters? If you feel that you have a thorough grasp on the story, if it's beginning to speak to you regularly, you may be able to piece it together scene by scene.

Screenplays are complex works made up of fleeting visual moments. You can easily become mired in details and lose sight of the whole entity. Perhaps the clearest way to choose between piecemeal and the other two methods is to ask, "What will you do when you forget where you're going?" If your answer is, "I'll look back through my research, reread my current scene, and find out," you may be able to choose the piecemeal method. If the prospect worries you at all, you may want to start with an outline.

From Lights to Camera to . . . ACTION!

Any 6-year-old knows how to tell a story. Human beings are born equipped with curiosity and a strong desire to understand what goes on around them. If you present an audience with a short film, secretly removing a key frame in the middle, most people will connect the images in some coherent fashion, regardless of the gap. They'll assume that it's supposed to make sense, and they'll inherently concoct a plot that explains it until they tire of the effort.

You may be surprised that many adults are afraid of the very idea of telling a story — suddenly unsure of their once-keen ability to do so. Yet with a few structural reminders, stories generate themselves. And the primary term to understand is *action*.

An *action* occurs when one event causes or allows another event to take place. Two events linked in a causal relationship comprise an action.

Screenplays subsist on action, and one action is really two linked events. Consider this example: I run away from home. This event in itself isn't an action. If I run away from home *and, therefore,* my mother calls the police — those two events together comprise an action. My mother calling the police (Event #1) can be the start of a new action if, for example, it causes the police department to begin a nationwide search (Event #2).

Want a film example? In the movie **Jaws,** a girl is eaten by a shark in the first scene. Although it's obviously the kickoff event, it nevertheless remains "something that happens" until her body is found on the beach, and the town panic begins. Then it becomes an action.

This distinction is especially important to make in film, where it would be simple to illustrate events without providing the information necessary to link them together. As a way to practice, try visualizing these events:

- ✔ A boy disappears.
- ✔ His mother passes away.
- ✔ His father leaves town.

These are three separate events. How might you link them to convert them into actions? I could rewrite them to read, "In despair over her only son's disappearance, a young mother dies weeping in her husband's arms. Unable to return to his now empty house, the boy's father quietly leaves town." I've now connected them through anguish, but there are many other possibilities. How would you do it?

So if an action is two causally linked events, what's all the other stuff that happens in a scene called?

Presenting both action and activity

Beginning writers often confuse action with anything that a character does in a scene. Yet movies are exactly what they advertise to be — pictures in motion. Some of that movement is action, and some is not. You will certainly construct scenes where people demonstrate hobbies, habits, professions, and idiosyncrasies. But these attributes don't all lead to action; in fact, most of them don't. A character may be cooking an omelet and planning the next corporate takeover in the same moment. Cooking omelets is an activity, or *business* in film lingo — it refers to a task that a character busies himself with, but that probably won't lead to anything other than a nice breakfast. Planning the next corporate takeover will probably cause other events to occur. It may even result in your next scene. So it's an action.

Really compelling scenes rely on *both* action and activities. Without action, your scene won't go anywhere; without activities, it'll be fairly boring to watch. Here are a few ways activities embellish a scene:

- ✔ **They reveal character information: habits, hobbies, and idiosyncrasies.** Does your character inline skate, paint, brush her hair 20 times before bed, or collect coins in her spare time? These activities add color, dimension, and an original sheen to your characters. They separate your romantic comedy from numerous others.

- ✔ **They quickly establish location or profession.** If your script takes place in a university during final exams, you may construct scenes in which students huddle together over books. If your character is a teacher, perhaps she's grading papers or preparing for class. Strategically chosen activities provide crucial establishing information in an efficient manner.

- ✔ **They offset and/or counter the way an audience views an action.** Humans often behave in ways that contradict their actions — it's in part what makes them fun to observe. Think about it: The man who is compassionate and well liked and causes only good things to occur won't interest an audience for long. But if that same man unwittingly causes his company's demise? I'll watch him then, and, moreover, I'll root for him to survive the disaster.

Constructing scenes in which the activities contradict the actions may be the key to dramatizing real life. In the film ***In the Line of Fire,*** John Malkovich plays a presidential assassin. In one key scene, he fishes alongside two local townsmen. The activity creates a serene, oddly safe environment. However, he's also fashioning a wooden gun in the scene — a gun he intends to use to kill the President. The casual activity of fishing makes his action all the more frightening; for a second, it lulls the audience into seeing him as the average man next door.

If you recognize the difference between an action and an activity, you can coordinate them in your own structure. The activities embellish your plot; the actions propel it.

Revisiting the story's time clock

If your average 6-year-old knows how to tell a story, he most certainly knows when the story is complete. And it's not generally complete just because he couldn't think of anything else to say or because his mouth grew tired. Every story moves to a fixed point. When the story reaches that point, it's over, or very nearly done. More importantly, every story has a problem the characters must struggle to solve. As I discuss in Chapter 5, the story's time clock refers to the amount of time you give them to do so.

Hopefully you've established your time clock in the first portion of your script, introduced the main characters and the central conflict, and thrown your audience a few hints as to where the film may be headed. As the story progresses, then time begins to run out. This phenomenon is based on a theatrical mandate known as *rising action*. The mandate suggests that a story's intensity escalates as it heads toward a conclusion. Rising action means that generally halfway through your second act, the pace of your film picks up.

Rising action refers to an increased momentum of the film's action as it progresses toward the main objective. As a film reaches a resolution, its pace usually increases, and the time clock shortens.

Rising action affects both your main plot and your subplots simultaneously. Each storyline has its own trajectory that bolsters the other ones. You may speed each plot along by using shorter scenes, by taking less time between important discoveries, or by making it more important that the characters achieve their goals. This last technique is called *raising the stakes*.

Raising the stakes refers to the increased amount of pressure that a writer puts on his characters to achieve their goals or solve a problem. The writer usually achieves this increased necessity by putting a human element at — a child, a family member, the main character's own life — and by shortening the time allotted to achieve success. When the stakes are raised, ultimate victory becomes a matter of life or death.

Ask yourself two questions as you revisit your time clock. First, are you starting scenes as close to the conflict as possible? Second, are you leading the audience through the most shocking, exciting, funny, or tragic portion of the characters' lives. In other words, the middle of a screenplay is a time when struggle increases and emotions run high. If you haven't written a full outline of the action, you'll want at least a general idea of how you plan to manipulate your time clock throughout, to propel us closer and closer to some climactic or revelatory close.

Status: Where's the Upper Hand?

Audiences thrive on competition. Think about it: The most exciting sporting events are those where the score fluctuates, when control of the game continually changes hands. If you want an invigorating game, watch two equally assertive, equally adept teams vie for one winning spot. Crowds love it; it's in their blood. If the favored team spends the whole game crushing the competition, fans will leave pleased but uninvested. After all, they hardly exerted themselves on their team's behalf. Their players didn't need support; it was an easy victory. If the opposing team dominates the game, fans will leave furious. Not only were their heroes beaten and humiliated, they hardly put up a fight.

Keep this dynamic in mind as you construct the middle of your script. Exciting cinema resembles a great basketball game. Power changes hands, control over precious cargo is won and lost, wars are fought on both a small and grand scale over top billing. A writer heightens this struggle; she brings it to an audience's attention, and drama is born. So, identify your hero, identify your villain, and determine how closely they're matched. What you're tracking here is that crucial and often elusive ingredient known as *status*.

Status refers to control. The person who dominates a scene physically, sexually, professionally, intellectually, or in some other way is in a position of *high status*. He controls the action. Those people he dominates are in a *low status* position. Status is based on power and control, not necessarily on expected social rank or class structures.

Status roles affect every kind of relationship, and an alert writer discovers exactly how. Writers act as sociologists in this way, pinpointing the type of relationship between two characters, determining who controls that relationship, and making educated guesses on what would happen if that control increased or diminished. Those guesses eventually become scenes.

Study the relationships around you and assess where the power lies. Those associations generally fall into one of the following categories:

- **Social:** Every culture consists of social classes. Even those groups that profess otherwise have some system with which to rank each other. Is that system based on money, political power, physical appearance? Is it an intimate system, employed within one circle of friends, or a complex cultural structure? Often, each tier of a social system can be similarly divided into high and low power roles. Within a group of servants, for example, one is the head of affairs, and the others answer to her. The Oscar-nominated film *Gosford Park* capitalizes on shifts in social status within the classes.

- **Professional:** Unless your character is self-employed and works alone, she's part of a pecking order in her professional world. Each profession ranks employees according to their credentials and provides standards for further advancement. Because people spend entire lifetimes trying to get that promotion, status shifts in the professional world, especially when abrupt, are full of dramatic possibility. ***Working Girl*** is a classic example of such a film.

✓ **Sexual:** In seduction, one person generally pursues the other. Sexual relationships, from the initial spark to the courtship to the marriage (if they go that far), are all about status games played by both parties. Romantic comedies like ***When Harry Met Sally*** are structured around those games.

✓ **Intellectual:** Intelligence exists in many forms. Characters may survive through academic achievement, biting wit, or an intuitive intelligence that's sometimes called street smarts. In films based on these relationships, the smartest people generally win, and if they don't, the audience wishes they had. ***The Untouchables*** works in this way.

✓ **Physical:** Here, the person in control is either the one with the most brute strength or the one holding the biggest gun. Action/adventure films rely on these relationships to proceed. ***The Terminator, Rambo,*** and ***The Godfather Trilogy*** are just a few of the many examples.

✓ **Personal:** This option refers to the relationship a character has with himself. He may be battling an individual trait, phobia, addiction, instinct, or, perhaps, a disability for control over his actions. The Oscar-winning drama ***A Beautiful Mind*** is a clear example of such a film.

The same characters may share several kinds of relationships in any given story. The bond between a king and a servant is one that's primarily defined by social rank. However, it may also become an intellectual relationship, or even a sexual one. A person plays many roles in any given day. For example, a woman who's at once a professor, a mother, and a wife may have unfettered control over her classroom (high status role) but remain timid and withdrawn at home (low status role). A shift in her personal status at home may well affect her teaching dynamic.

So how does status affect the action of a film? Status shifts, no matter how slight, create tension between family and friends, community, or rivals. This tension, however palpable, propels action. Characters will fight to heighten or alleviate that tension, and, usually, the fight to regain stability drives the story forward. If you thrust someone who's unaccustomed to power into the spotlight, he'll either fight to maintain notoriety or fight to escape it. If you strip someone of power that they're used to wielding, that person will fight to get it back. This quest is, in part, what drives Al Capone to distraction in ***The Untouchables.*** Whether the characters shift toward or away from control, the change makes them active and compelling to watch.

Writers also continually shift status between the audience and the characters. When characters have the upper hand, they know something that the audience doesn't. If this secret is alluded to or suggested, the audience will wait to discover what it is. They'll participate in the action by searching for clues to the undivulged information. When an audience gains the upper hand, it knows something that the character doesn't. The result is a tension known as *dramatic irony*.

Dramatic irony occurs when the audience knows more than the characters. It raises the audience to a position of advanced knowledge in which they'll wait for the character to discover what they know. It adds a level of dramatic tension to a scene that would otherwise not be present.

If the audience knows something that a character remains ignorant of, the audience will participate in that character's well-being, fearing for his safety or cheering him toward discovery. In **Jaws,** the audience is aware of the killer shark, but the crowds of tourists are not. The tension mounts as they plunge into the water unaware of the danger below. This tension is crucial in a horror film where the writer wants his audience glued to the action. It also exists in comedy. In **Gold Rush,** a starving man imagines that he sees a gigantic chicken in front of him. The audience knows that it's actually Charlie Chaplin and will wait to see what happens when he tries to eat him. In both cases, audiences wait for the moment of discovery when the character discovers what they already know. They're immediately invested in the action.

So, if the script is your sporting event, the audience is your referee. Shifts in status help an audience keep score. If your players are well crafted and the trophy worth attaining, everyone will stick around to see who the ultimate victor will be.

What's Your Problem? Introducing Conflicts and Obstacles

The dynamic of sporting events is comparable to that of films (see preceding section). So, too, are their structures. Generally, both venues consist of the following:

- A team or player to root for
- A team or player to heckle
- One ultimate goal that both teams are invested in
- Conditions under which players can achieve that goal

In stories, the player we cheer for is known as the *protagonist* or the *hero.* Anyone standing in her way (that person we jeer at or hiss) is the *antagonist.* The goal is what each character wants. It may be a grand, admirable goal, or it may be interesting to only your protagonist. It's only important that the characters feel that they won't survive without achieving it. The conditions under which the players achieve that goal are the rules of your film: where the struggle takes place, each character's moral code, the allotted time clock, and so on. The antagonist is the most important element on this list because she is generally the first obstacle you'll introduce.

An *obstacle* is anything that prevents your protagonist from achieving her goal or at least makes it difficult for her to do so. An obstacle results in tension, as the character struggles to overcome it. That tension is known as *conflict*.

Whereas a ballgame has one antagonist in the opposing player or team, movies employ all sorts of adversaries. A strong film antagonist may be any of the following:

- ✔ **One person (also known as the villain):** Darth Vader, for example, in the *Star Wars Trilogy.*
- ✔ **A community or nation:** Amity village, for example, in the first half of *Jaws.*
- ✔ **The environment or a force of nature:** The multiple cyclones, for example, in the movie *Twister.*
- ✔ **The protagonist himself:** For example, John Forbes Nash, Jr. in *A Beautiful Mind.*

Any one of these rivals, or perhaps a few in combination, can prohibit a protagonist from attaining his goal. The goal may be power, justice, love, or a seat on the stock exchange. What matters is how committed your characters are to attaining it. The more important the goal is to both the audience and the main character, the more terrifying the antagonist's power becomes. As a writer, the more power you give your antagonist, the more interesting the struggle becomes. The first three obstacles that I mention in the previous list are external, but when the protagonist is working against himself, as the final option in that list suggests, you're constructing an internal obstacle. Internal obstacles may be

- ✔ A phobia
- ✔ An addiction
- ✔ A psychological or physical illness
- ✔ An overbearing or embarrassing personality trait
- ✔ A debilitating state of mind, such as depression, jealousy, defeat, anger, or indecision

The most compelling films employ both internal and external obstacles. In *Jaws,* the police chief battles a killer shark (external obstacle) despite the fact that he's afraid of the water (internal obstacle). The film *Arachnophobia* is a perfect example of this fusion; poisonous spiders attack the town, and what do you suppose the main character can't stand? You guessed it — spiders.

An easy victory or a quick defeat offers little satisfaction. Audiences want heroes to beat the odds, to win under seemingly impossible circumstances. Internal obstacles give your characters something to overcome in themselves while the physical action ensues. In a way, that's two conflicts for the price of one.

Keep in mind that obstacles are goal related; they prevent a character from achieving something he desperately wants to achieve. If your obstacle isn't strong enough to do so, if it's the heavy traffic or the rising temperature or the misplaced car keys, it may only be an annoyance or a bother. These irritations may color your action, but don't rely on them to propel it.

Exposition: From Clunky to Creative

It's sometimes easy to forget that your audiences begin this journey knowing virtually nothing about your plot. You've thoroughly researched the subject, and you've spent weeks (if not months) with the characters — you're a field expert here. But your audience? Sure, they've arrived at the theater for a reason; they may have seen a trailer or read a review. But trailers are 30 seconds long, and reviews are generally subjective. The likelihood is that they probably don't know much about your film at all. Audiences need *exposition* in order to understand the story that you already know so much about.

Exposition refers to information that the audience needs in order to understand the present story. The information may concern a character's relationship to others or historical details surrounding an event. One or all the characters generally already know this information. Exposition differs from backstory. Backstory encompasses everything that you've imagined about these characters and their pasts. An audience won't need all this information to follow the story. Exposition strictly refers to details of backstory without which an audience will be confused.

Exposition is often difficult to reveal in a natural manner. On first try, it tends to feel awkward or forced, like a stutter in an otherwise fluent speech. It breaks the scene's momentum. Why does this difficulty arise? In large part, exposition is awkward to present because it rarely occurs in real life. Most of your characters will share a past, and when you share common experiences with people, you rarely have to retell the whole story to remember it correctly. You discuss those memories with the acquired shorthand that exists among friends, family, and partners in crime. However, stories are written for an audience. The audience didn't experience everything that took place in the backstory, so they'll need more explanation. The challenge lies in providing that information in a natural way, through believable dialogue, consistent action, or strong images.

Exposition comes in two types:

- ✔ Information the audience needs but everyone else knows
- ✔ Information the audience needs but only a few characters know

Sharing info the characters know

The first kind of information presents a distinct problem. In most stories, characters already share information about each other, so writers must concoct reasons for them to reveal or relive it. This important info may concern their relationships with other characters or details of events that they were all a part of — in any case, it's old news for them. The world of the audience doesn't concern them; they aren't aware that it exists. So how do you construct scenes that smoke the details out into the open?

Many writers use their opening sequence to handle exposition. Scenes introducing main characters may visually suggest the types of relationships shared, as well as present their professions, possible desires, and/or their goals. The first ten minutes may be a series of time jumps that guide an audience through key moments in the past before beginning the present action. In this way, the audience shares past experiences with the characters and begins on the same page (so to speak). You may use a narrator for the same purpose — to alert viewers to details they may otherwise miss — but that technique is often too easy to produce great drama. In any case, you can't possibly pack every piece of expository information into the first sequence, nor would you want to. Your opening would then be instructive instead of intriguing. So, in crafting your second act, keep in mind these pieces of information that you may need to clarify:

- ✔ A character's past successes and failures
- ✔ A character's secret feelings or opinions of another character
- ✔ A character's secret feelings or opinions of an event
- ✔ A character's personal tendencies, including fantasies, addictions, hopes, fears, and regrets
- ✔ Past events that continue to haunt your characters
- ✔ Basic information about any new character you introduce

Remember that any information you share should remain on a need-to-know basis. You may uncover details that, while fascinating, aren't necessary. Exposition is *relevant* information, without which an audience would be confused about the action. For this reason, you need to try to reveal the information at the moment that it's most helpful. In ***Jaws,*** for example, I need to know right away that it's Fourth of July weekend in a town that survives on tourism in order to understand the fierce resistance the police chief faces when he suggests closing the beaches. I don't, however, need to know that the chief's afraid of water until later when the shark swims past his son, and he stands powerless to help. If you divulge too many details in advance, those details may distract me from pertinent action in the moment, and I may forget them well before they become important.

Sharing info the characters may not know

The second type of exposition is less difficult to maneuver because it suggests more dramatic possibilities. If one character knows something that the others don't, eventually, that character will confide in someone, and the audience will be privy to that conversation. The character may also have the job of presenting information as needed. In **Jaws,** Richard Dreyfuss plays a marine biologist and a shark expert. The writer lets Dreyfuss's character provide the data on what sort of a creature the town's up against. Both the other characters and the audience need this information because the remainder of the film takes place on the water in combat against the beast.

Study films with an eye toward exposition and note how they convey necessary information. Does the writer alert an audience to pertinent facts through flashback scenes? Through character confessions? Or does the writer weave the information in gradually, explaining behavior and action as it seems necessary to do so instead of at the onset. Many screenwriters solve the problem in similar ways. The most successful films strive to do the following:

- ✔ Convey as much as possible through visual images rather than relying on dialogue
- ✔ Drop the information in a moment of extreme conflict or humor
- ✔ Only say what's necessary when necessary
- ✔ Avoid didactic speeches
- ✔ Force the characters to work for the information

For a clear example of an entertaining way to convey otherwise didactic information, look at **Back To The Future.** In this film, Doc needs to explain his time travel plan to Marty. Rather than simply describing it in a rather flat manner, he creates a scale model of their town square and demonstrates his plans with a miniature DeLorean. The audience (and Marty) can absorb the information more easily because they can visualize the explanation.

A little information goes a long way. Extraneous details make for unimportant action and won't hold your audience's attention for long.

Note also the difference between exposition and *dramatic secrets*. Secrets are details the writer intends for everyone to discover together, characters and audience alike. That withheld information isn't crucial to the audience's understanding of the script. It comes as a satisfying surprise; it may be something an audience waits for, but the audience understands the drama without it. With exposition, you plant the information when the time is right and get back to the action as quickly as possible. If you're crafty, you can find a way for the information to fuel an event, thereby making it an action in itself.

Determining What to Write from What You've Already Written

Many writers, beginning and veteran alike, panic at the thought of generating 100 to 120 pages of compelling drama. Yet this dread often exists because they're constantly looking forward, straining to see what comes next and afraid that nothing will occur to them. However, much of the writing has been done for you after you craft your opening sequence. You just have to revisit it and see what you've already done.

Every portion of your screenplay will consist of a few moments that ring above the rest. By *ring,* I mean that they seem to be prominent or important in the scene for a reason that may be unknown even to you as you write. As you begin the process, you may want to record a few scenes as you see them unfolding and return afterward, noting anything out of the ordinary. You're looking for items known as *dramatic plants.* And though it sounds this way, I'm not talking about potted greens with a flair for theatrics.

 A *plant* (in film lingo) is a piece of evidence or information that's strategically placed in a scene in order to be discovered later on. In literary circles, the term *foreshadowing* is used as well, as plants hint at events down the road. As the action progresses, the plant assumes new meaning and may then be reincorporated for greater effect in an ensuing scene. The moment of renewed discovery is called the *payoff.* A dramatic plant may be any of the following:

- ✔ A key image
- ✔ A line of dialogue
- ✔ A motion or a gesture
- ✔ An object
- ✔ A costume piece
- ✔ A song or intriguing sound effect

The key to every strong plant isn't necessarily what it *is,* but rather how you *reincorporate* it into the action later on. Suppose that I construct a scene in which a mother warns her children not to play near the china cabinet, pointing out one bowl in particular that's a family heirloom. That bowl is the plant. You know what has to happen later, don't you? That bowl has to break. Every time a child moves near it, the tension mounts. If it breaks in the next scene, I've robbed my audience of that tension. But if I construct a few scenes in which it nearly breaks, I'm reminding the audience to watch for the impending disaster. And if the mother finally breaks it, I've found a surprising conclusion, but one that's perhaps satisfying in its irony.

You'll want to place distance between the plant and the payoff to ensure that the plant has time to acquire meaning. In **Good Will Hunting,** Robin Williams tells Matt Damon a story about missing the World Series to go on a date with his future wife. When Damon inquires what excuse he gave his friends for missing the event, Williams says, "I told them I had to go see about a girl." This line rings at the time because it's well constructed and because it ends the story. It doesn't show up again until the final moment of the film when Damon decides to leave town to track down his love interest. The note he leaves for Williams says the same thing. Throughout the story, numerous experts try to break through Damon's stubborn veneer and teach him something. Although this line is funny the first time an audience hears it, by the end, it stands as proof that Williams taught him something.

Take a look at your opening sequence and circle anything that you might reincorporate later. If you've introduced more than one character, you'll probably want those characters to meet at some point. If you begin with a crucial image, perhaps you'll revisit it later; if danger lurks in your first moments, you'll want it to return in a different, perhaps stronger guise. If you repeat this process with every scene you write, future moments may suggest themselves to you. You'll worry less about what to write next and concentrate instead on how to get there. The next step is to craft plants from the start and place them in a scene with some advance sense of how you'll use them later.

Don't confuse *reincorporation* with *repetition,* though. When you repeat a line, gesture, or image, you return to it in its original shape. If it gains importance the second or third time around, the action has shifted around it, but the image remains intact. The key line in **Good Will Hunting** remains the same even though the character who speaks it changes. The students in the **Blair Witch Project** return to the same clearing in the woods several times before their demise. Because the location never changes, the characters and the audience both begin to feel that they must be lost, and panic sets in. By the third time, the clearing takes on a menacing quality.

In contrast, you can *reincorporate* a plant in many ways. One of the first scenes in **American Beauty** takes place around a dinner table. This dinner ritual is the plant. The conversation is clipped, tense, and restrained. When the characters return to the dinner table several days later, the scene explodes with accusations and rebuttals. The characters' lives have fallen apart, and so has their false custom. Alan Ball, the screenwriter, continually returns to clichéd family rituals, but he alters them slightly each time to suggest that the changes that have gone on outside the house.

Here's a quick way to define the difference between the two devices:

- ✔ **In repetition:** The plant remains the same, but the action alters around it.

- ✔ **In reincorporation:** The plant changes shape to suggest changes that have occurred in the action.

Plants establish a pattern; the payoff represents the satisfying end to that pattern. Returning to an unaltered image or event several times (repetition), lets the audience view it again, hopefully in a different way. The audience discovers new information as the film progresses, so the image acquires new meaning the second time around. Returning to a slightly altered image or event (reincorporation) helps the audience understand changes in the story as a whole. The image becomes a way to gauge the action. Whether you return to an event or image several times or only once, the process of revisiting grants audiences a way to assess the action and generally results in a feeling of completion. You'll want to track the plants through your second act to determine which ones you use to enhance your story, and which ones you ultimately employ to conclude it.

Continuing Success: Tracking Three Successful Movie Middles

In Chapter 6, I detail three very different but equally compelling movie openings. So here, I break *Jaws, The Untouchables,* and *American Beauty* into their ensuing actions, obstacles, key exposition, and status fluctuations. If you haven't seen any of these films, you may want to rent them before reading the next section, or the outlines may ruin a future surprise.

If you rent these films, I encourage you to break them into the individual story components of status, obstacle, actions, and exposition. The pieces will undoubtedly overlap; obstacles cause actions, status shifts result in more obstacles, and so on. Yet by focusing your attention on one task at a time, you soon garner a familiarity with plot structure as a whole. Hopefully, it'll make the construction of your second act less daunting.

Jaws

Key actions: The second act of this script takes place in two major parts that are separated by location. The first portion takes place in town; the second takes place on the water. Here are the key actions in chronological order.

The mayor decides to keep the beaches open, claiming that the initial death was due to a boating accident. The shark kills a young boy, and his mother offers a $3,000 reward for its capture. A shark hunter named Captain Quint says that he'll kill the creature for $10,000. The marine biologist, Matt Hooper, arrives and discovers the false boating accident report. A tiger shark is captured, prompting the mayor to announce the threat is gone. The mother finds out that Police Chief Brody knew about the shark and failed to alert anyone. She publicly blames him for the death of her son. Brody and Hooper discover that the tiger shark isn't the killer, but the mayor refuses to listen. Another man is killed the next day in the same area where both Brody's son and the mayor's children are swimming. The mayor signs an agreement to let Brody and Hooper hire Quint to kill the shark. The trio sail out to kill the shark, and it puts up a formidable fight — sinking the boat, separating Hooper from Brody, and eating Quint in the process. When the second act ends, Brody must face the shark alone.

Obstacles: The town and the shark are the two primary antagonists and external obstacles. They present the first obstacle by refusing to close the beaches to the tourists. This conflict becomes more prominent when the tiger shark is caught, and everyone assumes that the waters are safe. Brody overcomes this obstacle when the shark threatens the mayor's own children, and he signs an order to destroy it. The battle with the shark is further complicated by the shark's size, strength, and (believe it or not) intelligence, a rickety boat, and a slightly crazy captain. The largest internal obstacle is Brody's fear of water and boats. He overcomes this terror to finish the job.

Exposition: The audience needs to know that it's the Fourth of July weekend, that Brody is afraid of water, that Hooper has never tracked a great white shark (especially one of this magnitude), and that Quint saw his entire crew get eaten by sharks after a submarine attack in the war. The first pieces of information are conveyed visually and through scattered lines of dialogue. The rest is revealed over the ship's table, moments before the final struggle with the shark.

Status: Status first alters in the political battle between the town and Brody. Brody ultimately triumphs. The battle among the three men is both social and intellectual. Quint owns the ship and has practical knowledge of sharks; Hooper has the scientific data and is equally stubborn. Brody allows them higher status until called upon to fight at the end. Their relationship with the shark is obviously a physical fight to the death — when the second act ends, no one knows which side will triumph.

The Untouchables

Key actions: The second act of this script can also be divided into two parts: one that takes place prior to the selection of Elliot Ness's crew and one that takes place after the crew is assembled.

Ness raids a factory that's supposedly smuggling liquor for Capone, based on a tip he receives. The tip is a false one, and he's publicly humiliated. He meets Officer Malone (Sean Connery) in passing and asks him to join the Treasury team. Malone at first declines, but he then changes his mind. They select the second team member, George Stone (Andy Garcia), and with the unwitting help of the Treasury's accountant, successfully raid a secret liquor warehouse. Capone brutally murders the man responsible for the mistake. His crony offers Ness a bribe, which Ness refuses. They threaten Ness's family, who are quickly moved to a safe location. The gang successfully stops an arms shipment and retrieves Capone's financial ledger in the process. Capone begins trial for income-tax evasion. Capone has the accountant killed, at which point Ness almost ends the fight in despair. Malone is also murdered, but he manages to relay information on how to nab Capone's bookkeeper before he dies. At the end of the second act, it remains uncertain whether Ness and Stone will be able to do so without the help of their friends.

Obstacles: The antagonist is obviously Al Capone and his mafia crew. However, Ness also fights corruption within the Treasury itself, the police department, and, eventually, in court. Internal conflicts include Malone's initial fear of death, Ness's devotion to his family, and his concern for their safety.

Exposition: The audience needs to know that Ness begins the journey on his first day on the job, his police experience is limited, his ethics are strong and sound, he desperately loves his wife and child, and his wife is pregnant. The audience discovers all this information in the first ten minutes. Later, it becomes important to know that Malone is a religious man, Stone is a stellar marksman, and Capone will kill his own people, if necessary. All these details arrive when you need them — not a moment sooner.

Status: The film works very much like a tennis match. First, Capone wins; then Ness, then Capone, and then Ness. They're evenly matched, and although the audience roots for Ness and loathes Capone, the victor remains uncertain.

American Beauty

Key actions: The second act exists in three parts. During the first part, Lester despises his life. In the second part, his life begins to change, and in the third part, he begins to enjoy it again. His wife Carolyn and daughter Jane go through similar changes at exactly the same moments.

Lester is told that he may lose his job unless he writes a report convincing them that he's a valuable employee. Carolyn fails miserably at selling a house. Jane meets the new boy across the street, Ricky Fitts. He silently films her. The audience meets his family — his silent, withdrawn mother and his father, a homophobic, retired military colonel. Lester meets Jane's seductive friend Angela. He becomes infatuated with her. He embarrasses his wife at a social function, leaving her to flirt with a rival real estate tycoon. Lester smokes pot with Ricky. He begins to work out and buy marijuana from Ricky on a regular basis. The family takes the first major turn. Lester blackmails his company into a great severance package and takes a job at a fast-food restaurant. Carolyn begins an affair with the tycoon. Jane begins seeing Ricky. Colonel Fitts suspects him of having sexual relations with Lester. Carolyn buys a gun and takes up shooting lessons. Lester reminds the audience that he'll be dead soon. Their lives take the second major turn. Lester discovers his wife's affair. Jane ends her friendship with Angela. Colonel Fitts kicks Ricky out of the house. Ricky and Jane decide to run away together. Angela decides to sleep with Lester.

Obstacles: Internal obstacles abound in this film, too many, in fact, to list. Suffice it to say that most of the characters are their own antagonists; much of the action involves altering their mindsets and thereby changing the course of their lives. Other obstacles include Colonel Fitts, Lester's boss, and Carolyn's career, but these external obstacles take a back seat to the internal conflicts.

Exposition: Lester provides most of the necessary exposition through his narration. He tells us what his life is like, he tells us what his flaws are, and he tells us what he'd like to change. Colonel Fitts's own comments suggest the homophobia, Ricky tells Jane that he's recently returned from a mental institution, and everything else is revealed visually in scenes or through narration.

Status: All sorts of power changes hands in this film. Sexual tension erupts between Jane and Ricky, Lester and Angela, and Carolyn and the tycoon. Lester defeats his boss; he and Carolyn square off time and again; Angela loses social control over Jane but gains sexual power over Lester; Ricky and his father pit intellect against brute strength. The score is always in flux.

Chapter 8

Plot Part III: Endings

• •

In This Chapter

▶ Pinpointing your story's conclusion

▶ Tracing your character arcs

▶ Protecting your script from destructive elements

▶ Taking a look at successful movie endings

• •

*H*ow do you know when your story's finished? It's finished when the characters triumph over adversity, the villain disappears, the conflicts are efficiently resolved, and everyone goes home smiling, of course. You don't believe me? What if I said that your story's finished when the characters, who have undergone so much turmoil that they can hardly stand, finally give up the effort entirely and let the world collapse around them? You still seem skeptical. Well, good for you because, for a strong script, neither of those endings fits the bill.

Regarding your story's conclusion, I have both good news and bad news. The good news is that if all your second-act pieces are in place — if you've crafted dynamic actions, intimidating obstacles, and formidable foes — your ending should write itself. The bad news is that at the end of a first draft, your second-act pieces are rarely in place.

A convincing conclusion is one in which the conflicts that you've inflated in Act II find resolution, the characters achieve their goals or stop vying for them, and the new world you've created makes some kind of sense — however unorthodox that sense may be. Your ending relies on every moment that precedes it. If the second act offers no solution, your only resort is a forced wave of the magic wand (so to speak) to sum things up, which will leave your audience dissatisfied and confused.

This chapter offers suggestions on ways to recheck both your opening and second act to steer them toward the appropriate finale and on how you may craft that finale when you get there. (For more info on crafting your first and second acts, see Chapters 6 and 7.)

How Do You Know When You're Done?

The end of your second act is a precarious place to be. Your protagonist is either embroiled in chaos and ready to abandon hope, or she's just beginning to acknowledge a bright and promising future. The antagonist is closing in, ready to fight to the death if need be, and time is running out. The only question left to answer is, "Will your protagonist be successful?" In other words, will she overcome the obstacles and achieve her goal? After you answer that question, proceed to the following questions. They may help guide you to a fitting conclusion for your script.

- ✔ Has your story been written before? If so, how does it differ from predecessors with a similar concept?

- ✔ Do you understand your characters more thoroughly now than when you began?

- ✔ Are your rules still intact? (See Chapter 6 where I discuss rules.)

- ✔ What have you discovered about your story so far?

- ✔ Have your story's central themes or questions changed? If so, what are they now?

- ✔ Does each portion of your story address those themes or questions in some way?

- ✔ Has your story reached the point you anticipated reaching? If not, are you content with where it is?

- ✔ Have your characters changed? Have their worlds altered? How?

- ✔ What has been gained and/or lost for the characters, the environment, and the audience?

The first six questions address elements of your opening and second act, which you may need to adjust in retrospect. If you've discovered a movie that shares too much in common with your own, you'll want to enhance the portions of your script that make it unique.

You should know more about your characters now than when you started. If you don't, your action is probably fueled by events rather than people. Go back and see what you can discover in hindsight.

The rules of your film refer to its consistency. In other words, are you writing the same film now that you were at the beginning? If not — if characters have mysteriously disappeared, the genre has changed, or the ultimate goal shifted — you'll want to check to see where the plot became muddled. The same note applies to your story's central themes and questions. You may find that the themes you arrive at are more compelling than those that began the journey. If that's the case, rewrite your beginning to match your end.

The final three questions on the list speak to the all-important aspects of any film — the elements of discovery and change. Unless your characters have learned something about themselves or the world in which they exist, and unless both venues have changed accordingly, you won't know how to end your story. The film's final moments rely on an acquired knowledge on the part of your characters and, hopefully, in the audience as well.

Tracking the change: What's different now?

A strong story chronicles the most important or compelling moments in a character's life. And the most compelling moments involve the most difficult and, therefore, enlightening transitions. Consider revelations in your own life — moments when you discovered something horrific or awe-inspiring about yourself or your environment. I'd venture to guess that they included or were followed by personal growth and maturity. Your characters will experience the same phenomenon as the script progresses, and what they learn will affect where you lead them, a journey known as the film's *dramatic arc*.

A *dramatic arc* refers to the trajectory of a character, a community, or an environment from one state of being to another. The transition can be monitored through changes in behavior, in points of view, or in moral codes that, in turn, alter the story's action.

Reconsidering your story's time clock

Your story's time clock refers to the grand event your script is tiptoeing or barreling toward. In Chapter 5, I discuss several different kinds of time clocks and their advantages, but regardless of which time clock you chose, you'll want to reconsider it now. If your story is moving toward an external event, as in *3:10 to Yuma*, the culminating moments will involve watching the 3:10 train pull into the station. If your story revolves around an internal crisis, as in the Nick Nolte film *Affliction*, your final moments will determine whether he bests the past that haunts him, or whether it destroys him.

Generally speaking, the film ends fairly quickly after the culminating event. So if you know what the story's time clock is, and if you've built a plot moving the viewers toward it, you'll know exactly what the final moments of your script should entail.

Tracking character arcs

Before you begin crafting a conclusion, look back at what your characters have undergone so far. Hopefully, they've altered dramatically as a result. You're tormenting them for a reason, right? And it's not so that they can remain passive or content. It's your job to challenge and, if necessary, harass your characters into a new way of life. They'll become the sum of all the experiences you toss at them, so keep track of those experiences and, more importantly, of their effects. In doing so, you'll discover the following:

✓ Whether the stages of transformation are clear and consistent

✓ Whether your audience has been privy to the transformation

✓ Whether you've omitted key moments

✓ Who your character may ultimately turn out to be

If your character exits one scene as a millionaire and appears two scenes later begging for change on a street corner, your audience won't trust the transformation. Why should they? *You* might know exactly how he got from one state of being to the next, but don't forget to let your audience in on the actions that brought him there. The most dramatic scenes in this scenario connect the character from wealthy Point A to impoverished Point B. If you show me his gambling habit, the demise of his business, and a hefty divorce settlement that favors his two ex-wives, I'll not only understand his monetary transition, I may even expect it.

The preceding scenario is an example of an external change, which is generally less difficult to dramatize. Other external changes may affect the following aspects of your character:

✓ Appearance

✓ Mode of expression

✓ Profession and/or financial status

✓ Circle of family and/or friends

✓ Habits, hobbies, and personal tendencies

Many external changes don't necessitate lengthy dialogue. If your main character begins his journey hobnobbing with the elite and ends warming his hands over a back-alley fire pit, I'll visually note the change in his social circle. In ***The Talented Mr. Ripley,*** Matt Damon transforms from a middle-class nobody to a mirror image of his upper-class idol with virtually no discussion at all.

External changes generally mark key stages in the story's dramatic arc. Lester Burnham of ***American Beauty*** begins working out just as his life begins to improve in all capacities. In ***Good Will Hunting,*** the protagonist initially speaks like a Boston construction worker, but in later scenes, he verbally holds his own with world-renowned scientists. However, shifts in the character's physical person or circumstances may also be the result of some internal transformation. Internal transformations include shifts in the character's

- Psychological health
- Confidence
- Anxiety
- Sexuality
- Opinions or beliefs
- Passions or dreams
- Awareness of others
- Compassion or lack thereof
- Religion or faith

External changes are simple to dramatize; internal shifts require more skill. Unless you visually re-create the mind or spirit of the character, much as the writers do in *Being John Malkovich,* it will be the character's altered behavior that clues me in to the transformation. Brody begins his journey in *Jaws* as a man desperately afraid of the water, yet by the end, he's battling the shark alone on the ocean, clutching a piece of driftwood for support. Spielberg illustrates the change in his phobia by scenes in which Brody moves closer and closer to the water. He then makes it a matter of life and death that Brody charter a boat.

You'll also want to track the internal and external shifts for the other characters — support staff included. Though many villains shift from bad to worse, even the slightest transition affects their actions. Capone may remain a monster to the end, but by the film's conclusion, he becomes a desperate monster, and he's learned an important lesson: He's not untouchable.

After you know what alterations your characters have undergone prior to your resolution, you should be able to determine what the last step in that transformation is and whether it will aid or prevent the character from achieving her goal. The scenes in which the characters experience that moment become your *climax,* which leads to the *resolution.*

The *climax* represents the most intense and, generally, the grandest scene of the film in which the protagonist makes one last attempt at achieving his goal. The climax is the culmination of any struggles or transformations the character has experienced prior to it; it marks the story's final battlefield.

The *resolution* occurs immediately after the climax and comprises the film's last scene. This is the time characters and audiences alike absorb the impact of the final battle. It marks the character's first walk as a changed person in the new world of your script. It also marks the end of your film. In some instances, all that remains of a film after the resolution are the end credits.

Altering the world of your script

Characters are so closely linked to their environments that it's often difficult to distinguish changes in one realm from changes in the other. The world of your script will shift as the characters shift; in fact, the world may directly reflect their changes, both internal and external. You want to track these transformations through the opening and second act as well in order to better predict where you'll ultimately end up. Here are two important questions to consider while constructing your final landscape:

✔ What sort of world have I crafted?

✔ Why have I led my audience to that world?

The first question speaks to your script's general climate. By climate, I mean both the actual landscapes and the social, political, and economic conditions, all of which may alter with the action. The climate may change in any of the following ways:

✔ Physically

✔ Politically

✔ Socially

✔ Spiritual

✔ Ethically

✔ Sexually

A change in climate makes something possible that wasn't possible before, or it removes a possibility entirely. In *Lord of the Rings,* a beautiful and serene setting becomes dark and ominous. The landscape shifts, and it becomes more difficult for good to prevail. In *The Green Mile,* the spiritual climate shifts. People who once did not believe in the supernatural find themselves witness to it. As a result, they view a convicted murderer with very different eyes. To further understand what I mean by climate, you may want to complete this phrase:

> "My story ends in a world where _____ is no longer possible/acceptable and where _____ can now occur."

You should be able to complete at least one part of that statement by the end of your script. At the end of *The Untouchables,* Chicago is a city where extortion is no longer acceptable and where justice can now occur. At the end of *A Beautiful Mind,* psychological stability is no longer possible, but an honest way of life can now occur. Bear in mind that a shift in one of these realms doesn't necessarily mean that the climate will change within the boundaries of your story. You may only be concerned with leading up to the shift itself; the repercussions may belong in a different script. However, a shift in one of the realms always suggests the possibility of a change in climate. You may explore that change on-screen, or let your audience imagine it long after the credits roll.

The second question speaks to your responsibility as a writer. You're not going on this journey alone; you're taking an audience with you. That audience expects to gain or feel something along the way — preferably something grander than disgust or lowbrow humor. It expects to leave the film changed in some way. You're giving the audience a gift of some kind — the gift of laughter, of knowledge, and even of extreme pain if enlightenment is the result. Spielberg's ***Schindler's List*** is an example of a world full of bigotry, destruction, and death. Yet at the film's conclusion, relatives of the deceased leave stones on the graves, honoring the victims together. The audience may leave feeling mortified and/or ashamed, but it will also remember the victims.

The world you craft need not be neat, predictable, or safe. Your audience members probably don't live in a world where all three of those conditions exist, and they might not believe it if they saw it. Your characters don't need to end up happy or more ethically sound; that phenomenon also rarely occurs in everyday life. However, in order to fully satisfy your audience, the ultimate world of your script should do a few things clearly:

- ✔ It should evolve out of the previous action.
- ✔ It should represent the changes that your main characters have undergone along the way.
- ✔ It should allow or prevent your characters from achieving their goals and/or solving their problems.
- ✔ It should offer hope in some direction.

The last item on that list also speaks to responsibility. Hopefully, your story represents a change for the better or offers that distinct possibility. Yes, your main character may die, but can that death lead to some ultimate good? Lester Burnham's death in ***American Beauty*** leaves the other characters (and possibly audiences) questioning bitterness in themselves and the life they take for granted.

Crafting your story's conclusion

An *epiphany* is a sudden intuitive realization, an unexpected comprehension of reality. The key words in that definition are unexpected and realization. In grand cases, epiphanies are accompanied by a sharp intake of breath and an awakening of the senses as they struggle to absorb a new way of understanding something about the world. In more subtle terms, an epiphany feels like a great "Aha!" and a mild relief at the solution to a mystery. Get to know this word epiphany. It's the heart of a strong conclusion.

You can conclude your film in numerous ways, yet the classiest endings seem to exist in two parts: the climax and the resolution. In a sense, the rising action runs you up the hill where you fight the final battle (known as the *climax*), and at the end, you roll down the other side of that hill into the resolution. By the end of the second act, you should know roughly what that resolution will be. Even if you're a writer who loathes outlines, you know what your characters want, and you know where they're going. Start painting a picture that tells your audience what *you* already know.

Climax — the final frontier

The climax marks the first and most important part of your story's conclusion. If you've done your job, audiences have some idea of what's coming next, and they're ready for it. Your action up to that point creates expectations that your climax will probably fulfill. But no pressure, right? With so much riding on this scene, it really helps to take it step by step.

A strong climax will do the following:

- **Be the grandest scene in your script in weight, scope, and action.** All scenes lead to this one, so don't disappoint your audience by skimming through the climax. Consider your genre. If your film is a romantic comedy, the romance blossoms or ends here. If your film is an action/adventure, the greatest, most exciting battle occurs here. If your film is a tragedy, the climax marks the time of greatest loss. Remember that time is running out; the actions that your characters once shied away from must happen now if they're to happen at all. If you make bold decisions anywhere, let it be here.

- **Toss your protagonist into a moment of choice.** Your characters have undergone changes for a reason. They've acquired skill and knowledge for a reason. They've done so because that expertise will be necessary in the climax. Place your characters in a moment of uncertainty when they must choose which way to act and let them use their newfound knowledge to decide what to do. If things simply happen to your main character, the audience will leave dissatisfied, uncertain whether she's truly strong enough to solve the problem or is simply lucky.

- **Begin at the moment that the protagonist experiences the greatest despair or the first indications of hope.** The choice you make here often determines whether you end triumphantly or with tragic repercussions. A character that begins the climax in anguish has nowhere to go but up. Something will happen in the next moment to convince him to turn things around, and he'll face the enemy refreshed or, at the very least, determined. On the flip side, a character who's full of great hope at the onset of the climax has the most to lose. The character will either experience that loss in the final scenes or experience it and then make a miraculous recovery at the end.

✔ **End when the protagonist resolves his problems.** Resolving the problem doesn't necessarily mean achieving the goal. However, if your character doesn't achieve his goal, his failure to do so should somehow solve the problem. Scarlett O'Hara doesn't find romantic fulfillment, but her inability to do so ends her false marriage and puts a dent in her unhealthy way of life. Luke Skywalker doesn't decisively defeat Darth Vader until the third film of the *Star Wars Trilogy,* but he solves the ultimate problems in the first two films.

Your character is waging a dual war in the climax:

✔ **A war with the external antagonist/villain.** Keep track of your villain or your chosen antagonist. That villain has learned alongside the hero, and that villain has acquired a support group alongside the protagonist. That villain is ready to win, as is the hero. They should be evenly matched.

✔ **A war with himself.** Something internal has been barring your character from complete success. He needs to overcome that something here or use it to his distinct advantage. In either case, overcoming this internal conflict becomes an important part of your protagonist's primary journey or arc.

Ask yourself what event would force these people together, where would they choose to wage a last war, and who is the strongest of the pair. That scene is your climax.

Your audience should leave your film satisfied. Notice that I don't say thrilled or grief-stricken, but satisfied. In Chapter 7, I speak about reincorporation, the art of weaving key bits of thematic information continuously through your story. Those bits culminate here. The climax marks the final reincorporation of images, ideas, skills, and traumas. Luke Skywalker loses his aunt and uncle, who act as his parents at the beginning of the *Star Wars* Trilogy; he finds his real father in the trilogy's final climax. George Lucas reincorporates the idea of parenting and guidance one last time, and somehow, the story feels complete. The *Sixth Sense* begins with a violent break-in and shooting in the protagonist's home. It's not until the final moments of the resolution that we discover the true ramifications of that beginning, and they affect how we look back at the entire plot. Your climax releases the tension that you've constructed between characters, and it completes some pattern, be it behavioral or thematic. The ending of that cycle is very satisfying.

Resolution — the final lap

Your film's resolution is the audience's final grace note, the time to linger with the characters just long enough to feel what's shifted in the world. Here are some final questions that may help you clarify that scene when you get there:

✔ **Where is your villain?** What kind of justice reigns in your finale? A truly formidable villain leaves a mark even after death, be it a physical scar on the hero's cheek or his wiser, more wary sensibility.

✔ **What has your protagonist lost and gained?** This loss or gain may be as specific as a love interest and as profound as stability, but something is missing from this world, and something exists now that was not there when you began. What is it?

✔ **Was it worth the trip?** Ask this question for the characters and for the audience. What can a human being gain from watching the action? The answer may be "an evening of laughter" or "an acute look at racism." If the audience has gained something or even left with an element of hope, you've done all right.

✔ **What story might begin the way yours now ends?** The ending of every script could mark the beginning of a new one (and possible sequel!). You're moving your characters from stability into chaos and back to a new (not necessarily secure) stability. One person's finale might be another's opening night.

Your resolution will most likely be short. After all, you solved the problem in the climax. You probably just have a few loose ends to tie up. After the explosive and revealing scene between Matt Damon and Robin Williams in *Good Will Hunting,* Damon must still quit his job, pack his belongings, and leave a final note for Williams. The audience needs to see his friends drive up to the house and discover him not there because it completes a pattern established earlier. But these scenes happen quickly. The pervading tension has already been released, and the epiphany has been reached — give us a calm scene or two and let the closing credits roll.

Danger Will Robinson: Threats to an Otherwise Healthy Plot

Much of a first draft is written in a feverish pitch and at a feverish pace. If you let your script sit around for too long in between writing marathons, anxiety will creep up on you along with every other thing you have to do before finishing the script. So, often, the best thing to do is to write the whole thing quickly while caught in the story's grip and wait until you've completed a draft to hunt for those elements trying to sabotage it from within. However, you now have a complete draft. You have a beginning, a middle, and — lo and behold — an ending. Now, you can begin to search for those things that make your plot go clunk in the night instead of zing.

Would that really happen? The probable versus the possible

When you write a script, you make a silent pact with an eventual audience; they're going to trust you, and you're going to preserve that trust. Audiences want you to succeed at your craft. They've paid $12 to be here (not to mention $12 on popcorn); they want your story to astound them, move them, affect them in some positive way. In other words, they're on your side. That is, they're on your side until the first line of dialogue doesn't ring true, until the first scene with a forced conclusion, until that long-lost character emerges to sum everything up, or until that senior citizen with the broken ankle manages to sprint up six flights of steps at record speed just in time to force his way into the dead-bolted room and defeat the sumo wrestler. Do you see where I'm headed? *Plausibility,* and lack thereof, will be the first thing to make or break your film.

Aristotle said that drama lies in that which is probable, rarely in that which is possible. Plausibility refers to holes in your story's logic, and the more probable your actions are, the fewer holes you'll have. You should ask yourself the same two questions that audiences will ask as they watch:

✔ Could this really happen?

✔ Could it really happen this way?

Audiences may not think to ask these questions until something in your script suggests that they should. They may pass over the first awkward moment because they've spent money here, and they want to enjoy themselves. The next few moments will set them on edge; they may begin looking for flaws, and by the fourth or fifth error, they'll pick your script apart on the drive home. What sort of moments might grab their attention? All sorts, actually.

A story becomes improbable when

✔ **It has glaring historical or factual errors.** Audiences shouldn't consider movies, historical or otherwise, to be entirely factual. They're built on drama, and drama takes liberties. However, if your script takes place in the 17th century and a car drives by in the distance, I would have a hard time buying the setting, if not the action itself.

✔ **The film's genre shifts or is in question.** The best films combine comedy with drama, romance with adventure, and so on. Yet at its core, a film lives in one area. If it doesn't, if it jumps evenly between two or more categories, it may feel like two films are vying for space, neither of which has time to be complete.

- ✔ **Crucial information arrives too easily.** I go to movies to see people struggle, to battle each other for control of something that they want. Your heroes are only strong because an audience witnesses their struggle. Nothing in life is easy. If your hero's life is simple and easy, not only will I refuse to believe it, I may resent it as well.

- ✔ **A character's actions contradict each other.** This item refers to consistency, and consistency refers to the ultimate goal. If your character always moves toward one goal, her actions remain consistent in their purpose. If her goal shifts, or if she behaves erratically for seemingly no reason, I'll leave the theater frustrated and bewildered.

- ✔ **A character disappears with hasty explanation or no explanation at all.** This phenomenon occurs either because, in crafting the protagonist, you've forgotten a smaller character or because you found that you had one too many people to track and didn't know how to write one out.

- ✔ **A character bursts onto the action with little or no setup.** This phenomenon occurs either because you knew this person was coming but failed to allow for it in your opening or because you need to solve a problem in the script and are hoping that a new character will do it for you.

- ✔ **Problems are solved without combat of any kind.** Characters are only interesting when they're making choices, gaining knowledge necessary to make choices, or acting on choices that they've already made. They should make events happen, not let events happen to them.

Your opening may solve some of your plausibility difficulties. Those first 15 to 30 pages establish what can and can't happen in the script. If you want me to believe in a car that travels through time, introduce me to its inventor right away (***Back to the Future***). If you want me to consider racial stereotypes immediately (***Crash***), open with two black teenagers walking through wealthy, suburban Los Angeles talking about how people assume that they're gangsters. If you intend to introduce a character much later, create a world in which I'm used to surprised visitors. You might also mention the character in earlier dialogue, so that the name precedes its owner.

There is a distinct difference between *suspension of disbelief* and improbability. *Suspension of disbelief* refers to an audience's willingness to believe fantastical or extraordinary situations out of a desire to enjoy the story. Audiences suspend their disbelief because they're enthralled by the plot, and they want to believe that it could happen. An improbable script presents something as fact that cannot be, but it does little to convince the audience of its worth. It often happens with the best intentions. Writers are on a tight deadline, desperate for a next payment, or they're furious with one stubborn portion of the script and ready to be done with it. In any case, they reach a point where a solution won't present itself, and they quickly formulate some device to solve it for them. In Greek drama, it appears as a *deus ex machina*. A god descends from the heavens to settle old scores and sum information up. In modern times, it appears as that lucky tip that happened to solve the case, the one door that happened to be unlocked, or those keys that happened to be left in a getaway car. These solutions are too easy; I feel the writer stepping in. When the writer's hand in the work becomes apparent, the audience's belief in the action diminishes.

How do you avoid implausible action? You may try one or several of the following:

- ✔ **Research, research, research.** The more familiar you are with the world, the less likely that historical or continuity mistakes will occur. You should know more about your story than the audience does. Prove it to them so that they can trust the story and relax.

- ✔ **Allow a character to express the audience's disbelief.** *Back to the Future* works, in part, because one of the characters is a skeptic. The character takes on the role of the audience in questioning the action. As he becomes convinced that the notion is possible, so, too, does the audience.

- ✔ **Prepare the audience for improbabilities in advance.** Those script rules are all-important. Look toward possible improbabilities and prepare an audience for them in advance. *Star Wars* tells the audience right away that this is a galaxy long ago and far away. Audiences are immediately prepared for a sci-fi adventure where impossible things are now possible.

- ✔ **Make characters work for information.** Any piece of data that arrives quickly and easily is suspect. Life doesn't work that way. You may write an element of luck into your script, but too much luck is unacceptable.

- ✔ **Let characters solve problems themselves, using skills or knowledge that the audience has witnessed them acquiring.** The audience wants to get to know your protagonists, to learn from them, and to be changed by them. It can't do so if the protagonists don't act for themselves or make choices and follow them through.

Implausibility maligns your audience's trust and makes the audience wary of you as a writer and of filmmaking in general. You want your audiences to continue expecting good films, not to be surprised when they finally see one. Eventually, it's your name on the work, and audiences will see the film as an extension of you. Take care with what you present.

Scenes where nothing happens: Two final threats to watch for

Two final threats occur when a writer overwhelms a reader with unrelated action or unimportant dialogue. I call the first threat *cascading,* and the second threat *banter.* Ever been to a movie with scene after scene of exciting action or cutting repartee that has little aim or direction? Many things can happen in a scene without anything really *happening.* How? Look at this scene breakdown:

> A man robs a bank.
>
> Police follow him to the harbor.
>
> A boat chase ensues.
>
> He is picked up by a helicopter.
>
> He flies to an airstrip, but detectives are waiting.
>
> He charters a jet.
>
> A plane chase ensues.

Aside from the obvious improbability, what's really happening here? A lot of movement, some exciting special effects no doubt, and an element of danger — but beyond that? Not much. When one action follows another with no sense of purpose, you're creating a paper chain, not compelling drama. This is cascading. You cascade a script when you forget to reincorporate knowledge or experience from one action into situations that follow it.

Suppose that a boy goes flying with his father in the opening shots; the audience can see that he idolizes his dad. In a following scene, he plays airplane with his younger brother, explaining how to fly just as he heard his dad explain it to him. So if, at the end of the film, a group of men chase him into the shed where they keep the plane, how do you think he'll escape? Well, if he skateboards out, I'll probably leave the theater. Here, each action builds into the next, and, at some point, previously acquired knowledge is reused. I could've said that the boy flies with his father, he plays airplanes with his brother, the family's attacked, he escapes to the woods, he's chased through town, and so on. But that would be a cascade. The action never lands; it just keeps on coming.

Cascading affects your scene-to-scene structure. Banter works in much the same way, but it affects your dialogue. Remember, I go to the theater to watch characters change and affect each other. I go, in part, to keep score. Consider the following dialogue between two coworkers:

"Hey Jackie, how's your work going?"

"Fine, Grace. And yours?"

"Fine. Great shindig last night."

"It was, wasn't it? How much do you think it cost?"

"I don't know, but it wasn't cheap."

"Was Harry there?"

"I think I saw him. I loved his speech the other day, didn't you?"

And so on. Who's winning in that scene, do you think? It's hard to tell. Any tension on the rise? Doubtful. The problem with the conversation, as it pertains to drama, is that nothing's changing. Neither woman gains or loses status, nor does the conversation seem to be code for another topic. If Jackie had just been fired and Grace was purposely hurting her feelings, social tension would exist. If Jackie was speaking as if her work was fine, but really she had just been fired, the scene would have *subtext,* which means a conversation would exist below what was actually being said. I'll watch that scene. As long as someone in the scene is being affected, if that person leaves the scene different (however slightly) than when she went in, you've done your job.

Ultimate Success: Tracking Three Movies through Their Triumphant Conclusions

In this section, I tell you how three films end, and moreover, I break down those endings. I just thought I'd warn you in case you don't already know how these movies end and would rather see or read the endings for yourself first. (Aren't I considerate?)

The three films I skim through here tackle different subjects and different environments and build completely different people, yet they share a tight, efficient structure. Every ten minutes, a routine is broken, and an action occurs. The characters gain skills that they use later to further the plot. Every main character, villains included, is given a resolution, if not a joyous one. If you begin analyzing all the films you watch in this manner, you may be amazed at what you discover.

Jaws

Rising Action: The final battle in this film must take place between Brody and the shark. Brody is the one with the fear of water, Brody was responsible for funding the expedition, and Brody is the one propelling the town to take these actions. So the rising action consists of getting him alone. Hooper descends into the water in his observation cage, armed with sedatives meant to end the creature when it approaches. This plan, of course, fails. The cage is destroyed, and Hooper barely escapes to hide behind a reef. Next up — Captain Quint. After destroying the radio in a fit of passion and destroying the boat in foolish pursuit of the shark, Quint takes one last stab at it with his gun and three barrels. He fails, and the shark eats him. Brody is left alone on a sinking ship, facing a very angry shark.

Climax: The shark has a tank of compressed oxygen caught in its mouth. It repeatedly batters the ship until it sinks entirely. Brody faces the beast with a shotgun. The shark turns around and begins swimming toward him. Brody shoots once. Nothing. He shoots again. Still nothing. He continues to shoot, as the shark heads right for him. Suddenly, a shot gets in, and the shark explodes.

Resolution: Hooper emerges from beneath the water. He greets an exhausted Brody. They fashion a makeshift raft from the leftover ship and swim back to shore.

The Untouchables

Rising Action: The climax of the film occurs between Ness and Capone, but the action leading to it suggests that Ness may not have gotten that far. It begins as Ness decides to give up the fight. The accountant is dead, his family's in hiding, his wife has just had a child, and he's exhausted. But Capone won't let him rest. Malone is brutally murdered. He dies in Ness's arms, but he's able to alert him about a train carrying Capone's bookkeeper in the seconds before his death. Now resolute to avenge his dear friend's death, Ness heads for the train station.

Climax: This film's climatic scene is one of the most tense and well-choreographed scenes in film history. Ness and Stone wait at the train station. At first, no one shows up. A woman begins dragging her baby carriage up the steep stone steps. Worried for her safety, Ness runs down to help her, just as Capone's men show up en masse. As he reaches the top step, the bookkeeper shows up, and the men begin to leave. A shot is fired by one of Capone's gang. The baby carriage tips with the baby inside it. As it clatters down the steps in slow motion, Ness and his sharpshooter comrade Stone proceed to kill all Capone's men but one, who uses the bookkeeper as a shield. In the final tense moment, Stone shoots Capone's man in the head, narrowly missing the bookkeeper.

Resolution: Though the climax is over, a few things still need to be solved before the film can end. First, Ness discovers Malone's murderer sitting in the courtroom. After a quick chase scene over the rooftops of Chicago, Ness pushes him off the high-rise onto a car below. Next, he discovers that Capone has bribed both the jury and the judge. He scares the judge into switching juries mid-trial. Capone is furious. Clearly, he'll be sent away. Ness is finally able to approach him in complete victory.

American Beauty

Rising Action: This film spends much of its time helping Lester Burnham take control of his life. When he finally does so, the climax and resolution occur very quickly. The rising action bounces between family members, so every character experiences a climax of some sort. Carolyn's affair comes to an end, her work is in shambles, and she's desperate for some sort of real connection. She purchases a gun. Ricky's father accuses him of seeing Lester, and he kicks him out of the house. Ricky and Jane decide to run away together. Colonel Fitts approaches Lester in the garage and kisses him. Lester tells him that he must have the wrong idea, and Fitts stumbles back home in the rain. Angela and Jane fight; Ricky accuses Angela of being the shallow person that she pretends to be. Angela, vulnerable and upset, decides to sleep with Lester. They try, but she admits that it's her first time, and Lester is unable to follow through with the encounter.

Climax: The final battle also takes place on many fronts. Angela washes her face in the bathroom, Jane and Ricky lie together upstairs, and Carolyn approaches the house with the gun in hand. Lester sits at the kitchen table. Suddenly, a gun goes off, and blood sprays on the white walls. Lester is dead.

Resolution: The final moments of the film are a sweep of sorts. The audience sees Ricky staring at Lester's vacant eyes. Angela turns to listen from upstairs, Carolyn clutches Lester's clothes in the closet, and Colonel Fitts rushes into his house covered in blood. The narration returns, asking us to cherish every moment of our mundane little lives. It is, at once, a tragic and a hopeful finale.

Chapter 9

Character Building

In This Chapter

▶ Building your character's physique and inner world

▶ Making your character's inner world cinematic

▶ Jogging your imagination

*I*f plot is a story's skeleton, characters are its heart. Astounding events rarely transpire organically; they occur because people make choices. Those choices require action or have consequences that result in action. Your audiences may be enthralled or shocked by a series of high-adventure situations, but they rarely invest in situations alone. Audiences invest in people — people scraping by, people braving the elements, people beating the odds. Without compelling characters, your story takes place, but to what end? The events may elicit raised eyebrows, some laughter, perhaps a gasp or two, but so what? Give me someone to care about, and I'll take your film home with me. I may even talk about it the next day.

Creating a character requires the artistry of a painter and the curiosity of an ace reporter. You must illustrate the person physically, crafting a form one brush stroke at a time; and you must interrogate that person, crafting a history one question at a time. Your goal? Create someone true. Whether you portray your character realistically remains to be seen, but I want to believe that he can exist. True characters have questions, and so will yours. True characters have strengths and weaknesses, and so will yours. True characters have distinct ways of moving through the world, and so will yours. This chapter provides tips on crafting such characters, while offering advice on how to allow your characters to propel the story as a whole.

Portrait of a Person: Constructing a Physical World

Character building has two primary approaches: from the outside in and from the inside out. No one method is correct, and, occasionally, a decision in one approach leads to a discovery in the other. For example, the scar on Harry Potter's forehead is the result of childhood trauma. This memory propels the entire series of books and the resulting film. In this way, a physical characteristic can allude to the emotional backstory. (See Chapter 5 for more on backstory.) The character-building approach you take depends on what kind of a writer you are and what part of the character suggests itself first. However, because film is a visual medium, audiences will base their first impressions on what they see physically, which I tackle first. Those visible components are the character's physical being and the character's physical environment.

Your character's physical being

You know the phrase "Never judge a book by its cover"? That sentiment is false as it pertains to character development. Audiences will judge characters by their appearance, and you want them to because it gives you a set of expectations to fulfill or contradict.

Think about it: A young woman stands on a busy sidewalk at night. She wears tight, revealing clothing, gaudy jewelry, and an excessive amount of makeup. She waves to several cars as they pass by, leaning into a few when they stop to talk. The immediate assumption is that she's either a woman of the night or an undercover cop. If you fulfill these expectations — if it turns out that this young lady is on assignment by the FBI or if she goes home with one of the drivers — audiences will appreciate your continuity, secure that their expectations were correct. If, however, she enters the next scene wearing a business suit and tries a winning case before a jury, audiences will watch to see how these images can both be part of the same person. Either way, you win. Audiences like surprises as much as they enjoy continuity.

The movie **Superman** is based on this premise. As Clark Kent, the protagonist is a mundane, bumbling young man. As Superman, he's the extreme opposite. The juxtaposition of the two types makes him dynamic. So although you know and may later prove that looks can be deceiving, you want audiences to go ahead and judge your characters by their covers. Physical appearance is the first piece of the character puzzle.

Ideally, you make every decision for a reason — from your character's name to the childhood secret he harbors. In films, an audience follows a character closely for three hours or less. You have to convey years of information in those three hours. Therefore, every choice has the potential to speak volumes. Choose wisely.

The following sections present a few physical attributes to consider.

Your character's name

What's in a name? Possibly everything. A well-chosen name has the capacity to impart pivotal character information quickly, often prior to the main action in a film. Perhaps the character's title matches his personality exactly. James Bond is a slick name, easy to repeat with a monetary connotation; James Bond is a slick man, spoken of often with an eye toward personal gain. Scarlett O'Hara is a volatile, melodramatic Southern belle whose name suggests those qualities. In other words, you may want to choose names based on the images they elicit. If you want to establish someone with a romantic flair quickly, Jane Smith is the wrong choice, but something like Francesca Romani may just fit the bill.

One of the most difficult and important things to do in film is to make internal qualities apparent. Some writers choose names that suggest emotional or psychological characteristics for this reason. These names often have a mythical air about them. George Lucas utilizes them throughout **Star Wars:** Luke Skywalker's destiny is apparent in his title, and Hans Solo's name encapsulates his aloof and distrusting personality.

Names can suggest cultural or ethnic backgrounds just as Vito Corleone does in the **Godfather** series. If your story is historically based, be aware that the names may already carry certain associations. The name Al Capone is linked to wealth and corruption. Amelia Earhardt's name conjures up adventure, daring, and mystery. Names of any kind, but especially those rooted in history, often attach images to your story before it's told. Your job is to use those images to your advantage or oppose them with images of your own.

In determining your character's name, consider three things:

- **Length:** The longer the name, the more eccentric, important, or complex the character seems. Shorter names tend to imply grounded, simple, or direct personalities.
- **Sound:** The sounds of the names you choose may suggest images or simply elicit an emotional response. Isabella Rossellini sounds elegant and a touch exotic. PeeWee Herman sounds immature and cartoonish. Also, try to script characters with very different-sounding names. Similar names become confusing for the reader and suggest the characters are similar in ways you probably don't intend.

✔ **Meaning:** If you want to suggest a theme or an internal trait with a name, numerous books detail both the history and the definition of personal titles. Baby books often categorize them into names based on cars, countries, animals, colors, gemstones, and so on.

Feeling overwhelmed? Here are some specific questions to help narrow the name search down:

✔ What's the story behind your character's name?

✔ Is your character named after a friend or relative?

✔ If so, did that person have a legacy?

✔ How does your character feel about the name?

Take some time and care with your decision. When a child comes into the world, a name is chosen based on personality, on relations, and on your personal feelings or aspirations for the child. A character name is no different. Give it some thought.

Your character's appearance

A character's appearance is made up of a variety of factors, including

✔ **His physique:** What does he look like physically? Is he short or tall, fat or thin? What color hair, skin, and eyes does he have? Is he physically fit? A character's physique may suggest anything from his worldview to his confidence or insecurities. The difference in size and weight is what initially makes Danny Devito and Arnold Schwarzenegger such an intriguing pair in the movie *Twins.*

✔ **Visible scars or physical disabilities:** Scars of any sort suggest history and maturity, and they affect how that character moves through the world. The bearer has been through some trauma and has survived, albeit slightly scathed. Scars may also represent an internal turmoil that has yet to be worked through. In *Pay It Forward,* Kevin Spacey plays a teacher who was badly burned as a child. His fight to mask the scars on his torso mimics his fight to remain emotionally removed from other people. In *V for Vendetta* the character V wears a mask to hide physical scars but also to ensure that he becomes a symbol of revolution.

✔ **The wardrobe:** Does your character dress to impress? Would I know what he does by what he wears? Is his sense of style or fashion slightly left of center, or do his clothes suggest a type? Molly Ringwald's character in *Pretty in Pink* is what she wears; so is her quirky friend Ducky. Films like *Pretty Woman* and *The Devil Wears Prada* thrive on the makeover of one character's sense of fashion and style. The general message here is what you wear affects how you're perceived and, therefore, who you are.

Appearance is perhaps most striking when it conveys the inner life of your character and the changes therein. Lester Burnham's initial appearance in *American Beauty* suggests a man who's average in all ways. He wears the same type of suit and tie every day, his body lacks muscle tone, and he's neither short nor tall. When he begins to turn his life around, his appearance changes. He alters his wardrobe, he begins to work out, and his posture improves; the physical alterations suggest the emotional shift.

When you consider your character's appearance, start by answering the following questions:

✔ How much time does your character take getting ready every day?

✔ What does your character do to get ready?

✔ What parts of his physique would your character hide and/or flaunt?

✔ Your character would be most comfortable wearing what?

✔ Your character is most often caught wearing what?

✔ What physical attribute does your character most admire and condemn in other people?

✔ What sort of an impression would your character like to make?

✔ How does your character feel about being noticed?

I spend a great deal of time envisioning my characters physically. First impressions are commonly based on appearance alone. The impressions of audiences are no different. I want their impressions to match my intentions.

Your character's physical environment

Characters spend time in certain places for three primary reasons:

✔ By choice

✔ Out of habit

✔ Out of necessity

Each reason suggests something different about your characters. If they choose to be in a location, that speaks to who they are and what they want. If they're used to being there, that speaks to their sense of security and routine. If they're forced to be there, that speaks to the lengths they'll go to in achieving success or to please someone else. When you peruse the following three environments, ask yourself not only where your character is but also how she feels about being there.

Your character at work

What does your character do for a living? Her work may be a step toward her career or something she does to put food on the table. She may be a novice or an expert in her field. If it's something she's good at or has done for a number of years, it will affect how she looks at the world and the way she speaks. It should also result in certain talents or access to information that will eventually come in handy. A seasoned waitress will be adept at handling unruly customers; photographers look at the world with selective eyes; a medical student may be too busy to assess the outside world at all. Indiana Jones's professorship in archaeology not only explains his expertise in historical relics, but it provides a nice contrast to his adventurous exploits as well. *Erin Brockovich* is, in part, about one woman's growing ability to collect information. In building a work environment, keep track of skills the job requires and the benefits it provides. You'll use both later on.

Try to envision the grand scope of each setting and then narrow your focus to specific details. You may imagine rows and rows of gray office cubicles with people in suits talking frantically over the phone, separated from their neighbors by plastic partitions. This is how Lester Burnham's office appears in *American Beauty.* A closer look may reveal photographs on the desk, a favorite poster hung haphazardly on the wall, particular books on the shelves, and so on. Lester's cubicle reveals a distinct lack of anything personal. Every detail offers another clue to the disposition behind it.

Pay particular attention to the relationships your character fosters at work. Who does she work for, and how long has she known her coworkers? Does she work amongst friends or rivals? These relationships may aid or thwart your character in her quest for success, so give them some thought.

Do I have some starter questions for this section? Of course I do. Try the following questions and then craft some of your own.

- Does your character work in an office or at home?
- How many jobs does your character have?
- What is the chain of command at work?
- What are your character's duties?
- What are your character's immediate and ultimate professional goals?
- What are the rewards for a job well done and the consequences of failure?

Your character at rest

Your character's home may be the most revealing location. By home, I'm referring to that place your character returns to at the end of the day. This place may be an apartment or house. It may be her place of work, someone else's house, a shelter, a box, or a hole in the ground. What matters is that it's uniquely hers, and it houses what belongings she has.

First, decide how secure the environment is. Is it a refuge or a war zone, some place to escape to or to avoid? If it's safe, what about it specifically offers comfort? Envision everything from the photos on the walls to the number of windows and the kind of light they allow. In *About a Boy*, the main character's flat is full of technological gadgets and little else. You get little sense of the man himself or anyone else in his life from the space. Perhaps this is because he has little sense of anyone other than himself at the story's beginning. If your character's home life is traumatic, it may explain behaviors in other areas of her life. It may even suggest what she dreams of pursuing.

TRY IT

From a list to a life: Building a generic physical world

Characters are the most personal part of your story. You will undoubtedly put most of your effort as a writer into constructing their forms and creating a world for them to walk through. When the process becomes overwhelming — and believe me, it — it helps to step away from your story and into another one, for however short a stint.

The following project combines several details chosen arbitrarily into a unique physical world. It's fun, it's fast, and best of all, it's just a project, so the pressure's off.

Chose answers for the following categories:

- Two colors
- Two numbers from 4–10
- A number between 80–400
- A song
- A country
- A weather condition
- A type of dwelling (house, barn, igloo, or whatever)
- Pick one body part (the head, the torso, the limbs, or the face)

Jotted something down? Here's how they fit together. The first four items pertain to your character's physique — the colors match the hair and eyes, the first set of numbers is the height, the second set is the weight, the song is both the character's physical rhythm and somehow pertains to his name. The country is where your story takes place, the weather condition depicts the climate, the type of dwelling may be home or work, and the body part refers to a physical disability. The exact nature of that disability is up to you; it affects the body part you selected.

After you've pieced this new and often crazy character together, take a second and imagine him in action. How does he interact with others, whom does he live with, and what does he do all day? You'll be surprised at the scenarios that occur to you when you concentrate on one small portion of an imaginary script.

Next, decide whether she lives alone or with someone else. If she lives alone, was everything in her home chosen and designed by her? If so, this is one of the fastest ways for an audience to assess a character. In ***Kissing Jessica Stein,*** Jessica lives in a well-lit loft, surrounded by books, her easel, and paints. She works as a reporter, but her apartment offers a first glimpse of her other love: art.

Anything chosen by the character becomes a reflection of the character in some way. If someone else has designed the home for her, I'll want to know which portions and why. If she lives with someone else, is it a lover, a room-mate, or family? This decision affects her responsibilities and ability to main-tain and juggle personal connections. Also, it provides an opportunity to illustrate a different side of your character — the mother or girlfriend side, perhaps.

Finally, what kind of feeling does the place arouse? Is it an uncomfortable space, original, traditional, eerie, or threatening? How should the audience feel when entering it? After you answer this question, determine what details in the setting suggest that atmosphere.

Here are a few questions that may clarify your character's home environment:

- ✔ Does your character live in a suburb or in a city?
- ✔ Does your character live in a house, an apartment, a shelter, or some-thing else?
- ✔ Is your character's home a stable or unstable place to be?
- ✔ How much pride does your character take in his home?
- ✔ How much personal effort has gone into the maintenance of the home?
- ✔ Why does your character live where he lives?

Your character in play

Play environments refer not only to those locations your character goes to in her free time but to any location other than home and work where she spends a reasonable amount of time. I say in play because these environ-ments are generally ones in which important action takes place. Play environ-ments include the various bars in ***Star Wars,*** the woods in ***Stand By Me,*** and the art museum in ***The Thomas Crown Affair.*** If your character goes to a library once, you don't need to spend much time detailing that library in your mind. If your character spends many scenes in that library, as Morgan Freeman's character does in ***Seven,*** you may want to explore it with a bit more depth.

As in-play environments vary drastically from film to film, I include four basic questions to help get you started. Add to the list as more occur to you. These questions will come in handy with each new script you write.

✔ Does your character have a circle of friends or one close friend?

✔ How does your character know his friends, and how did they meet?

✔ Where does your character go to relax?

✔ Given your plot, where might the character need to return to for information or aid?

The Good, the Bad, and the Ugly: Constructing an Internal World

Audiences base their first impressions of a character on the physical world that you construct; the internal world provides a steadily unfolding mystery that eventually proves those impressions true or false. Consider the metaphor of a fancy car. The body of the vehicle may suggest high-class elegance and durability. If the car handles well and lasts 25 years, your impressions of it were correct. The car is exactly what it advertises to be. If, however, you lift the hood to discover a leaky engine and missing parts, your assumptions were incorrect. The car is a dud in disguise. With characters, you may just as easily discover that the beat-up old Pinto has the engine of a new Corvette. It all depends on how you envision the internal working with the external. In creating a vibrant internal life for your characters, you're "lifting their hoods" in a sense, revealing what lies beneath.

If you've done your job composing a backstory (see Chapter 5), you already know the following things about your character:

✔ Her educational background, if any

✔ Her family background, if any

✔ Some key memories, including past successes and failures

✔ Her childhood dreams and aspirations

✔ The key events that led her to the threshold of your story

Now, you can construct the sum of these parts. Simply put: Who is the person those details have become? Your character's inner world is complex and ever shifting. Portions of it should change dramatically over the course of the film. For now, concentrate on one element at a time, painting each with bold strokes. The stronger your choices today, the stronger and more intriguing your character's choices will be tomorrow.

I discuss the primary elements of your character's inner world in the next four sections.

Dreams, desires, and passions

In order to generate a dynamic script, you must know three things:

- ✔ What your character wants
- ✔ How badly your character wants it
- ✔ What your character's prepared to do to get it

Compelling characters establish themselves early in the film with a dream or a desire, and that longing fuels the ensuing action — all of it. The dream may have originated in the past. Perhaps the character's harbored it for years, and your story is his opportunity to pursue it. Perhaps the character's forgotten all about it, and you're about to jog his memory. The desire may begin as a subtle tug at the character's heart and grow in urgency as the story progresses, or it may be urgent from the start and become more desperate with every scene. In other words, it moves from a desire to a need, as important to your character as life or death. In **Rear Window,** Jimmy Stewart's curiosity over events he witnesses in a neighbor's apartment steadily becomes an obsession and, finally, a frantic need to stop what he thinks has transpired. By contrast, Jake La Motta (played by Robert De Niro) in **Raging Bull** begins his journey with a passion to become the greatest prizefighter in America; that passion immediately underscores all his dialogue and action. How you manipulate the desire is up to you, but your character must have one. Without that overriding passion, your character is like a car without any gas for the trip.

Talents and expertise

Your characters are good at something, and if they're not, they will be by the end of your film. This is one of the fastest ways to show a *character arc,* or how he evolves through the story. Remember, audiences go to the movies to see people with extraordinary skills braving extraordinary circumstances or to see people utilizing average skills to survive extraordinary circumstances. Did you catch the comparison? Both scenarios require skills of some kind.

A character's skills may be any of the following or a combination of several:

- ✔ Artistic
- ✔ Athletic
- ✔ Technological
- ✔ Academic
- ✔ Mechanical
- ✔ Interpersonal

- ✔ Parental
- ✔ Financial
- ✔ Medical/scientific
- ✔ Strategic
- ✔ Political
- ✔ Magical (including intuition and psychic and supernatural ability)

Your character may be good at many things. Novelists fill pages with descriptions of the characters' talents. In a film, though, time is money. Choose pertinent skills that will advance your story's action. The young girl in **Jurassic Park** may be good at checkers for all I know, but checkers won't save her and the others from the raptor. On the other hand, her computer skills will, so that's the skill highlighted in the film.

Your character's talent may be his personality. Main characters need not be likable. Likeable characters are often dull. They may.be power-hungry brokers, unscrupulous lawyers, manipulative seductresses, or deadbeat dads — if they're in some way compelling, I'll watch them.

If your character doesn't excel in any one area, audiences love to see that character learn. The training sequences in **Zorro, Star Wars,** and **Million Dollar Baby** are capitalize on this technique. These films allow the audience to train beside the character, to assess firsthand any changes that he may undergo in the process. The **Harry Potter** series is charming, in part, because the characters are studying the art of magic. The audience observes them using a broomstick and practicing spells for the first time, and learns along with them.

Internal obstacles

No true character is perfect. Characters who are talented, intelligent, funny, good-looking, and well-off without personal flaws to balance them out aren't only impossible to believe, they're also maddening. Every person in your script, no matter how surreal or magical your landscape, has some internal demon to wrestle with before the story is over. This demon may be

- ✔ **A mental or emotional illness:** Does your character suffer from depression, a learning disability, insomnia, amnesia, or some similar problem? These illnesses can serve as metaphors for other problems in your character's life. They also clearly set restrictions on that character's behavior and outlook on life.

- ✔ **A past trauma:** Perhaps something from your character's backstory (see Chapter 5) still haunts her. This may be a memory or trait she's always struggled to overcome, or something revived by events in the current plotline.

✔ **An addiction or obsession:** Any urge your character can't control has the power to be destructive. Addictions and obsessions can determine what and whom your character notices, and they can manipulate everything that the character says and does.

✔ **An overriding passion:** Like the previous item, passions here refer to emotions so strong that they control your character's ability to think and act rationally. These passions can include anger, fear, lust, vengeance, greed, indolence, ignorance, and envy, among others. Anger and fear are the two most common overriding passions in films today.

Often, these obstacles provide your character with his main objective. Coupled with external conflicts that the antagonists provide, these inner flaws create the tension that holds your action together. Main characters generally face up to and/or conquer the primary obstacles in the film's climax.

Your character's argument

When constructing your characters, bear this in mind: It's not your job to judge them on the page. It's your job to show them in action and to let the audience be the judge. Perhaps your character is a hit-man who has trained himself to murder without forethought or emotion. You may loathe this character, but your job is to find a way to jump inside his mind for a little while and to discover what allows him to act as he does.

How would an assassin justify his profession — to himself or to someone else, someone like you perhaps, who loathes what he does? If you can answer that question, you'll be able to craft a complex character. If you can let him answer it, in his own words, you may also have the beginnings of a scene.

Want an example? Look at the movie *Seven,* where Kevin Spacey plays a serial killer who targets victims he believes exemplify one of the seven deadly sins. In a scene toward the end, Spacey tells the officers holding him that they shouldn't judge his behavior too quickly. After all, he suggests, everyone knows people who shouldn't really exist in this world, people doing more harm than good. The only difference between him and the officers is that he gets rid of those people, thereby doing the world a service. Not only does the writer depict this character's point of view for a few minutes, he suggests that we all may have something in common with this madman. The result is that much more disturbing.

Your villains don't necessarily know they're villains or see themselves that way. Everybody has reasons for the way they behave. You may not agree with those reasons, but you should know what they are.

More questions to get you started

By the time you're finished constructing your character, you may feel that you've put him through the Spanish Inquisition. That's all right. In this case, your character will be stronger for it. Here are a few starter questions concerning the inner life of your character. Again, keep a running list of other questions that you come up with as you write.

Dreams, wants, and passions

- ✔ What does your character want to achieve financially, ethically, and spiritually?

- ✔ Would your character pursue these goals on her own, or would it take some effort to convince or force her to do so?

- ✔ Is your character pursuing these goals for herself, for her friends or family, or for a cause?

Talents and expertise

- ✔ What skills has your character acquired at work?

- ✔ What talents was your character born with?

- ✔ What skills will your character need to attain in order to survive your plot?

- ✔ Who, if anyone, can provide training or expertise for your character?

Internal obstacles

- ✔ Does your character drink, smoke, or use narcotics? Why?

- ✔ Who/what does your character adore and why?

- ✔ Who/what does your character loathe and why?

- ✔ What is the most trivial thing that your character is afraid of?

- ✔ What is the most significant thing that your character is afraid of?

- ✔ How would you describe your character's self-esteem?

- ✔ What specifically brings your character great joy or great sorrow?

From the Inside Out: Making the Inner World Visible

One of the screenwriter's greatest challenges lies in finding ways to suggest a character's inner world visually. In plays, characters reveal their fears, feelings, and regrets through dialogue. Novelists fill pages with descriptions of their characters' emotional states. Screenplays, however, unfold pictorially, and a person's inner world is often physically imperceptible. Your character may expend remarkable amounts of energy maintaining a serene front when, in fact, he's dying inside. He may manage anger by donning a stoic facade or use humor to ward off fear. So how does a writer visually reveal what lies beneath the physique? The following techniques may help answer that question.

Balancing character dialogue with character action

Sometimes, characters reveal themselves, and sometimes, they're revealed by others. Generally, audiences grow to understand them in three primary ways:

- ✔ Through what they say about themselves
- ✔ Through what other people say about them
- ✔ Through what they do

The first two options rely on dialogue, so bear in mind that characters need a motivation to speak. In screen life, as in real life, people rarely offer information, especially personal information, without some incentive. They're cajoled, threatened, or seduced into doing so. They gain something by revealing themselves.

In *Jaws,* Captain Quint seems like a drunken and slightly mad fisherman with a penchant for catching sharks. For much of the film, he seems to hunt the beast solely for money, yet his growing obsession begins to suggest otherwise. Finally, Quinn relays the story of the crew of his ship that was consumed by sharks before his eyes. This crucial piece of information explains his erratic behavior throughout. Yet the writers wait until moments before the climax to reveal it. Why? It's stronger storytelling. Quinn doesn't trust easily; he wouldn't logically have revealed that information earlier. The other characters must joke him into confession. He tells the story almost without meaning to. The result is a powerful, realistic scene. So before your characters talk about themselves or about others, ask yourself this question: What's in it for them?

Also, bear in mind that audiences like to earn the story as well. Easy information is unrealistic and generally disappointing. Never provide a piece of the puzzle until you're sure that someone's after it. The information is worth more if a character and, therefore, the audience have to work to acquire it. The discovery is only as grand as the search itself.

Of the three methods, the third is the strongest. The phrase "actions speak louder than words" is a screenwriting mantra. A character's actions are always based on some inner need. Therefore, they offer the most honest glimpse of his personality. Here's an example: You meet a young man. He looks kindhearted. He speaks at great length about the good deeds he's done. His friends and neighbors swear that he's a man of his word. Yet an hour later, he kills two elderly women and steals their money. What have you discovered? He's a killer and a liar. Other characters may not know that, but you do. You've seen him in action.

After you determine what character detail you want to divulge, consider who might reveal it and how an audience will know that it's true. When in doubt, rely on action and save your breath.

Crafting concrete character goals

If your characters seek happiness, revenge, true love, justice, power, or retribution, they're in the market for an *abstract goal.* Abstract goals are theoretical or ethical in nature and lack a specific form. Is there something wrong with that? Yes and no. When a character is after something that's solely abstract, tracking his success rate can be difficult. He wants to be happy; that's fine, but how will I know when he gets there? Happy means many things to many people. So, for that matter, do power, love, and revenge. They're grand, undefined desires.

For this reason, I encourage you to make your goals concrete. By *concrete,* I mean give them a form, define specifically what "happy" looks like in your film. In *Braveheart,* Mel Gibson's character seeks retribution for the treatment of his people and the murder of his wife. Retribution is his abstract goal. He'll achieve it when the law grants his people the right to manage their own land and when the villain is dead. Those goals are his concrete goals, his definition of retribution. Concrete goals allow audiences to track how close or far away the hero is from success.

Concrete goals suggest their abstract counterparts. Elliot Ness wants to rid Chicago of corruption. In putting Al Capone and his henchmen behind bars, he achieves the abstract goal of justice. Think of one as the physical form of the other. Without a concrete goal, your character may win or lose without your audience even knowing.

Providing character opportunities

You've already determined your characters' talents. Now, craft opportunities in which they can utilize them. In *Gone with the Wind,* Scarlett O'Hara is an accomplished flirt. She demonstrates her prowess when she surrounds herself with men at a gala, making them compete to see who can fetch her dessert. Ferris Bueller, from the film *Ferris Bueller's Day Off,* is an expert liar. He feigns a temperature; he impersonates his girlfriend's father; he lies to friends, family, and authority figures alike in order to avoid going to school. If your character begins the journey with skills or expertise, find a way to demonstrate their ability early on.

If your character acquires skills during the story, provide an opportunity for him to use those new skills later — preferably while fighting the antagonist. These scenes become checkpoints for the audience as they track how your characters are changing.

Be aware that a growing talent also suggests a growth in maturity and spirit. Luke Skywalker becomes a Jedi knight over time — every other scene tests his skills — and as his expertise grows, so does his confidence and determination. So equip your characters with some original talent, prepare them to acquire more, and then decide what opportunities might reveal and eventually test those skills.

Establishing routines that change

In *About a Boy,* Hugh Grant plays a character who spends his afternoons watching television alone in his flat. One day, a young boy blackmails his way into that routine until, eventually, Grant can't spend the afternoon without him. This routine and the shift therein both suggest his emotional journey from a man more comfortable alone to a man who relies on others.

Habits and routines provide instant access to a character's true nature. People engage in them because they always have, and because doing so is comforting. These routines are glimpses into a character's past or current emotional state. As your characters change, their habits change; they may eventually abandon those habits altogether. After you know your character fairly well, crafting routines is a simple and satisfying way to make the inner world visible.

Forcing your characters to choose

Characters aren't just what they do; they're what they choose to do. In other words, don't let life happen to your characters; let your characters happen to life. A character's inner strengths and weaknesses are instantly apparent when he's confronted with a difficult choice. Audiences assess characters by the choices they make. Here's a look at how the process works:

- ✔ **The film:** *The Untouchables*
- ✔ **The character:** Elliot Ness, Chicago Treasury officer
- ✔ **The choices:** To accept a bribe from Al Capone and back off the case or to refuse the bribe, thereby incurring Capone's wrath but maintaining moral dignity.
- ✔ **The decision:** Ness refuses the bribe in front of witnesses.
- ✔ **The audience's verdict:** Ness is a man of honor and his word. He's committed to putting Capone away and brave enough to start the fight.

Your goal with this technique is twofold. First, make the choice a difficult one. If Ness takes the bribe, Capone leaves him alone, and his family lives comfortably for a long time. With a wife he loves and a new child on the way, it's a tough decision. Second, put something personal at risk. If Ness takes the bribe, he loses his dignity and self-respect; if he doesn't, he may lose his life. Tough decisions beg the question, "What would you do?" and involve an audience in rooting for an outcome. One choice has the power to clearly define a character. Craft options that test the character's strength, ethics, and spirit throughout your script.

Using a mentor

A mentor or confidante provides interesting avenues into the main character. A mentor has an inherently higher status; he knows something that the character wants or needs to know. This places the hero in a state of vulnerability, in which all sorts of inner conflicts might arise. In *Good Will Hunting,* Matt Damon plays Will, a genius consumed by quiet anger rooted in his childhood. With everyone else, he is aloof, funny, or indifferent. He's vulnerable only with his psychiatrist, played by Robin Williams, and only then after many angry sessions. Through Williams, audiences glimpse a younger, more hopeful side of Will that they may otherwise not have seen.

A mentor is in a position to teach the hero a new ability or way of life. The audience learns along with the hero, becoming an active part of the adventure. Through Mr. Miyagi in *The Karate Kid,* you learn control; through Gandalf in *Lord of the Rings,* you learn the bravery of a selfless act; and through Obi One Kenobi in *Star Wars,* you learn to fight for the good. In tutoring the hero, mentors educate the audience as well.

Finally, a mentor forces the hero to answer for himself and to make difficult choices. A strong mentor expects the protagonist's weaknesses to become strengths. In training the protagonist, those weaknesses emerge. A mentor removes facades that a protagonist might don in other settings and forces him to rethink past behaviors and habits. The resulting interrogation may tax the hero beyond endurance, but it's a dynamic way for the audience to get to know your character at his core.

Using a narrator

Narration is challenging to maneuver gracefully, and, unfortunately, it's a device that's often abused. Narrators are commonly the protagonists, though on occasion someone else chimes in. For example, the narrator in *Election* alternates between Reese Witherspoon's teenage character and her teacher, played by Matthew Broderick. If you can relay the story any other way, avoid narration. The strongest narrators, such as Lester Burnham in **American Beauty,** have a desperate need to speak directly to the audience. They're delivering a message. Lester tells the story immediately after his death, as if on his way out of consciousness. His message is both a warning and a hopeful prayer, and it certainly warrants a direct voice. He's an exception.

Many writers utilize narrators because they don't know how to convey plot information. Narrators become an easy way to introduce characters, to relay backstory, to explain events. In most instances, this information would be better told in action. Film is, after all, a visual medium. Why *tell* me something when you can *show* me something equally compelling? For example, **Radio Flyer** begins and ends with narration, but the meat of the film stands without it. It seems a weaker choice in this film because you so readily forget the narrator's presence. If you're interested in a clear example of how a film changes as a result of narration, compare the original **Blade Runner,** which uses narration, with the director's cut where it's been removed.

If you're thinking about using a narrator, give her a reason to speak, a unique voice, and a vibrant perspective. If these details don't readily present themselves, consider a different technique.

Crafting secondary characters

Guess what? Just as villains don't necessarily know they're villains, your secondary characters don't know they're secondary. In fact, they probably assume that they're the main characters, so it will help you to craft them that way.

Secondary characters, also known as supporting roles, should be created with the same attention to physical and psychological attributes that you use in crafting the main characters. They should have their own goals, their own routines, their own talents and their own obstacles. The only difference is that the decisions you make for them will somehow support or thwart the main character's journey through the script.

In **When Harry Met Sally,** the best friends of each main character meet, fall in love, and get married. Their storyline is complete in its own right, but it primarily serves to encourage Harry and Sally to fall in love with each other. Consider the best friends the support staff. You'll construct lives for each of them, but you'll only dramatize the parts of their lives that support your main character's story.

Chapter 10

Say What? Constructing Dynamic Dialogue

Dialogue: What is it? It's words, it's sounds, it's rhythm — simply put, it's music. Perhaps this is why great dialogue, like great music, soars off the page, and why awkward dialogue clunks about or flat-lines halfway through a scene. Your script is a symphony. When a symphonic composer wants a section of the music to swell, he calls upon the strings. Should he require a wail, a squeak, or a piercing melodic line, the reeds are close at hand. And if the piece demands a backbeat or punctuation, he looks to the percussionist.

Much of a writer's orchestra is made up of characters. Their words, silences, the pace and quality with which they speak — these are their instruments. A skilled screenwriter knows which voices together or in succession produce the most compelling moments. He knows which words escalate a conflict and which diffuse it. He knows that words spoken by one character may cause friction, but when spoken by another, they offer solace. All in all, he knows who to point the baton at to create the desired effect. Powerful dialogue springs from character. If you're comfortable with your musicians, you'll eventually conduct them with clarity, depth, and precision.

This chapter breaks dialogue into two components — diction and music — and then suggests effective ways to pull them together in conversation.

Diction: What's in a Word?

If scores consisted of similar instruments playing similar notes, the resulting music would be rather dull. Rather dull? It would be downright monotonous. The same principle holds true for films. The quality of your dialogue depends on a combination of unique voices singing different tunes. The key word here is *unique,* and a unique voice begins with a unique vocabulary. If you can envision your character in detail, if you've jotted down her background, her social life, and her inner qualities, the time's come to let her speak. What she finally says is known as diction.

Diction, as it pertains to films, refers to a character's distinct choice and use of words. Factors determining this vocabulary include the character's education, profession, geographic location, and overriding emotional state.

Find a comfortable seat in any public place and eavesdrop for awhile. You'll notice the same conversations being held in a variety of ways. Consider this selection based on a woman speaking to her young child in a fast-food restaurant:

> "Quit it, Sammy. I said put that thing down. I ain't sayin' it again, you heard me the last four times, I know you did. Now, I can take it, or I can break it — what's it gonna be?"

It may not be verbal fireworks, but it's a distinct voice fueled by a clear frustration. Now, I'll rewrite the clip in an alternate diction. See whether you can pinpoint the distinction.

> "Now Samuel, stop that this instant. I would appreciate it if you would put that thing away. I've asked you nicely several times, and I'm certain you've heard each request. Now, you have a choice. You can either give me the toy, or I can toss it in the garbage."

Hear the difference? The first woman says exactly what she feels without ornamentation. Her words are short and clipped. As a result, her anger comes across loud and clear. The second woman speaks with larger words and complete sentences, which contain her irritation. Her speech is orderly and precise, as if chosen in advance or pulled from a book on parent-child confrontation. Yet the two women are saying essentially the same thing.

Understanding diction is like discovering a new language. Listening for the variations in that language is the first stage. The second stage involves understanding what those variations convey to a listener. In other words, what does a character's diction suggest about him as a person?

Isn't versus ain't: Diction's determining factors

How do you craft a character's diction? If you've spent time researching her background and illustrating her present circumstances, you have all the information that you need. Diction is the natural next step and is primarily determined by these four factors:

- ✔ Education
- ✔ Profession
- ✔ Geographic location (past and present)
- ✔ Overriding emotion

Every character discovery you've made can be suggested with a variety of words and phrases. The remaining process involves selecting which of those words communicate these discoveries to an audience. As I detail each factor individually, revisit your research and listen. Character voices either behave as shy children or eager participants. In any case, consider yourself a reporter searching for the perfect quote. Have a pencil handy.

Your character's education

Intelligence comes in many forms. The character Mark Van Doren in *Quiz Show* is a college professor from a renowned literary family. Reporter Dick Goodwin, in that same film, may not hail from an Ivy League school, but he uncovers a historical scandal most newspapers overlooked. The characters in *The Sting* successfully con a league of con artists. The young man in *Finding Forrester* survives the inner city to become a successful novelist. Are these men equally intelligent? Yes, in different ways.

In establishing your character's education, contemplate which of the following forms of intelligence matches his own.

- ✔ **Academic:** How much schooling does your character have? Someone with a grade-school education may speak differently from someone with a doctoral degree. What subjects in particular catch his fancy? The literature buff, the math whiz, and the aeronautical engineer — these people express themselves in diverse ways. Degrees of academic intelligence are often delineated by verbal complexity or lack thereof. For example, if a character speaks primarily with one or two syllable words, limited vocabulary, and incorrect grammar, such as Billy Bob Thornton's character in *Sling Blade,* an audience will assume that his schooling has been minimal.

✔ **Intuitive:** Some characters possess an instinctual intelligence, a sort of sixth sense that they're born with or gain through traumatic experience. From Sherlock Holmes to Yoda, these characters act on spontaneous impulse, rarely on lessons learned in school. Reporters, detectives, and responsible parents often demonstrate this strength; characters in horror films, tragically, do not. For this reason, reporters and detectives in other film genres generally uncover the crime, while characters in horror films become the victims of one.

✔ **Acquired:** This type of intelligence is also called "survival sense." Characters who possess it choose their words carefully, certain that what they say could result in trouble or heartache. Any child who survives the inner city of a John Singleton or a Spike Lee film does so because he's acquired street smarts. Francis Capra's character in *A Bronx Tale* and Frankie in *Frankie and Johnny* dodge the Mafia and a life of physical abuse, respectively. Those experiences mold their vocabulary.

Obviously, these types of intelligences may overlap. A duality of language makes characters mysterious and compelling. Matt Damon's character in *Good Will Hunting* has a blue-collar, poverty-stricken background, a grade-school education, and the intelligence of a Rhodes scholar. He can maintain a conversation with his working-class Boston friends and college physicists alike. The switch from one diction to another keeps the audience and other characters on their toes.

Your character's profession

Your character's choice of work often defines how she views the world and, therefore, what she has to say. A writer, for example, may speak in metaphors or have a highly developed vocabulary. Politicians speak in triumphant yet noncommittal phrases to avoid offending voters. A rhyme that I've adopted over the years goes, "If a job affects your point of view, it probably affects your diction, too." In other words, let what your characters do for a living color how they express views, opinions, and beliefs. This is often true in real life, and so could be true on-screen.

Specific professions also require specialized or technical language, known as jargon. If I can determine your character's profession by her vocabulary, you've probably correctly identified that jargon. These Jargon Alert icons in the margins throughout the book, for example, define screenwriting terminology; a character's jargon reveals her line of work.

Every occupation comes with a list of terms and phrases learned on the job or required to do the job. Here are a few examples of phrases commonly heard in certain work professions:

- **Wait staff:** "The usual," "He's a regular," "cup of joe," "table four," "order up," "stiffed the tip," "over-easy or sunny side up," "soup du jour," "straight-up or on the rocks"

- **Actor:** "upstaged," "on cue," "heads up," "black-list," "hit your mark," "from the top," "ingénue," "blocking," to "go up" on your lines, "curtain," "flies," "wing space," "apron," "understudy," "dark night," "talent on the set," "slate"

- **Lawyer:** "verdict," "approach the bench," "plea bargain," "manslaughter," "assault and battery," "hung jury," "beat the rap," "the jury will disregard," "stricken from the record," "take the stand," "pro bono," "objection."

Do you know what these terms mean? If you're writing about waitresses, actors, or lawyers you should. What would the television show ***E.R.*** be without medical lingo, or ***The Wire*** be without police terminology. Sci-fi adventures like ***Star Wars*** and ***Star Trek*** are believable, in part, because of that jargon and the confidence with which it's delivered. Audiences buy it because the writers took it seriously.

Some writers believe that jargon suggests a stereotype rather than a three-dimensional person. They contend that lawyers, doctors, teachers, and so on speak in ways that generally have nothing to do with their jobs. This argument is valid, and over-reliance on jargon may rob characters of their distinct voices. However, screenwriting is not life, it's art. Writers choose professions for their characters for a reason — to help define behavior and personality. If you're not familiar with the necessary terms, if you don't employ them when required, audiences may dismiss your characters as phony or incomplete.

Jargon is meant to augment your character's dialogue, but a little goes a long way. Over-reliance on jargon may make it difficult for audiences to understand your characters at all, which is not usually the effect you're going for. Also, everything your characters say, jargon or otherwise, should move the action forward.

Your character's geographic location

Where your character grew up and where he's from now may affect the way he speaks. As a general rule, I don't advise spelling out a dialect — you're liable to wind up with dialogue like:

> "I'ma goin' ta hafta take that there knife away from ya'll, do ya hear? Ifn ya don't put it away right quick."

I'm exaggerating a bit, but I have encountered phrases that I'm sure the writer understood, but which resemble hieroglyphics to anyone else. Sounding out dialects and transcribing them to the page slows readers down and irritates actors. However, certain regions yield colorful phrases, phrases like "not the brightest porch light on the block" and "a shuffle short of a winning card," for examples. These colloquialisms are known as slang, and to miss them is to miss a verbal gold mine. If you simply want the character to speak with an accent, consider including that direction in a parenthetical such as (speaks with a Southern drawl) below the character's name.

Slang refers to nontraditional language that's specific to a certain culture and/or geographical region. It consists of words and phrases peculiar to that group of people.

The only way to really absorb the language of a group of people is to immerse yourself in it for a length of time. If it's impossible to visit the region, track down interviews or recordings made by people from the area. Read literature from the region or make a phone call and talk to a local. If you're creating slang for a fictional group, listen to conversations in your own neighborhood and record any slang you hear. Those recordings should give your fictitious expressions a hint of authenticity, though the phrases themselves are unique.

Certain regions or peer groups add, abbreviate, or drop words from sentences entirely. Canadians, for example, often end sentences with "eh?" Pittsburgh natives say "don and arond" instead of "down and around" and "yins" instead of "you guys." In some places the words "like" or "all" may replace the verb "to say," and "totally" may become an adverb for all seasons, as in the sentence:

> She was like "you should totally do this," and I was all "you totally know I just can't."

Again, I'm exaggerating for effect here, but sentences like this one abound amid the younger generation. Movies like *Heathers* and *Clueless* capitalized on expressions like these and were unexpected hits. They took an unusual vocabulary and stretched it to ridiculous proportions. Utilizing slang when necessary lends credibility to both your characters and their environments.

Your character's overriding emotion

Characters exhibit a wide range of emotions over the course of a film. However, most human beings have one emotional state that they return to in between dramatic events. I call this their overriding emotion their default state of mind, and it certainly affects how they communicate.

Consider whether your character adopts any of the following dominant emotional states:

- Anger
- Fear
- Hope

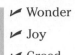

> ✔ Wonder
>
> ✔ Joy
>
> ✔ Greed

Cautious personalities generally say little, and when they do speak, they use carefully chosen neutral words. Many angry people curse their way through life. David Mamet's characters capitalize on this colorful, albeit potentially offensive, language time and again. Artistic or particularly vibrant personalities may use words that call up images of grandeur. Norma Desmond of **Sunset Boulevard** fame was one such character; Orson Welles himself was another. Revolutionaries and politicians share this tendency, which is why many speeches include image-based metaphors like "a bridge to the future," "soar like the eagle," or "smoke the enemy out of his hole." Audiences can see these phrases, which makes them particularly effective, especially in film.

In many situations, your characters will assume a vocabulary that they don't usually employ. Perhaps, as Carolyn does in **American Beauty,** they want to impress someone whom they admire. Maybe they do so out of a desire to fit in, as Shannon Dougherty does in **Heathers.** Whatever your character's reasons for altering her vocabulary, knowing what base diction she'll return to when the façade deteriorates is helpful to you as writer.

The way your character speaks will also be determined by her relationship to the sound of her own voice. In other words, is she an introvert or an extrovert? Does she enjoy hearing herself talk, or is she deathly afraid of exposing herself that way. Who is she comfortable speaking to, and who makes her nervous? After you've made decisions about her education, profession, location, and over-riding emotion, the next step is to consider how often she speaks up.

The highs and the lows of language

Human beings can be classified by a variety of conditions — finances, social status, political power, physical appearance, and so on. Each one of these classifications exists on a scale. Those people with the "most" and "least" of that condition make up the respective ends of the scale, and most everyone else falls somewhere in the middle. Language is no exception to this rule. Words, like people, can be classified into groups: High diction and low diction mark the ends of the scale with middle-grade words in between. These groups are based on education, profession, and upbringing.

Most people speak with a combination of dictions, called *middle diction.* Middle diction is a more common way of speaking, but it doesn't jump off the page or the screen as readily as high and low diction. If you want an immediately distinct character voice, a character I can identify with my eyes closed, you may want to look at other options. You're a writer, and words are your tools. If you have a clear understanding of the weight and scope of each word, you'll craft unique voices.

High diction: The prince

In politics or economics, the level of status is determined by the degree of power or the amount of money that a person controls. With appearance, the person deemed most attractive holds court, and so on. With language, the classification of "high" vocabulary doesn't necessarily determine a character's power or prestige. It can, however, suggest a degree of education, professional training, a historical setting, and, perhaps, a privileged lifestyle.

Consider the following example. In speaking to a friend, I might say:

> "You know, I just finished a book that you have to read. It was great."

This is not an example of particularly high diction; it's rather neutral or middle range, in fact. It is hard to distinguish my education, profession, or socio-economic standing from that sentence. Now I'll rewrite it, using high diction:

> "I have just completed the most tremendous novella. You simply must peruse it when you have a moment to spare; it is undeniably compelling and persuasive."

Although I may not imagine this person in detail, the words "novella," "peruse," and "persuasive" suggest character. Most people don't speak this way today, so if your story takes place now, this character will most definitely stand out. And what if you're writing a period piece? Might a Victorian lady use these words? Perhaps your character spent her childhood obsessed with language; perhaps she enjoys showing off her verbal prowess or likes to hear herself speak. There are innumerable reasons for choosing high diction, and it's worth picking up a dictionary just to have these words at your disposal.

A quick way to differentiate between high and low diction is to note the word's structural degree of complexity. High-diction words are generally multisyllabic, technically verbose, or ornate in style. They generally comprise the carefully chosen phrases of the elite, the academic flourishes of a professor, and the technical jargon of a lawyer or renowned physicist. They expectedly fuel the literary Van Dorens of **Quiz Show,** but they may also come from an unlikely source. In **Good Will Hunting,** Matt Damon spends much of the film speaking in middle-grade, everyday diction. However, in a classroom setting, he uses high diction, surprising university professors, award-winning theorists, and possibly the audience.

Allowing characters to speak against expectation is a quick way to grab an audience's attention.

Low diction: The pauper

Low diction, by contrast, is strictly functional; it gets the job done with little or no flourish. Characters who speak with low diction may have little schooling or may not care to draw attention to what schooling they've had. They often hold down unpretentious, blue-collar jobs. They speak with direct, monosyllabic words and without artifice.

Low diction is rarely concerned with grammatical precision and tends to rely heavily on slang. Low diction is often associated with street language for this reason. It's not a language picked up in school; it's picked up by necessity and experience. It may be passed down by friends and family. Low diction is the language of the main characters in *Sling Blade,* of Tony Soprano in *The Sopranos,* and of Sylvester Stallone in *Rocky.* An example of low diction may be

> "Hey. Cut that out. You gonna talk to me 'cause I ain't got all day. You best say what you have to say, man. I've got places to be, you dig?"

Notice that I'm spelling certain words to read the way I hear them? That's another way to distinguish between high and low diction. High diction is concerned with precision of speech; low diction is not. Don't worry if it's not clear right now. The distinction between high and low diction often comes after a great deal of comparison. Here are a few examples of words from both categories to get you started.

Low Diction	*High Diction*
Nice	Astounding, divine, splendid
Hate	Loathe, detest, despise
Glad	Delighted, elated, jubilant
Bad	Unfavorable, detrimental, atrocious
Mean	Nasty, spiteful, vicious

Bear in mind that a character's level of diction isn't always an indication of true intelligence, prestige, or profession. The wisest person in the room may be the working-class servant, as is the case in *Gosford Park.* Someone with the diction of a scholar may, in fact, work as a janitor, as Will does in *Good Will Hunting.* Your character may choose a lower diction than she is capable of to blend in, nab information, or avoid pretension. Yet at some point, her true verbal palette will emerge. That palette may be a mixture of the two dictions.

Putting words in your character's mouth

Here's a fun and simple way to generate the beginning of a clear diction. Take a look at this list of a few neutral phrases. (By neutral, I mean that they don't suggest any type or level of diction.) Now, give yourself two or three minutes on each one, jotting down as many different ways to express the thought as you can think of in the allotted time. Feel free to make up expressions if they occur to you.

✔ Hello

✔ Goodbye

✔ I love you

✔ I hate you

✔ Get lost

✔ That's great

✔ Have a nice day

After you complete the lists, think about your character. Circle any of the phrases that you came up with that your character might use. If you can't find one that fits, think of one now. Try this project with other neutral phrases. Eventually, your character's voice should emerge.

Name That Tune: Crafting Your Character's Music

A well-crafted verbal exchange is like a catchy song. Diction provides the lyrics; music provides the tune. Dialogue relies on the sounds of words as well as their definitions, on the rhythm of a conversation as well as its meaning. If you block the literal significance of a discussion and isolate the sounds that it's made up of, you discover a rhythm holding the entire exchange together. Shakespeare wrote in the unstressed-stressed pattern of iambic pentameter. Why? Because it mimics the cadence of natural speech. The dialogue of David Mamet and Oliver Stone explodes off the page. Why? They use explosive words in an explosive way. The result is verbal fireworks.

Compare these two examples. The first is from **Under Milkwood,** a radio play by Dylan Thomas. The second is from Sam Shepard's **Cowboy Mouth.**

"It is Spring, moonless night in the small town, starless and bible-black, the cobblestreets silent and the hunched courters-and-rabbits wood limping invisible down to the sloeblack, slow, black, crowblack, fishing-boat bobbing sea."

"I don't need no black baby lamb with a bell in its tail and I ain't gettin' no cradle for no dead crow. I have a baby! My own baby! With its own cradle! You've stolen me away from my baby's cradle!"

Out of context, these passages may make no sense, yet each one has a distinct sound and rhythm. The first one is not unlike a lullaby, lilting and slow. The second passage uses hard consonants and repetition to drive its meaning home. Both selections are held together by the sound of each word in conjunction with the others, by the felt melody those sounds create together. They're held together, in part, by music.

The music component of dialogue is responsible for any mounting tension or emotional undercurrent in a scene. After you know what types of phrases your character utters, rework them with an ear toward melody and percussion. Which voices enhance each other? Which are combative? What is the character's state of mind as he speaks? Joy, fear, anger, grief, awe — these emotions have unmistakable rhythms; listen for them around you, examine their form, and then try to recreate them on the page. Like a catchy song, eventually, they'll stick with you.

Sound 101: Using poetry as a guide

The terms *alliteration* and *assonance* are often used in poetry, where an ill-chosen sound can make or break the piece. Alliteration refers to the repetition of consonants and the effect of that repetition on the listener's ear. Imagine a tiny percussionist sitting inside each word, matching an instrument to each consonant and sounding them in succession. Perhaps he pounds the hard "d's" out on a kettledrum and taps the "t's" out on a snare. In any case, he repeats the sounds of each word in such a way that they produce an audible rhythm. That rhythm is alliteration.

Consider these examples:

> "Hollywood is jam-packed with professional people pounding on doors." The repeated "p" here creates the sound of those people in action.

> "The wind whistles through the willow tree." The "wh" sound here becomes the wind.

> "Terrific, I say. Terrific. It's utterly and totally terrific." This sentence is explosive in part because of the resounding "t's."

Alliteration is helpful when you want to punch a line or emphasize it for your audience. It also tends to speed a line up. Alliteration can produce the biting anger of Don Corleone or Michael Palin's stutter in **A Fish Called Wanda**.

If it's percussion that you're after, alliteration's your approach. If you're trying to produce a specific tone, it's assonance you're after.

Assonance is the repetition of a vowel sound within a phrase. Assonance creates the pitch or timbre of a conversation.

When repeated in direct succession, vowels can mimic the human voice. A sentence full of vowels may produce a subtle moan, wail, squeal, or cry. In this way, assonance helps to create an emotional soundscape for a phrase, a speech, and possibly an entire conversation.

Consider these examples:

"Don't go. I won't know what to do with myself all alone." The long "o's" in this sentence underscore its mournful request. They prolong the phrase so that the other character, and, therefore, an audience, can hear it.

"It rained on my birthday. A cold rain that refused to abate until the guests had gone away." The long "a" sounds here emphasize the sadness of the speaker.

"I will fly higher than ever before. I will fly until your eyes cannot detect me and I become the sky itself." The repeated long "i's" here accentuate the speaker's determination. The phrase has the sound of a victory cry.

If alliteration speeds a sentence up, assonance slows it down. If alliteration provides a backbeat for the conversation, assonance heightens the mood. Together, they help a writer generate a distinct palette and rhythm for a character's voice. Your audience may not always be aware of how you're using these tools, but they'll certainly feel their effects.

Fascinating rhythm: Crafting your script's pulse

Clichés abound depicting the body's physical response to a grand emotion. When struck by love, hearts beat wildly against the chest, and knees grow weak. When scared, a person's pulse begins to race; angry people stomp and growl or stare coldly ahead with no expression. All these responses are easy to see, but what if you close your eyes? Would you hear them as well? Chances are that you would because every emotion has an accompanying verbal pulse — a rhythm that gives it away.

Of course, every sentiment sounds different in different mouths, but something about the way a character speaks should eventually suggest the way that he really feels. As you eavesdrop on conversations around you, listen for a few key rhythmic elements:

- ✔ Punctuation
- ✔ Repetition
- ✔ The use of silence

Punctuation

Punctuation, or lack thereof, is often considered the key to realistic-sounding dialogue. First consider interruption, which appears in your script as a dash. People often interrupt themselves mid-sentence. Why? Perhaps they're excited over something and get ahead of themselves as they speak.

> "I can't begin to tell you how wonderful it all was — did I mention the food, oh the food was just — and the wine? Out of this world — and the service?"

You get the picture. The speaker can't relay the information as fast as her brain recalls it.

Another form of interruption occurs when people think ideas through as they talk:

> "It's best if the reception starts at noon, yes noon — or maybe one. That might be better. And the cake should be chocolate — oh, but Sal can't eat chocolate, better make it vanilla. I called the musicians — wait, did I call the musicians?"

See how this one works? The more thoughts that occur to this character, the more interruptions required.

A trail off, represented in a script by an ellipses (. . .) also punctuates every-day conversation. The trail off is generally used when a person forgets what she's trying to say or is searching for just the right phrase. If your character frequently trails off mid-thought, she may also be a dreamer.

T The punctuation and grammar of your dialogue need not be technically cor-rect. Phrases that look like questions may end forcefully with an exclamation point. Nouns may replace verbs in sentence structure and vice versa. People speak in fragments; so will your characters. So don't dot all your i's or cross all your t's. Unless your character's an English buff, an aristocrat, or a robot, doing so will sound unnatural. Again, I emphasize that this rule holds true for dialogue. You'll probably want other portions of your screenplay — your scene descriptions, for example — to remain grammatically correct. (See Chapter 4 for info on punctuating your script.)

Repetition: You can say that again

Repetition is a valuable and multifaceted tool. It may be used to emphasize a point:

> "We get the job done, do you hear me? We get. The job. Done."

It may be used to create the stutter of confusion, love, or fear:

> "What I meant was, what I meant to say just then, was to ask, that is I would like to know, I would like very much to know if you might consider, just consider mind you, going out sometime."

It may be also be used to portray eagerness or demand:

> "Did you get it? Well? Did you? Did you get the job?"

As a writer, you must find a way to create heightened and carefully selected dialogue under the guise of naturalistic conversation. Punctuation and repetition make that task considerably easier.

The sound of silence

Dialogue isn't made up of words alone. Silences are as important and, sometimes, more important for conveying intent on-screen. If words are implied, a silence may take the place of an entire conversation. However, bear in mind that silences in film are usually conveyed through action or gesture. Characters do something instead of saying something.

I should distinguish between a natural pause in conversation and the pauses that you'll use throughout your script in place of words. If I wrote in every natural pause, I'd add at least ten unnecessary pages to my screenplay. Leave natural pauses to the actors. If your scenario is strong enough and your character voices clear, a good actor will know how to say the line.

Pauses are scripted when a writer wants to do one of two things:

- ✔ Highlight the last line spoken
- ✔ Suggest to readers and audience alike that some nonverbal exchange is taking place.

If your last line is a humdinger, if you want your audience to remember it, script a pause after it. This pause allows the line to linger before the next action directs attention elsewhere. Practice rewriting generic or otherwise neutral dialogue with these three musical elements, or layer them into a scene from your script. You should be able to say essentially the same thing with different emotions in mind and, therefore, with varying rhythms.

Listening: The Other Half of Conversation

With all this talk about talk, it's easy to forget that conversations also involve listening, and the way your character listens will affect the rhythm and quality of his dialogue. In life, people generally listen in one of five ways:

✔ **Noncommital listening:** Noncommital listeners are either not interested in what's being said, or they're too distracted to hear it. This type of listening often results in vague responses or abrupt switches in conversation. For example:

"So, I had lunch with Daphne the other day."

"Uh-huh."

"She mentioned you hadn't talked to her in awhile."

"Oh?"

"She seemed upset about it actually."

"You don't say."

Noncommital listeners are only pretending to listen; in reality, they're just waiting for the other person to stop talking.

✔ **Selective listening:** Selective listeners have their own agenda. They hear the parts of conversation that relate that agenda and nothing more. Selective listeners commonly interrupt each other, especially when in the throes of some grand passion. One person's thought is triggered by a word or phrase directly before it. For example:

"So, I had lunch with Daphne the other day, and —"

"Daphne. I haven't seen her in, well I can't think of the last time we —"

"She mentioned you hadn't called. I told her you were busy and —"

"Of course she did. She always was one to keep track of —"

"Now, now. There's no need to start in on —"

"Really though. What right has she to talk about our friendship with —"

"The same right as you, I suppose."

Can you sense the trigger words? The urge to speak generally occurs well before the current speaker is finished talking. This is because selective listeners only hear half, if not less, of what's said to them.

✔ **Selfish listening:** Selfish listeners find a way to relate the conversation to their own experience. They believe they're being helpful, when in reality they're using one person's concerns as an invitation to talk about themselves.

"So, I had lunch with Daphne the other day. It sounds like she may be getting a divorce."

"I don't envy her. My divorce was awful. Did I ever tell you how I finally made the decision to leave?"

"No. I don't think you did. But Daphne seems okay with it."

"She may feel that way now. But give it time. When I first got divorced, I thought things would get easier. . . ."

You get the picture. While selfish listeners may have good intentions, they really only have one person in mind.

- ✔ **Attentive listening:** Attentive listeners actually care about the person speaking, and they don't have an agenda of their own. They don't usually offer advice or anecdotes; they're content to simply be present for the other person. Psychiatrists and counselors of any kind often fall into this category.

- ✔ **Active listening:** Active listeners take part in the conversation. They might repeat or paraphrase what the speaker is saying. They often ask questions that clarify or encourage the speaker to elaborate.

"So I had lunch with Daphne the other day."

"You had lunch with Daphne? How does she look?"

"Not well. She may be getting a divorce."

"No! That's horrible. Did she say why?"

Active listeners are so called because they take an active part in drawing conversation out of someone else. For this reason, you might see active listening between life-long friends, reporters, or police officers trying to obtain information for a case.

How your character listens will vary according to who he's listening to and what the subject matter is. However, this attribute is as important as how your character talks. It contributes as much to dialogue as the words do.

Putting It Together: Letting Your Characters Speak

Okay, you've chosen a vocabulary, a sound, and a rhythm for your characters. You're ready to write an entire scene. Where do you begin? You might simply start writing and see where the discourse takes you. However, if you're pressed for time or want to approach the task in a more organized fashion, you may find it helpful to outline a few things about the scene before you start writing.

Setting the scene

Here are a few elements to consider immediately before you write any scene, but especially one with dialogue.

- **Which roles are your characters playing now?** Each character plays a variety of different roles throughout her day. Each role speaks in a different way. Your protagonist may be a mother, a friend, and a boss. As the mother, she may be nurturing and kind; as a boss, demanding and curt. Before crafting your scene, determine what relationship the characters have and how that relationship affects their dialogue.

- **What is the status or perceived status between the characters?** When a veteran employee addresses the new hire, he may instantly assume higher status. After all, he knows the company fairly well, so he has knowledge to impart. His dialogue may be pompous, authoritative, or stern. If he later discovers that the new hire will soon be his boss, that diction may change. Determine the perceived level of status between the characters in advance.

- **What does each character want?** What your characters say in a scene is determined by what they hope to gain from each other. Your characters may flat out demand what they want, or the dialogue may code for what's really being discussed. Before you start writing, try to determine what each character wants and who, if anyone, will get it.

- **What will change during, or as a result of, the exchange?** Every strong scene relies on tension, on risk, or on mystery. Scenes in which friends discuss the weather are dull no one is being changed by the experience. If they're talking about the weather to avoid talking about an impending medical operation, the scene becomes more interesting. This technique is known as subtext.

People rarely say exactly what they mean. Instead they employ a variety of tactics to glean the information they're after. When one character talks about one subject in order to avoid talking or to ascertain information about another, *subtext* is present. *Subtext* is everything that's not being stated explicitly between characters, and which therefore underscores the entire scene.

After you've outlined these four things, you're ready to write. By this time, the characters should have plenty to say. After all, they've waited all this time to say it. However, if you get stuck, you can always return to one component of their voices — the diction, the music, or the rhythm — and see what's lacking. You also have an outline of the scene's action and objective to keep you afloat.

Dialogue do's and don'ts

The challenge of great dialogue is that it has to accomplish specific tasks while drawing little attention to itself. Remember that you're creating the illusion of average conversation, but there's really nothing average about it. Characters perform extraordinary actions, and they're also able to articulate thoughts and emotions that many people never express.

Developing good dialogue

Strong dialogue does the following:

- ✔ Combines distinct voices
- ✔ Reveals character and character relationships
- ✔ Propels the action forward
- ✔ Conveys pertinent information or exposition
- ✔ Prepares an audience for events to come
- ✔ Grows out of events in the past

If your dialogue seems flat or uninteresting, check to see whether it's accomplishing at least two of these goals. If it's not, revise it with another one in mind. If it is accomplishing two things on this list but it still feels flat, look at the character relationships more closely. Most dialogue feels flat because, in a sense, it's not moving forward. In other words, the lines don't know what they want to accomplish, so they're not accomplishing anything. In the most interesting dialogue, characters want something from each other, and they switch tactics according to how close or far they are from obtaining it. Can your characters more actively try to acquire, convince, elicit, or demand some response from the others? If you know what your language is doing in each scene, it won't remain flat for long.

Crafting a scene with these dialogue goals in mind is helpful. However, you can enhance one or two facets of the exchange after you've written it. Here are a few ways to rework it:

- ✔ **Speak it out loud.** Always test your dialogue by speaking it out loud yourself. If you stumble over the words, an actor will, too.

- ✔ **Let other people read it out loud.** Sometimes, you can't tell what's wrong with an exchange until you've heard it. The dialogue may sound great in your head and lousy out loud. See what an objective reader has to say.

✔ **Build your scene toward some point.** Every line, every speech, and every scene culminates in some resounding moment. Know what shift your scene is building toward and eliminate any detail that distracts an audience from it. If the man gets the girl at the end of the scene, make it difficult for him to do so, but not impossible.

✔ **When in doubt, cut it out.** Too many images, silences, or words clutter up the action. You have minutes (sometimes seconds) of screen time for every scene. One image can speak volumes; one well-phrased line may resonate for pages. Try not to repeat yourself. Keep your story moving aggressively forward.

Avoiding bad dialogue

If you know what kind of dialogue to avoid in advance, you may be better equipped to write a convincing scene. Take a look at these top five dialogue offenders, so that you can avoid these pitfalls:

1) Too "on the money"

This type of dialogue tells rather than suggests. In these scenes, characters divulge information with seemingly no reason to do so. As a result, the dialogue sounds manufactured instead of organic.

> "Dad, I can't tell you how glad I am that you called. I've been waiting all these years for some sign that you missed me."

> "Of course I missed you, honey. I've been so miserable here alone. Just hearing your voice makes me want to cry."

The conversation would sound more natural with silences, hesitancy to speak, or awkward stops and starts. They're speaking for the first time after an extended absence — how comfortable can they be? Here's how I might rework it:

> "Dad, I can't tell you how . . . I mean, it's been so long, you know? I guess I'm just really glad you called."

> "I know. I've missed you too."

Note that what's left unsaid is often inherent in what's said. The daughter doesn't need to tell her dad that she's waited all these years for a sign from him, because it's inherent in how difficult it is for her to speak with him. The subtext of the scene makes it all worthwhile.

2) Too repetitious

Repetition is a great tool for crafting rhythms. However, like any technique, it can become overbearing. Repetition of first names, phrases, or ideas has a tendency to slip into first-draft dialogue uninvited and overlooked.

> "Larry, can you hand me that wrench?"
>
> "This wrench? Sure thing, Phil, I'd be happy to."
>
> "Thanks, Lar, this wrench works on everything."
>
> "No problem, Phil. I've got a wrench like that at home."

We rarely use first names more than once or twice in everyday conversations. They slow down your line, so strike them whenever you can. Also, make sure every line of the dialogue takes you somewhere else. This exchange sounds better if you keep the first line and a few words more and then alter the rest. For example:

> "Hey, Larry. Can you hand me that wrench?"
>
> "Sure thing. Careful though, it's Dad's."
>
> "Right. He used this to fix just about everything when we were young, didn't he?"
>
> "Pretty much. Everything except his marriage, that is."

Now the speech patterns resemble those of a real conversation, and the conversation becomes about something more important than a wrench.

3) Too similar

When characters begin to sound alike, scenes become about information and not about people. If I can close my eyes and identify a speaker by the sound of her voice, you've done a good job crafting the dialogue. If all the characters sound alike, you've got work to do.

> "Did you go to the party last night?"
>
> "Yeah. Were you there?"
>
> "Yeah. It was great, huh?"
>
> "Pretty great, yeah."

First of all, nothing's happening in the scene. Also, both characters have the same voice. Here's a tip: If you glance at your page and notice that every character has roughly the same number of lines in each section, your characters probably need some help.

Here's a potential rewrite:

> "Did you go to the party last night?"
>
> "Hell yes. Never miss a party, man. Never, never miss a party. Were you there?
>
> "Yeah. It was okay"
>
> "Okay? Man, what's wrong with you, that party was stellar from jump."

Again, the dramatic potential is iffy, but at least there are two distinct voices in this conversation.

4) Too long or wordy

Lengthy dialogue often suggests a novice writer. You don't need many words in film because pictures do most of the work. Opinionated discourse and philosophical discussions have no place in drama unless the fate of the world rests on the outcome of that debate. Characters raving about a cause or standing on a soapbox should be sent home.

> "The campus didn't act on this one because the administration doesn't care. Most large organizations are so adept at sending messengers to do their work for them, or putting someone on hold while they grab lunch, or nodding and looking the other direction that they've forgotten how to act. Nothing happens anymore without red tape. If a question doesn't come with red tape, they'll put some on it and hire someone to take it off. This wasn't always the case, but it is now. Good luck trying to get the campus to act; I'll be surprised if you even get a foot in the door."

This entire speech is one opinion. Nothing new is said after the second line. If you cut it by a third and give the person a clear reason for ranting, the speech may get interesting. Here's a potential reworking:

> "The campus didn't act, because the administration doesn't care. You think they'll listen to you now? No way. They'll get some secretary to intercept you, they'll put you on hold, by the time they're done with you, you'll be nothing but a mound of red tape. No, it's a lost cause tryin' to get this administration to act. Won't even get your foot in the door."

If you find yourself getting overly wordy, break the language up with lines of action or description to remind the audiences what's happening visually. You don't ever want them to forget what's happening on the screen.

5) Too flat

By flat I mean that no one's in control of the scene. When characters have the same amount of power, their conversations tend to be dull.

> "He shouldn't have gone behind my back."
>
> "That's true. He shouldn't have done that. And we'll tell him."
>
> "Yeah. We'll show him who's boss."

Active dialogue often depends on two people vying for control of the scene. If you pit these two characters against each other, the scene is more exciting. Notice how conflict enhances dialogue as vividly as it enhances action.

> "You had no right to go behind my back."
>
> "You're right. I'm sorry. It was stupid to even try."
>
> "Damn straight. And you'll pay for it, too."
>
> "Or you could just let it go. After all, you owe me. Remember?"

TRY IT

Who's in control? Letting status enhance your scene

Power dynamics and the changes therein are the most important elements of any cinematic exchange. Why? Because the moment status shifts between two people is the moment a scene becomes active. We don't go to the movies just to hear people talk; we go to watch them win or lose or both in rapid succession. And while you can always go back and revise scenes with status in mind, it helps to spin a scene around it from the start. The following exercises are meant to help you do just that.

One-Upmanship

The formula for this scene is simple. Create two characters, quickly imagine what their relationship is, and set them in a location. Public locations are often better when you start, as the possibility of humiliation is high, but really any space will do. Now I want you to imagine that status will shift in this scene EVERY TIME a character speaks. In other words, if Character A begins in control of the power, she'll lose it or gain more the moment Character B opens his mouth. For example, consider this dramatic set-up:

Amy is head librarian at a prestigious university. Ben is her relatively new assistant. The two of them are placing labels on a large stack of books at the main desk. The following are five lines of dialogue in which status shifts every time:

AMY: Ben, really, you might consider taking some pride in your work.

BEN: And you might consider loosening up.

AMY: And you might consider that I am your superior, and insubordination is not tolerated here.

BEN: So fire me. I dare you.

AMY: Don't think I won't. Just because your father owns this university does not mean there won't be a consequence for your every action.

In this example, each character regains power on their line. Bear in mind it's just as much fun to let one character continue to relinquish power while the other continues to take it:

AMY: Ben, you really might consider taking some pride in your work.

BEN: You're right. I'm a complete failure at organization.

AMY: I've tried not to mention it, but it's true. I don't know anyone less competent at his job than you are.

BEN: Oh it doesn't stop there. I'm a failure at everything I attempt. Look at me, I'm a wreck!

One Swipe at a Time

The formula for this scene is similar to One-Upmanship, with one exception. You allow Character A to remain in power for a little while, script in a natural pause, and then let Character B take control immediately after. For example:

AMY: Ben, you're completely inept at this job. And I'm sorry, really, to have to be the one to tell you this. I'm sorry to rain on your seemingly unending parade, but if not me, then who? Are you listening to me?

BEN: I'm listening, yes.

Ben begins to stamp library books with surprising gusto. One after another after another after. . . .

AMY: Because that's another thing. Your attitude is pathetic. We took a chance on you here, and it was a gift, let me tell you. There were other people up for this job, people more qualified and, frankly, more interesting. People I'd be happy to see on a daily basis.

Ben pushes the pile of books off the desk with one swipe of his hand. The resulting crash echoes through the space for a moment.

BEN: Were you born a monster, or is that an acquired skill?

In this scenario, Ben has just taken control of the scene. He may remain in control for awhile before Amy regains it, or this line may mark the end of the moment.

Both formulas can be attempted at any stage of your writing process. They're helpful when you're just beginning to flesh out your characters, and when you're trying to revise a scene that seems stagnant. The important thing is that power is always changing hands. If a character's actions are motivated by a desire to win or a fear of losing, something will always be happening in each scene.

Chapter 11

The Nontraditional Film

Most screenwriting books will tell you that there's only one way to structure a film — in three acts, which follow one main character chronologically forward toward a grand conclusion. It's true that this is the most common formula in the industry, and many successful films have been forged upon it. It's such a popular structure, in fact, that I dedicate my entire Chapter 16 to the subject.

However, just as life doesn't arrive in any one pattern, neither does art. Your film will always have a beginning, a middle, and an end, but just because your film about a great white shark terrorizing a resort town moves steadily forward in time doesn't mean your film in which a character relives his last five years will follow suit. Your characters and your subject matter eventually dictate how your story gets told. So while it helps to familiarize yourself with the industry standards — and I'd certainly suggest a novice screenwriter begin with them — I'd be the last person to tell you there's only one way to spin a yarn.

This chapter gives you an overview of some alternative plot structures and provides several examples from popular cinema. I also concentrate on films that branch away from traditional realism into the world of high style. Movie musicals and films in which time runs some way other than forward all fall into this category.

Breaking with Tradition — Other Ways to Get the Job Done

In traditional story structure, writers spend the first act introducing the characters and the central conflict, the second act getting to know those characters and enhancing that conflict, and the third act forcing the characters to face the conflict resulting in great failure or great success.

If I were to draw this structure on a chalkboard, it would look like the big hill on a roller coaster. We start on the ground and work our way up to a great height, gaining speed and tension as we ride, and after we've been pushed to our limit, we plunge laughing or screaming back to earth again. The entirety of a three-act screenplay works toward the moment before the fall; everything that comes after the fall is wrap-up. (See Chapter 16 for more on this structure and its proven success rate.) But before you run off and pen your screenplay, consider the Titanic.

Everyone knows the Titanic sank. There's no great mystery to the conclusion of a film about the Titanic. You may want to begin that film as if the audience doesn't know what happens and work your way toward the tragedy, or you may want to begin your film with the ship sinking and spend the rest of the film showing viewers how it happened. The former version follows traditional structure; the latter version follows cyclical structure — which is one of three nontraditional ways to construct a screenplay:

- ✔ **Cyclical structure:** The movie ends where it begins. The Titanic sinks in the first scene, we flash back to see how we get there, and we watch it sink again at the conclusion. Cyclical films suggest the what of the story at the onset so that audiences can concentrate on the how.

  Why use this structure? You want your story to feel inevitable. You want your audience to see a moment in the first scene and understand it by the end. You believe that people don't actually learn from their mistakes, but rather keep repeating them throughout their lives.

- ✔ **Parallel structure:** The movie follows several equally complex plotlines simultaneously. *The Hours* is a good example of a movie crafted this way. The film follows three generations of women, all of whom are affected by suicide. Each woman's story is fully realized, each has its own conflicts, its own secondary characters, its own conclusion. However, audiences learn more about these women by comparing their lives than they would by following each woman individually.

  Virtually all Robert Altman films employ parallel structure, but *Short Cuts* is the clearest example. This film follows at least five plotlines. Occasionally, the characters weave in and out of each other's lives, but they're primarily connected by location. As a result, audiences feel they've experienced a day in the life of an entire neighborhood.

✔ **Pattern structure:** The movie is comprised of many scenes that exist independently of each other, connected only by one element. If each scene in your story takes place in a different hotel room, as in the film *Four Rooms,* you have a pattern film. The idea of a hotel room, and all that can occur there, is the element that holds the film together. The Hal Hartley movie *Flirt* is pattern script. The same events occur three times in that film — though the locations, the time frames, and even the genders of the characters change. The plot points are the pattern. How they occur and who they occur to differ throughout. *Paris Je T'aime* is similar in this regard. All 18 stories take place in Paris, and each tackles the question of romantic love.

Sometimes pattern films feel like parallel films, but here's the difference: Parallel films follow a few storylines from start to finish, and occasionally those storylines interact. Pattern films show you glimpses of stories, all connected by one element. The characters in those glimpses rarely (if ever) interact, and an audience rarely (if ever) gets more than the glimpse.

Screenwriters aren't always strict in their adherence to any one of these structures. Many films have moments of cyclical structure, moments where stories run parallel to each other, and moments where patterns emerge. *Groundhog Day* is a film where the main character, played by Bill Murray, seems trapped in a never-ending cycle of events. He relives the same day at least five times in that film. However, he's aware of the cycle, and the film attempts to demonstrate what it takes for him to break it. The first scene is therefore not the same as the last, but audiences wonder throughout if it will be. James Cameron's version of *The Titanic* is essentially a flashback. It therefore has the feeling of a cycle script, but in reality is traditional in design. So please take note: I offer you these formulas not to suggest you base an entire screenplay on them (though you could), but because they're other ways you can tell your story.

Thinking Out of Time

Most films are *linear,* meaning that they move chronologically forward in time. Even movies that employ flashbacks are essentially linear. I may pause in the course of my day to recall the hour my child was born, but my day will pick up again when the reverie passes.

If you've ever wanted to retract something you've said or see how life may have panned out if only you'd stayed with that certain someone, you're in luck. You can do that in film, if necessary. However, before you stray from the linear path, ask yourself why your story is better told out of sequence.

Here are some reasons you may decide to tangle with time:

- **You want to highlight a pivotal decision in your character's life by dramatizing the road taken as well as the road, well, not.** These films either reveal both possible storylines simultaneously, or we live one with the character and then live the other. *Sliding Doors* is an example of such a film. Audiences follow Helen, played by Gwyneth Paltrow, through her day twice — once in which she catches the evening train and catches her boyfriend cheating on her, and one in which she misses the train entirely.

- **You want to trace an outcome back to its inciting event.** These films present a conclusion in the first act and work backward to reveal what led to that conclusion. *Memento* is a clear example of this technique. The film's protagonist wants to solve his wife's murder. Unfortunately, he suffers from short-term memory loss and must write himself memos to keep track of the facts. The film moves backward, note by note, until he is forced to confront the reason his wife died. Notice that the decision to move backward is far from arbitrary. It stems from the protagonist's infliction, and it methodically drives an audience toward his final, extremely personal, revelation.

- **You want to analyze an event in the way an academic analyzes history.** Films structured this way feel like a slide presentation or a documentary. Audiences are given all the information surrounding an event, but they don't necessarily receive it in order. These stories are often narrated; they pause and rewind as desired, speed through events or skip them entirely, and provide expert testimony as needed to prove a point. Christopher Guest's mock-umentaries, *Waiting for Guffman, Best in Show,* and *A Mighty Wind,* work this way. Each is a pretend documentary and jumps in time and between narrators quite often. Alexander Payne's *Election* is also structured in this way: One high school teacher pits himself against a student in the upcoming school election. They take turns trying to justify their actions to the audience, citing some hilarious reasoning as they go.

- **You want your character to be able to retract her actions and try again.** You know the expression, "Hindsight is 20-20?" Here's your opportunity to allow characters to relive a moment once, twice, even three times with renewed vision. *Run Lola Run* works this way. Lola has 20 minutes to find a certain sum of money for her boyfriend, before he robs a store for the cash. Audiences see three alternative endings to this plotline, every variation of which is based on a tiny change in her run for the money.

So how common is cinematic time twisting? As you may have guessed from the examples, it's fairly common, and films that succeed here keep audiences guessing what'll happen next.

Bear in mind that you can confuse an audience or lose them entirely this way as well. If you're unclear about portions of your plot or conflicted about your characters' motivations, don't try manipulating time just yet. Wait until you're confident in those arenas before manipulating time at all.

Map your screenplay out as if it's linear in design. Doing so reveals the pivotal events in your plot and any holes therein. Again, your story will always essentially have three acts — a beginning, middle, and end — so it can't hurt to see what those acts would look like if you gave them to us chronologically. You can always reverse the events or manipulate them after that clarification. This tip is also useful if you plan to layer another artistic medium on top of your story — a medium such as song perhaps.

Song and Dance: The Movie Musical

Crafting a movie musical is similar to crafting any story, with one exception: Certain portions of these films are better told in song. Let me emphasize that last point. Song is not simply a fun way to enhance your story; in musicals, it's the best way certain pieces of information can be communicated. Yes, I know, there are any number of instances where characters in musicals simply give us information or tell us a story in a song. That's true, but I would argue it doesn't make for the most compelling musical scene.

The most successful musicals are ones in which songs are a necessity, and characters break into them for one of the following reasons:

✔ They're consumed by emotion, and words alone no longer suffice.

✔ They're saying one thing, but feeling another.

✔ They're thinking out loud, and music suggests their internal landscape.

Sense a pattern here? In each instance, music provides the emotional impact of the scene. Writers rely on song to burst forth where language alone falls short, to reveal the subtext of a scene, or to lead us into the character's mind. Either way, it's working with the character to enhance a moment emotionally, or it's working against him, to reveal his true sentiments to an audience. It's wise to consider what role music will play in your story in advance, because it will make conversations you have with your collaborators that much easier. Oh, yes, here's the other part of this process that differs from the norm: You'll most likely be working with a lyricist and a librettist.

In film, as onstage, musical scripts generally have three collaborators: the *composer,* the *lyricist,* and the *librettist.* The composer is in charge of the music; the lyricist is in charge of the words to the songs; and the librettist is in charge of the general story, otherwise known as the *book.*

Often, these roles overlap. Stephen Sondheim wrote the music and the lyrics for *Sweeney Todd,* for which Hugh Wheeler wrote the original book and John Logan wrote the screenplay. Baz Luhrmann and Craig Pearce share credit for the screenplay of *Moulin Rouge,* but the music was pulled from a variety of different artists. *Sweeney Todd* was also an adaptation while *Moulin Rouge* was an original piece.

A musical is simply a story with song. You're still crafting a plot that needs to be active, characters who require motivation, conflicts that need to be faced, and protagonists who will fail or succeed. Music is one more element to consider, and it should be a necessary addition, but the writing process is much the same as any other.

Original musicals

Some of the most exciting original musicals include *Moulin Rouge,* Julie Taymor's *Across The Universe, Singin' in the Rain, Meet Me in St. Louis, The Wizard of Oz,* and virtually every animated Disney film to date. *High School Musical* may be the most successful original musical to date. It began as a Disney television movie in 2006, but a sequel soon followed, as well as a successful stage-musical. A quick glance through these examples suggests three distinct formulas for original pieces:

- ✔ An original book with acquired music
- ✔ An adapted book with original music and lyrics
- ✔ An original book with original music and lyrics

Moulin Rouge and *Across the Universe* take songs from popular artists and craft them into a script. *Moulin Rouge,* the story of a famous showgirl and her forbidden love affair with a young composer, includes songs by Elton John, David Bowie, and Madonna. The entire plot of *Across The Universe* was constructed around music from The Beatles. Taymor uses their songs to walk through history, specifically the drafting of unwilling youth into the Vietnam War. If you're interested in writing a musical, but aren't a composer yourself, consider which songwriters interest you and why. You may be able to construct an idea for a film around those artists. Because rights are involved here, you'll want to approach someone with the idea before writing the screenplay, but you can sell a story this way.

The Wizard of Oz and Disney's animated films follow the second formula. The writers chose fictional material, adapted it into a screenplay, and collaborated with composers and lyricists for the music. This route is perhaps easier to follow for the novice screenwriter. First, the story's already there for the taking. You have to figure out how to transfer it to film, but you're not responsible for devising all the plot points yourself. Second, it's often easier to see where to place songs when looking at someone else's material. Finally, it's easier to market these musicals because the primary material is usually pulled from popular literature. And anything that's easier to market is easier to sell, which is good news for the screenwriter.

The third formula is the rarest of the three, in large part because it requires the most intense collaborations. It's also the one most likely to fail in process or at the box office, because all the material is original, and several artists are working on the product simultaneously. ***High School Musical, Singin' in the Rain,*** and ***Meet Me in St. Louis*** are examples of this form. All three were immediate hits, but they were created by artists who had worked together before in studios that had past experience with the form. In other words, they had a lot of help, and they spoke the same creative language. If you decide to go this route, more power to you. Make sure that you and your collaborators have agreed on which story you're writing and have a similar aesthetic for the piece in mind.

Musical adaptations

Adapting a musical is by far the more common way to write one. ***Sweeney Todd, Chicago, The Producers, Hairspray, Mamma Mia!, Grease, Annie*** — the list of successful musical adaptations is endless. I talk in detail about adapting one medium into another in Chapter 18, but here are a few things to consider if you're interested in this type of musical:

- **Know the pros and cons of the original medium.** If your primary source was a Broadway show, one set-may serve several locations, or a chorus of people play multiple roles, or grand song and dance numbers, all of which need to be altered to make sense on-screen. Know which parts of the original medium will be a help to you in this endeavor, and which will be a hindrance.

- **Know which characters you want to keep, and which you can lose.** You may convert an entire chorus into one on-screen role. The original piece may have two villains while your film may have only one. You may eliminate entire secondary characters in fiction so that audiences can concentrate on the main story in the two hours allotted them. However you do it, make sure that you know which characters interest you, and which get in the way.

- **Be familiar enough with the original plot to know which three to five events will become the skeleton of your film.** You don't need to use more than that, though many writers do. If you can narrow your focus down to five events, you can rearrange their order until the screenplay version reveals itself to you.

- **Let the music be your guide.** You don't need to script every scene in the original if you've accurately captured the quality of the show. The Broadway version of ***Sweeney Todd,*** for example, begins with a chorus of ghosts telling us about the life of the protagonist. It then deposits us on the boat, which carries Sweeney himself back to London. The film version skips that introductory song and opens with the boat. This alteration works because the film becomes the tale of Sweeney Todd; we don't need a choral rendition of the plot in advance.

✔ **Allow the music to tell you what that quality of the film should be.** The dark corruption of *Chicago* stands in stark contrast to the technicolor mania of *Grease,* not simply because the subject matter demands it. The music conveys that difference before any words are even spoken.

In order to adapt material into a musical, you must first own the rights. I go over the process of acquiring rights in Chapter 18, but it's important to consider it in advance. If you're adapting a stage musical for the screen (as in *Chicago* or *Grease*), you'll need control of the primary source. If you have an original story but would like to enhance it with songs by contemporary artists (as in *Moulin Rouge*), you'll need to acquire rights for each song. While the process can be a complicated one, consider it now. You don't want to script a musical you won't be legally allowed to market.

Musical techniques for nonmusical projects

Whether you're writing a musical or not, considering its structure may help craft the project you are working on. Here are three techniques I borrow from musicals on a regular basis when writing screenplays with songs or without:

✔ **Write to a soundtrack.** Find songs that reflect the pace and feel of your larger scenes and write them with that song playing in the background. You won't include these songs in those scenes, necessarily, but often the quality of each one finds its way into your work as you write.

✔ **Choose musical themes for your characters.** In musicals, each character is often underscored with their own riff. This choice is meant to immediately convey personality and intention. You should know what your characters themes would be, whether you use them in the script or not.

✔ **Consider crafting any grand activity, long speech, or extended silence in the same way you'd write a song.** Each moment is its own story, and each moment can't be conveyed any other way. The best songs are the ones characters have no choice but to sing. Your nonsung moments should feel the same way.

✔ **Borrow the traditions.** Musicals are traditionally broken down into male and female solos, boy numbers and girl numbers, dance breaks, the show-stopping song, choral moments, and reprises. Does your script have this variety? Do you include private moments for the lead roles? Are they balanced out with crowd scenes? Do you have sequences of pure activity and story-stopping speeches?

Just because most musicals structure themselves a certain way, doesn't mean you can't use the techniques to inspire your high-octane political thriller or your off-beat romantic comedy. Every form teaches you something about the others.

Chapter 12

Maintaining an Audience's Trust

- -

In This Chapter

▶ Remaining true to an audience and the work

▶ Tackling difficult material with integrity

▶ Understanding audience expectations

- -

Cinema is fast becoming a medium in which any visual effect is both technologically and financially possible. Its audience also extends beyond that of other mediums, reaching millions of people every year. These elements in combination make film an incredibly exciting art form but a potentially dangerous one as well.

Why dangerous? Perhaps you've heard the saying "With power comes responsibility" or a variation of it. Nowhere is that sentiment more applicable than in film, and the responsibility falls to the screenwriter first. Every time you begin a project, the resulting work may affect children, adolescents, and adults from differing cultures and educational backgrounds. What you write may be seen, heard, and, quite possibly, believed by those viewers. And your name's on the material.

So before you toss a script out there, take another look through it. Have you written a responsible script? If you're not sure, read this chapter, which explores what a writer's duties may or may not be and how to shape a work so that it remains true to the subject and to its audience.

Screenwriting and Ethics

Because film is so accessible, so much like a window to the world, it's easy to assume that screenwriters should strive above all to create the illusion of reality. In other words, the more real the action appears, the more successful the script seems to be. Yet in truth, the screenwriter's objective isn't always simply to mirror reality, nor should it be. The screenwriter's job isn't to re-create life but to design it. The difference between these tasks is subtle but vast.

If I record the conversations around me and transcribe them onto the page, I'm re-creating life. The result may sound convincing, but it begs the question: So what? I'm not writing the discourse; I'm simply writing it down — a big difference. But if I spend time replaying the conversations, weighing one section against another, selecting between them, and then reconnecting those portions, I'm designing life. I have a grand scheme in mind. Writers create a text in this way. Even when they're adapting from a source or pulling from historical events, they're selecting which pieces to include and how to present them with a grand scheme in mind.

Responsible writers ask two central questions at some point in their process:

- ✔ What kind of world do I want to design?
- ✔ Why design that world in place of others?

Implicit in these questions is the idea of choice. Between you and every creative decision lie at least three options. Will your character survive, perish, or simply leave the story? Should you kill a character on-screen or off-screen or begin the action and then cut to another moment? Do you set the scene in Paris, Prague, or Rome? Sometimes, you make a choice based on logic — he's Italian, so the memory scenes take place in Florence. Sometimes, you make a choice based on style — that dark alleyway fits the *film noir* genre better than a crowded street because film noir is a style that relies heavily on shadow and mystique. These decisions often take care of themselves; they just make sense. The more difficult choices — how do you kill a character on-screen, how explicit is your language, is a scene funny or offensive — are based on ethics.

Artists sometimes bristle at the word *ethics*. And yet, every script exists in an ethical realm. The study of ethics is the study of human motivation. You're presenting work to an audience, and that audience will weigh the choices that you've made therein. They'll search for motivations for each character action, and they'll judge those characters accordingly. Are the characters honorable or despicable, do they elicit praise or disdain, are they trustworthy or two-faced, why do they behave the way that they do? These questions are ethical questions, and because it's your job to guide an audience through your piece, they merit your attention.

Unfortunately, ethical has come to mean "family oriented" or "innocuous." Under this definition, films with violence, cursing, and sexual content become unethical, forcing artists to censor themselves in undesirable ways. I'm not using the term in this way. Many of the most troublesome and thought-provoking films are written for ethical purposes. Charlie Chaplin's ***The Great Dictator*** and Steven Spielberg's ***Schindler's List*** tackle the Holocaust in ethical ways. They're not meant to be comfortable or easy to watch; they're meant to invite debate. ***Crash*** challenged racial and economic stereotypes throughout. The controversy around this film also created *buzz,* or Hollywood attention, which helped it win the Oscar. These films aren't designed to make audiences comfortable, but they're written for ethical reasons. Because film is a social medium designed to elicit audience response, screenwriting is an inherently ethical craft. Screenwriters, then, are automatically moralists as well as storytellers.

Screenwriting and Responsibility

So what do ethics have to do with responsibility? Well, in a sense, you're responsible for considering what ethics you present. Why? Someone's going to watch them; you're not on this journey alone. In other words, be aware of what you suggest. Know why you're writing the script. Screenwriters have a threefold responsibility. They have to consider themselves, the material, and the audience.

If you write an irresponsible script, all three of these entities suffer, but consider this: The medium itself also suffers. Audiences enter a theater wanting to enjoy themselves and wanting to discover something along the way. They enter with expectations. If you fulfill those expectations, even in a small way, they're more likely to trust that the next film will, too. If I see three action films in a row that offer special effects and little else, I'm likely to assume that the whole genre's lost its touch.

What are you willing to put your name on?

Right now, the script is yours and within your control. It may not be yours in the near future; it may be *optioned* (purchased for temporary consideration) or purchased for production outright, and what it becomes after that sale is out of your hands. But right now, it's your story. How do you want to tell it? What do you want it to say? Because you're putting your name on this script, you need to be responsible to yourself in this way first.

Writers approach material for any number of reasons, and they usually hope to interest an audience in the same things. What affects you in the material may similarly affect an audience. Moreover, you can enhance those qualities in your script so that they have the desired effect.

Being responsible to yourself also means remembering why you're writing the story and maintaining the integrity of its ideal. What's sacred in your script? The depth of character? The thoughts and opinions expressed? The way that certain events transpire? List those details now and make sure that you accomplish them. Just as actors sign contracts stipulating what they will and will not do on-screen, writers make an agreement with themselves. That agreement may include the following statements:

✔ I will write stories that I believe in.

✔ I will entertain several options before I choose one.

✔ I will keep my audience in mind.

✔ I will remember what drew me to the story in the first place.

✔ I will do the best that I can.

Your intentions may shift along the way. Let them. This story is your opportunity to explore a new world, to ask difficult questions, to inspire yourself and others. This vision may change radically in the hands of business executives, but a responsibly written script is more likely to become a responsible film.

Approaching difficult subject matter

So you're writing a film about warring gangs in the inner city. Right away, the subject matter evokes images of guns, blood, drugs, murder, and danger on multiple levels. You may feel the need to include these details for the sake of accuracy, but before you craft scenes full of graphic violence, ask yourself, "How is the story best served?" To tell a story clearly, you have to consider both the material and the audience. On-screen violence may seem realistic, but if audiences spend two hours with their eyes closed, they'll miss your story. The question, "How do I approach that material responsibly?" really asks, "How do I do justice to the story?"

Violence, abrasive language, and sexual content offer distinct challenges. If you err on the side of caution, you risk credibility. If you opt for completely realistic, you risk distancing your audience from the narrative. I usually ask writers to consider three truths before choosing an approach:

✔ **Images linger.** I've said it before, and I'll say it again: Film is a visual medium. Your audiences are more likely to leave the theater with a series of images in their minds than they are to leave considering a grand message. Which images do you want them to retain? Is your film really about a naked actress, or is it about two people falling in love? Do you want them to remember a gunshot to the head, or two children huddled together listening to that gunshot? Is it important to watch a man strike a woman, or to see her walking through public places wearing sunglasses and covering her mouth with one hand? The images that linger come to represent the story itself. How is your story best served?

✔ **Words have weight.** The film *RKO 281* contains a line that suggests that great speeches change the world. And they do. Why are presidential speeches so important? Why choose the wording on advertisements with so much care? Words are a writer's tools. They're the vehicle between your mind and someone else's. They're active and can, therefore, inspire action.

As cinema is a public forum, the language that your characters use also enters a collective vocabulary. Those words not only remain with audiences, they also become more common as they're used more frequently. So consider your language carefully. Again, you're not re-creating life, you're designing it. This task isn't an easy one, especially where language is concerned. If you're simply pounding out words without consideration, you're writing carelessly. Many screenwriters seem to have forgotten this fact.

✔ **What attracts also distracts.** Many films these days openly advertise graphic violence and sexual content. Why? Because sex and violence sell tickets. Advertising agencies know it; so do film executives. Although using these elements may make sense for financiers, it's a dangerous practice for screenwriters, whose first priority is to a story, not a violent moment or a sexual scene. Consider the problem of nudity. Audiences may flock to a film to see Brad Pitt's backside. But the moment that the scene occurs, those people are thinking, "That's Brad Pitt's backside." They're not involved in the story.

Screenwriters must walk a fine line between what draws an audience in and out of a narrative. Assess current films like *Crash, Kill Bill I & II,* and *The History of Violence* to discover where that line lies. That knowledge will come in handy when it's time to craft an intimate scene of your own.

The Immunity Factor

When you first see a film, everything's new. You watch in a state of naiveté, during which many things may surprise, shock, or intrigue you. In other words, you're actively involved. After a while, you become more sophisticated about its design, and you develop certain expectations. If those expectations aren't circumvented, the film eventually becomes old hat, and you begin to imagine events before they actually transpire. You may cease to think about the movie; you may even begin planning the rest of your day. You've become immune to any potential impact that the film may otherwise have had.

It's an aging process of sorts and can be detrimental to any artist who doesn't foresee it and plan accordingly. This immunity can happen to entire genres just as it happens during the course of a single film. The phrase "If you've seen one action film, you've seen them all" speaks to the dilemma, and it becomes dangerous where difficult subject matter is concerned. You probably don't want audiences saying, "If you've seen one drive-by shooting, you've seen them all," and yet films with excessive violence inoculate audiences to its effects in just this way. After several scenes where cursing prevails, I cease to hear the words. In movies with high sexual content, intimacy may lose meaning altogether.

So how do you protect your work against this process? Begin by asking yourself these questions:

- ✐ What do you want an audience to simply accept?
- ✐ What do you want an audience to hear and/or remember?
- ✐ What surprises do you have in store?
- ✐ What facts might be more powerful suggested rather than presented outright?

Part of your responsibility, to both the story and to audiences, is to wake them up. With a nudge in the right direction, people's imaginations will concoct scenes more gruesome, delightful, terrifying, or inspiring than you may be capable of writing. Never underestimate the power of suggested violence or sexual contact, and whatever you do, don't let audiences become immune to the very thing that you need to convey. Write a film that challenges their expectations or demands that they create new ones.

Finally, before you send a script anywhere, imagine different kinds of audience members for it. Imagine a child in the theater, a young woman, an elderly man. Imagine a victim of violence or sexual abuse. Imagine someone who's fought a war or lived through the events that you're dramatizing. Will they be adversely affected by what they see? This procedure doesn't mean that you'll change the script to fit their needs; you may not. You may feel strongly that it's important in your piece to dramatize war in a graphic, realistic way. *Saving Private Ryan* and *Platoon* are examples of such films. However, if you've thought about the audience that this subject matter may disturb, you can craft a marketing strategy that warns the audience in advance. You might put it on your list of priorities when speaking to executives about the film. After a script hits production, the advertising campaign may be out of your hands. But it's your script first, so the responsibility for your audience begins with you.

A strong script is probably written for several kinds of audiences. But if you know who it's not intended for in advance, you'll be better able to market the script responsibly later on. You'll want to consider agents and studios in the same way. Match your material to the industry professional. (For more on selling your script, see Part IV.)

Part III
Turning Your Story into a Script

The 5th Wave   By Rich Tennant

"Do you use these 3x5 cards for anything other than charting your screenplay, or does the creature actually make a pineapple bundt cake at this point in the movie?"

In this part . . .

Here's where the process gets technical. You've developed an idea into a story. You know what's going to happen, who it's happening to, and how it's going to end. Fantastic. So what makes that story a screenplay? Its organization, artistically and technically, that's what. This part is about mapping the story out and piecing it together on the page. From setting your margins and pounding out a draft to revising it until you're satisfied. This is where the story becomes a film.

Chapter 13

Mapping Out Your Screenplay

. . . .

In This Chapter

▶ Telling your story in a nutshell

▶ Treating your story to a treatment

▶ Choosing the outline that's right for you

. . . .

Writers spend months constructing characters, choosing locations, researching events, and conceptualizing the look or angle that their stories will take. Yet, despite this preparation, few screenwriters jump immediately into composing a first draft. Why? They don't know where to start. Or they know where to start, but they don't know what comes directly after or what the first scenes are moving toward. More often, they've envisioned the beginning, middle, and end of the story, but they have only a vague idea of how to get from point to point.

A full-length screenplay is a vast project, generally between 90 to 120 pages long, hinged together by countless visual moments. Ideally, no detail is wasted; the writer reveals every piece of information for a reason. Can you visualize all those pieces? If the answer is no, don't worry. Most seasoned writers can't, either. It's a lot to consider all at once. So when you complete the initial research, you have two choices: start writing immediately and risk staring at a computer screen for hours, wondering what comes next, or plot out the story in advance.

This chapter is all about the second choice. I show you how to plot out your story, from the initial premise to a working outline. You'll still stare at the screen for hours — even an outline can't cure that — but at least you won't be wondering what comes next.

Conceptualizing Your Concept

If your script makes it to an agent or a producer, here are a few questions that you'll hear quite often:

- ✔ What's the hook?
- ✔ Does it have audience appeal?
- ✔ Remind me again — it's like what two films?
- ✔ Where's the big event?
- ✔ Yeah, but, what's it about?

These questions are really asking the same thing: What's your film's concept? The *hook* is a detail from your story that ropes an audience in. The *big event* is usually the first major turning point in the protagonist's journey. In some films, the hook and the big event are the same thing. In *Jurassic Park,* a man who resembles a zookeeper is eaten by a creature as he tries to load it into a pen. While we don't realize until later that the creature is a dinosaur, it's clear from the opening shot that it's unlike anything we've seen. That hook is clearly linked to the premise of the dangers of some scientific research.

After all your research, you may find it odd to return to the beginning, but before you map out a script, you have to revisit the original idea. Do you have a three- to five-sentence *nutshell synopsis?* (See Chapter 5 if you don't have one and want to know how to create one.) If so, now's the time to turn that synopsis into one of two things: a logline or a question. You may want to take a stab at both.

A *logline* is a one- or two-sentence encapsulation of your story. It highlights character, conflict, and those aspects of your piece that make it unique. It's significantly shorter than a synopsis.

Here are a few examples from established films. I include both a logline and a question for each:

- ✔ *E.T.:* When an alien lands in a young boy's backyard, that boy and his family struggle to send it back home before it's too late.

  or: What happens when an alien lands in a young boy's backyard and finds itself unable to get back home?

- ✔ *Juno:* When a teenage girl becomes pregnant, she must figure out her own values in order to find the right parents for her child.

  or: Young Juno MacGuff has just discovered that she's pregnant. Who exactly will she choose to raise her child?

Even epic-length films can be whittled down to size:

✔ ***Lord of the Rings:*** A ring of power surfaces after years in hiding, and many forces seek its dark authority. The fate of Middle Earth depends on the hobbit Frodo, bearer of the ring, and his decision over its demise.

or: The dark ring of power is entrusted to the hobbit Frodo. Will he find a way to destroy it? Will it be lost along the way? Or will its power turn him toward the evil?

✔ ***Raiders of the Lost Ark:*** Artifacts unearthed in Egypt reveal the whereabouts of the mythic Lost Ark of the Covenant. Only one man stands between Hitler's Nazi regime and the Ark's fabled power — archaeologist and university professor Indiana Jones.

or: Artifacts unearthed in Egypt reveal the whereabouts of the mythic Lost Ark of the Covenant, an object fabled to possess measureless power. Will Hitler and his Nazi regime find the Ark and harness this power? Or will Indiana Jones beat them to it?

Do you see how these snippets depict the crux of each film? These snippets are film concepts. From a business perspective, more films are bought and sold over concept than on full drafts, outlines, or other literature combined. From an artistic perspective, the concept is your greatest ally when writing the first draft. It keeps you on track when the story eludes you. It also fuels the eventual outline.

So after you condense the story into a few sentences, or a well-phrased question, double-check that the following elements are true:

✔ Your concept is clear and easily understood.

✔ It suggests the largest conflict in the film.

✔ It suggests a cast of characters.

✔ It suggests what's unique about the story.

✔ It suggests what may be familiar to an audience.

✔ It suggests what's easily marketable in the story.

✔ It suggests dynamic action.

As a final challenge, layer in character motivation. In other words, your characters want something for a reason. What is that reason? Elliot Ness is ethically opposed to Al Capone. Frodo must destroy the ring or be destroyed himself. Usually, your film provides life-or-death consequences. Add those consequences to your premise. And take your time. A clear concept provides the foundation for every draft of the script that you write thereafter.

How to Treat Your Treatment

If you had to write reports in school, you're probably familiar with a *treatment*. Most class projects require a cover page that explains what topics the report includes and what it ultimately proves. A treatment is the screenwriting equivalent of that cover page, albeit more entertaining.

To be more specific, a *treatment* is a narrative summation of your story. It's part synopsis and part short story. It runs anywhere from 4–20 pages in length, depending on the scope of your film, and it describes each act of your script in chronological order. It does not, however, include dialogue examples, unless that exchange is pivotal to the story.

In five-page treatments, Page 1 is generally dedicated to Act I, Pages 2 through 4 illustrate Act II, and Page 5 sums up Act III. A film's second act is twice as long as the first or third and therefore requires more explanation. Most screenplay treatments run 15–20 pages in length. If your film is three hours long, or includes several subplots, it may require a few more pages.

Treatments that run longer than 20 pages are generally overwritten and overwhelming to the eye. After all, most first acts are about 30 pages; you may as well start writing the script.

Before you begin

Two kinds of treatments exist: the one that you write for studios or agents and the one that you write for yourself. I talk about marketing treatments in Chapter 19. In this chapter, you're writing this first treatment for you, so concentrate on depicting the following elements clearly:

- ✔ **A brief description of your main characters (villains included):**
  Character introductions are important. Your audience will judge the character's initial actions on that introduction. The characters will also change as your story unfolds. If they make strong first impressions, you'll be better able to recognize those changes as they occur. So think: What do your characters look like? How do they spend time? How do they communicate, verbally or otherwise? In other words, what are they like when they first enter the scene in five sentences or less?

- ✔ **An immediate sense of their goals and motivations:** Most stories entail what people want and how they're going to get it. You'll probably want to reveal the first part of that statement, the "what people want" bit, early on. If you establish character goals quickly, you'll have more time to pursue them.

✔ **The platform:** What is your protagonist's life like prior to the first big event? What is her routine? This routine includes job, family, friendships, romantic involvements, hobbies, and so on — basically, anything that constitutes a normal way of life for your protagonist.

✔ **The catalyst:** What event changes that routine forever? What event launches the film? This event may be as large as a military invasion or as simple as a first kiss. If it topples your character's sense of normal, it's a catalyst.

✔ **Plot Point I:** What event forces the character into action? At what point does he or she commit to the journey? This event is generally the time when your character decides to pursue her goal. Whether or not she does so willingly is up to you.

✔ **Plot Point II:** What event determines whether or not the character decides to face the primary conflict once and for all? This is generally a moment of great pressure for your character. He may want to give up, or a pivotal event may strengthen his resolve to continue forging ahead.

✔ **Climax:** What scene or series of scenes depicts the final battle? Pay particular attention to your antagonist or your villain here. How does that force behave in these scenes?

✔ **Resolution:** What is the outcome of that battle? What does the world of the film look like now?

I discuss these plot considerations at greater length in Chapter 16, but this list provides an overall sense of what to include. If you envision a number of important events, touch upon as many as you can. If your story has subplots, scatter the information, albeit briefly, for those characters and situations throughout. Consider this first treatment as a personal test. How well do you know your characters? Are their goals strong enough to maintain an entire script? Where is the action unclear? If you find that you need more information, do some more research and layer it in. A treatment sorts through your drama. It immediately reveals any holes in your storyline. You may find yourself tweaking it with each act of your first draft or constructing a new one entirely before a big rewrite. After you're comfortable with the process, you'll find it to be invaluable to your writing.

Putting it on the page

Like the concept, you're constructing this treatment with two minds. Artistically, you want people to visualize the plot and to fall in love with the characters. From a business standpoint, you want to emphasize marketability. So although you can write a treatment any way that you want, the following guidelines usually apply:

✔ Treatments are written in the present tense, so that they're active and immediately accessible. This guideline remains true even if the story takes place in the past.

✔ They're written in brief paragraphs, spaced on the page so as not to become overwhelming to a reader.

✔ They're not meant for personal commentary, psychological analysis, or editorials; include only what you intend to put on the screen.

✔ They may be written in the style of the film.

✔ They may include bits of dialogue, especially those written for comedies. (Dialogue in a treatment is placed in quotes, unlike dialogue in a script, which is not.) However, use dialogue sparingly and only if necessary.

✔ They emphasize the visual action of each scene.

✔ They share the goals of a first draft, namely:

- To grab a reader's attention

- To elicit emotion

- To create a specific world and atmosphere

- To communicate genre

- To highlight aspects that are particularly unique as well as those that are familiar to a target audience

✔ The shorter your treatment is, the better. However, don't skimp on description in an attempt to be brief. The treatment should help your readers see the film in advance.

You can flip to Chapter 19 for more info on the business treatment, but for now, concentrate on clarifying the story for yourself. This process takes a while, so don't give up. It helps you assess the strengths of your idea as well as its drawbacks. It reveals which characters jump off of the page, and which remain vague. It provides information for you to return to as you piece together your first draft, and eventually, it may help you sell your script.

Exploring the Ins and Outs of an Outline

An *outline* is a further breakdown of the treatment into individual scenes. If you're writing an outline without a treatment, think of it as a chronological list of the actions in a given scene or an entire script. I encourage you to write a treatment first, though — if only because, in doing so, many smaller actions and images may emerge. However, sometimes, research reveals them as well.

Outlines come in several types, and the structure of each differs according to individual preference. Like the initial treatment, this outline is for you. You aren't likely to be asked to submit a scene outline to studios initially. This request is usually made well after the completion of a first draft. The outline is an integral part of the screenwriter's process; it allows you to write the bulk of the script with a sense of purpose and destination. It troubleshoots many of the story flaws in advance, preventing innumerable bouts of writer's block. It also serves as a formatting liaison between the prose of a treatment and the technical lingo of a screenplay.

So choose the form that feels right and mold it to fit your needs. The goal is to become comfortable pouring information onto the page, so that you can later convert it into coherent cinema.

One sentence at a time

A *sentence outline,* also known as a *beat sheet,* is a sentence-by-sentence list of the action in any scene. You can practice this outline form off the page as well as on. Watch the people around you and choose someone engaged in an interesting activity. Can you break that activity into separate moments? Try it. Convert each detail into a sentence. For example, I'm watching a woman give a campus tour. My imagined outline may look like this:

> The tour guide corrals the crowd into a designated area.
>
> She rattles off information about the architecture on campus.
>
> She's interrupted by a boy on a bicycle who calls out her name and waves as he rides by.
>
> She watches him, temporarily forgetting that her tour group exists.

In four sentences, I suggest two characters (the tour guide and the boy), a location (a university campus), and something that makes the moment memorable (the attention she gives him). The scene is brief — it may take less than a minute of screen time — but it conveys a slew of information. It also raises a few questions — namely, who are these people to each other, and what may happen between them?

A sentence outline follows exactly the same process with a few additions:

- ✔ It includes the Act number, the location, and the time of every scene.
- ✔ The actions of one scene inspire the actions of another.

Hopefully, you can envision the story's conclusion. With that end in mind, you can highlight the moments that take you there within each scene. To rewrite my previous example then, I must decide where that moment may lead. When I imagine the tour guide's raging crush on this boy and determine that this event propels her to ask him out, I can add the scene to my outline. The rewritten version might look like this:

> **Act I, Scene — Ext. Campus Street — Day**
>
> A tour guide wearily corrals the crowd into a designated area.
>
> She recites various facts about the architecture on campus.
>
> Suddenly, she is interrupted by a boy on a bike. He calls out her name and waves.
>
> He passes her, as if in slow motion, revealing in detail his blue eyes and dazzling smile.
>
> She watches him ride off, oblivious to the group she's in charge of.
>
> She finally looks at them for a second, then takes off after him, calling his name as she runs.

The heading of each scene in an outline corresponds to the slug line that will eventually appear in your script. Slug lines include the basic information needed to set up a shot. I talk about them at greater length in Chapter 15, if you want the whole scoop, but for your purposes here, just remember to include a rough indication of where the scene fits in the chronology of your story, a sense of location, and a sense of time. If the following scene in the tour guide drama takes place in the bookstore where she tracks the boy down, the next portion of the outline should begin:

> **Act I, Scene 7 — Int. Bookstore — Day**

If you want to be even more specific about time here, the next bit may read

> **Act I, Scene 7 — Int. Bookstore — Moments later**

Outlines help you organize the action. Planning so much may seem odd at first, but eventually, this blueprint becomes second nature and, in many cases, necessary.

A sentence outline (or beat sheet) does the following:

- ✔ Runs in chronological order from Act I through Act III
- ✔ Is broken into sequences introduced by the act number, the location, and the time of day

✔ Is broken down within each sequence into individual actions. Each action gets one or two sentences of description

✔ Highlights the characters, situation, and the pace of each scene

Think that's the only kind of outline to explore? Think again. The next example fleshes the story out even further.

One step at a time

The sentence outline is like a writer's grocery list. It's typed directly into the computer or written into a notepad. Some writers post it by their desks, some carry it around, and many check off the scenes as they go. One of the strengths of the sentence outline is that it exists in one piece. Eventually, however, you may want greater flexibility with your outline. You may want to switch scenes around or remove some entirely and watch the story change accordingly. When and if this becomes the case for your story, the time's arrived for the step outline.

Step outlines are traditionally written with 3 x 5 note cards. This technique allows you to rearrange the order of events, as well as quickly eliminate or add scenes. I talk about index cards later in this chapter, but know that step outlines are usually when they're most handy. The slug line or scene heading goes somewhere at the top, followed by a short description of the action in that moment. For example:

Act I, Scene 8 — Int. School Hallway — Day

Miriam approaches her locker. It appears to have been broken into. The door has a giant dent, and her books and papers are strewn across the floor. Worse, the letter is no longer taped to the inside wall.

What's the difference between this form and the last one? Detail. In the sentence outline, you summarize the action in each scene. In a step-by-step outline, you envision every visual moment that makes up those actions. For instance, consider the moment where the tour guide sees the boy on the bike smile at her. This one sentence may be made up of several fleeting bits: A shot of her turning around to watch him ride by, a shot of his face, a shot of his mouth calling her name, a close shot of his eyes as he winks, and then a shot of him riding down the street. Each one of those flashes might receive an individual note card in the step-by-step outline.

In the example of Miriam at her locker, the card concentrates on the locker from one person's point of view. If someone taps Miriam on the shoulder and she whirls around, the ensuing interaction merits a new card.

Some writers further classify each card in the following ways:

- **Organization by location:** Several moments may take place in one location. If you add that location at the top of each card, you can tell how many shots make up each sequence. The "living room" sequence may be made up of several note cards.

- **A character list:** Try recording the characters in each scene on the card. This log lets you determine how often a character speaks, when she may need to speak, and who she interacts with on a regular basis. The list also helps you track each character's journey individually.

- **A note on plot:** Is this scene pivotal to the main plot or to a subplot? Indicating that information on each card helps to determine when a subplot scene may be necessary, when the subplot has been overextended, and when two plots intersect.

- **Scene strength:** You may want to delineate the strength of each scene in a word or two on each card. For instance, is the scene primarily fueled by character, dialogue, plot, exposition, or theme?

How much or how little you include on each card is up to you. For some writers, three or four sentences of description are enough; other writers go so far as to color code their cards by act, strong point, or sequence locale. Directors and cinematographers create storyboards for the film. They break the film down into pictures that will become each shot.

This step-by-step outline is your storyboard. Do you need to use 3 x 5 cards? Absolutely not. This method allows you to rearrange individual parts, however. The ability to spread the scenes out in front of you and mix and match until you're satisfied with a chronology is invaluable. You may choose to cut and paste on a computer or use a page per action instead, but whatever you do, choose a form that can be easily rearranged.

What to Do When the Outline's Through

If you're satisfied with your story at this point, the next step is to start writing. However, few writers complete an outline satisfied. If you don't have large portions of the script to be reworked, you almost certainly have moments that are missing entirely. Here are a few questions to ask yourself after you've completed one or both of the previously mentioned outlines:

✔ Do you have long sequences of dialogue or action? How might you break these sequences up so that they don't become monotonous?

✔ Are the characters' goals clear? Are they obtained in the end?

✔ Do your characters acquire new skills or information along the way? In which scenes?

✔ What relationships exist at the end that did not exist at the beginning? Do you have enough scenes to plausibly support that interaction?

✔ Is your villain fully represented?

✔ Are your subplots represented? Do they support the main plot?

✔ Is each scene motivated by a preceding scene or moment? In other words, does every scene inspire another to occur?

✔ Does each scene propel a reader to the climax in some way?

✔ Is enough backstory introduced to successfully frame the action?

✔ Does the choice of location strengthen the theme or the action?

✔ Does your script contain surprises? If so, where are they?

Be on the alert for too many scenes in one location, or of one quality in succession. Your script is like a visual symphony, too much of one melodic line quickly becomes repetitive. Break up action-packed scenes with moments of budding character relationships. Break up image with dialogue. Find any way you can to vary the form and content of your story.

Also, beware of action that happens to or around the protagonist. You want the protagonist to happen to the script, not the other way around. Force your character to make choices, and the scenes will become active and dynamic.

When you're finished, spread the cards out in front of you and sit with them for a few hours. Even if you're satisfied with a sequence of events, try rearranging one or two cards. Try envisioning your piece with alternate opening and closing images. Force yourself to remove three moments. Which three will they be? You're creating a visual piece, so being able to see the entire project in front of you is very helpful. Tell the story out loud and see how it sounds, based on your short descriptions of each moment. It may take a week, it may take a month. By the time you're finished pouring through the cards, you'll know the story inside and out — which is convenient because the next step is composing a first draft!

Outlining someone else's story

This project is familiar to many television writers who rely on it to acquire a feel for any new series. It's helpful to feature-film writers as well, especially because outlining someone else's script is easier than outlining your own.

Tape an episode of your favorite TV show or rent your favorite film. You can do this project with a piece of paper or with note cards. If it's a TV show, watch the whole thing once through; if it's a film, choose a portion of it to watch. Take note of the following details:

✔ Order of locations

✔ Character introductions

✔ Major events

✔ Minor events

✔ Actions that caused other actions

When you're through, watch the piece again. Keep the pause button handy for this part. See if you can construct a sentence or a step-by-step outline of what you see. Finally, watch the sequence again with outline in hand to see what you missed. By the time you're through with this project, you'll know the story, the genre, and the structure of the piece that you selected. You'll also know how to approach an outline of your own work.

Chapter 14

Surviving Writer's Block

*I*f you've ever taken up exercise, you know what writer's block feels like. You're running on that treadmill, your pulse rate is high, your breathing is steady, you feel invigorated and alive. "This is easy," you think, and for a while, it is. Then, all of a sudden — bam! Your muscles tense up, your legs give way, you're winded, and you have to stop. The impetus and the desire to run are gone, seemingly forever. The next day, beginning again is infinitely more difficult, if not impossible.

Writers experience this same cycle. One minute, characters speak unbidden, and images fly across the page; the next minute nothing, no pictures, no voices, no sense of what comes next. It's called *writer's block,* the not-so-great equalizer. It strikes without discrimination and without warning, and it strikes the best writers in the business. It leaves you uncertain of how to proceed and panicked that you can't proceed at all.

But what is writer's block really? Is it an affliction or a natural part of the creative process? Is it to be feared or embraced? Can you do anything to avoid it? And what, oh what, do you do when it finds you? If you've ever experienced writer's block, or if you're curious about how to handle it when you do, you're in the right place. This chapter takes on all those questions and more.

From Panic to Peace: Switching Mind-Sets

In conversation, writer's block sounds like a disease. It certainly has all the symptoms: confusion, lightheadedness, loss of appetite, insomnia, restlessness, headaches, and nausea. I know a writer who hyperventilates at the mere thought of writer's block, and another writer who swears that she can sense its approach by the twitch in her left hand.

Every year, a student asks me whether I believe that writer's block is contagious. I usually say, "No, I do not," but I know why they're uneasy. Writer's block seems to carry more legends than any other part of the artistic process. Horror stories abound, from novelists unable to complete more than one novel to dramatists with award-winning ideas who abandon projects halfway through the first draft. People hear these stories and develop all sorts of misconceptions. A few years ago, I began compiling a list of these fallacies. The following are among the most common:

- ✔ Writer's block means that you're a bad writer.
- ✔ Writer's block means that your story isn't worth telling.
- ✔ If you enjoy time away from your work, you're not really a writer.
- ✔ Some writers don't experience writer's block.
- ✔ Writer's block means that you're not psychologically ready to write this story yet.
- ✔ After you've written several screenplays, writer's block disappears.
- ✔ If you ignore the problem, it will go away.
- ✔ If you tell people that you're experiencing a block, they'll think that you're inexperienced or mediocre at your craft.
- ✔ If you don't find a way around writer's block, you'll never be able to accept work with a deadline.
- ✔ Writer's block is something you have to face alone.

None of these things are true, yet they're only a few of the beliefs circulating among writers. With all this bad press, it's no wonder people fear the ordeal.

Surprisingly, though, writer's block isn't something to fear. In fact, fear is the problem. Look at other professions. Would anyone expect a doctor to offer diagnosis after diagnosis without pausing for thought? I doubt it. Would anyone expect a teacher to understand students at a glance or fault her for puzzling over them until she determines how each one should be taught? I hope not. Yet many writers expect to maintain a breakneck pace and a rigorous schedule without allowing for an occasional question, a pause or, heaven forbid, a moment of indecision. Why? Because they're afraid, and thus, they're artistically exhausted. Fear is the culprit behind virtually all forms of writer's block. If you look closely, you can see it lurking behind each one.

The top ten reasons for writer's block

Writing is a private process, so finding an explanation for every creative obstacle is difficult. However, as most writers experience the same stages of the creative process, they share the problems with each process as well. You can, therefore, trace the most frequent blocks to one of the following causes:

- **Something about the story needs to change.** After you've outlined a script, you'll probably write it scene by scene. However, stories change as you write them, and you'll probably deviate from that outline a bit, sometimes a great deal. Unfortunately, tracking larger changes in structure can be difficult when you're entrenched in the details of scene work, and you may finish one scene only to find yourself confused as to how the next should look.

- **You've written past your initial design.** Your story develops as you write, so the landscape and the characters in the second portion may not match their original images. Writers often become frustrated by plot and character inconsistencies halfway through a script, fearing that the story has gotten away from them.

- **You're under a strict deadline.** Some people work well under pressure; others do not. Although deadlines provide clear artistic goals, they also require a strict schedule and a pace that allows little time to daydream — let alone question a script. The pressure of meeting those demands often makes it impossible to do so.

- **Your expectations are unreasonable.** Writers aren't robots, so you shouldn't be expected to churn out the same material in the same way every time you write. Some days, you'll produce a lot of work; other days, you'll produce none. Some days, your writing will be palpable and precise; other days, it will drag across the page begging you to hit the Delete key. Impossible expectations put undue pressure on you, as an artist, and they virtually ensure failure of some sort.

- **The last thing you wrote was fantastic/wretched.** The last thing you wrote was successful, so this one might be a flop. The last thing you wrote was unique, so this one might be clichéd. The first script was horrific; this one might be worse. If thoughts of what your script "might be" keep you from writing, these thoughts "might be" your block.

✔ **You're unable to admit uncertainty.** Today's society doesn't applaud indecision, and it certainly doesn't reward hesitation. People feel a need to provide answers instead of asking questions. Writers are no exception. Without a ready answer, many writers panic and can't write at all.

✔ **You're a perfectionist.** Your script is never going to be perfect, and it won't even be close when you first start writing. If you worry about perfection, you'll never get past the first page. Rather than worry about it, consider it a relief that you don't have to and just get something, anything, onto the page. You can tweak it later.

✔ **You're facing a pivotal script decision.** When facing a pivotal decision, some writers trace each option through the remainder of the story as if it were a game of chess. They're afraid of making the "wrong" choices, so they don't make any. This deliberation often lasts a long time, and, as a result, little work gets done.

✔ **You write quickly.** I know what you're thinking: If writing quickly is a problem, send it your way. Writing quickly can be an asset, but it can just as easily be a curse. In your artistic frenzy, you may lose sight of the story as a whole. When you finally do come up for air, you may have to take a while to assess what you've written and what to write next.

✔ **You're overwhelmed by the prospect.** When you first start writing any script, it can feel like an impossible task. Please bear in mind you're not sitting down to write the entire screenplay. You're sitting down to write one small part of it. Break your project into manageable pieces. Then script one at a time. Eventually, the entire story will emerge.

✔ **You're constantly interrupted.** Few people can write in the 15 minutes between phone calls and meetings. Your imagination needs time to shift into working mode, to focus on your characters again and determine where you left off. Interruptions make it impossible to switch into working mode and, as a result, work at all.

✔ **You don't allow time for a personal life.** Although you need uninterrupted time alone with your work, you also need time away from it. Many writers view free time as wasted time and fear that they'll lose momentum if they don't spend every minute with the characters. Yet without time off, you may end up with one-dimensional characters and contrived plot points.

Notice a pattern? Unrealistic expectations, excessive pressure to succeed, lack of personal time — these factors underscore the entire list, and they're all fueled by fear. You're afraid to fail, or afraid to succeed, or afraid to succeed and then fail. In any case, fear is what's stopping your pen.

Can you avoid this predicament? No, but you can survive it. The first order of business involves a change in attitude. Despite the symptoms, writer's block is not a disease; it's a natural part of the creative process — maybe even an important part. Nine times out of ten, writer's block means that you're on the verge of some discovery. Tedious and irritating as it may be, writer's block may be beneficial. Here are a few things that it may suggest:

- **Your abilities as a storyteller are improving.** Writers sharpen their skills as they write. Perhaps you're becoming more adept at the craft, and your imagination needs time to adjust. If you stop and reread your work, you may be able to catch the improvement on the page.

- **The characters have something unexpected to say.** When people spend enough time together, they can close their eyes and re-create the sound of the other person's voice. The same process occurs as you get to know your characters. If you spend enough time with them, they'll start speaking to you. You know them better now than when you first began writing, so don't be surprised if they're telling you something new.

- **Your reason for writing the story has changed.** Some people have a clear reason for writing from the very beginning. Others do not. Events that you discover as you write quite possibly may change your reason for finishing the project. If you didn't have a reason when you began, you'll probably find one as you go. Use the extra time that writer's block bestows on you to reconsider that position.

- **Your subplot is becoming more important.** Subplots have a way of becoming more dynamic as a script develops. As subplots tend to carry the movie's theme, they often threaten to overshadow the main plot. Your creative block may be fueled by that subplot, tugging at your sleeve for attention.

- **You forgot a critical piece of information.** If you're entrenched in the work and writing at a fast pace, you can easily lose sight of backstory and exposition. After all, you understand the story; you don't need that piece of information. Your audience will need it, though. Double-check that you've included all the information that an audience needs to understand the world of your script.

Creative blocks are like red flags meant to catch your attention. If you ignore them, they just get larger. If you become angry with them, you exhaust yourself beating them down. Instead, consider them a warning and try to discover what they have to say. Maybe — and this is most often the case — you just need to relax. Take a breath. You have nothing to fear; if anything, something exciting is in store for you and your story. You're about to learn something new.

A survival guide

Are you breathing? Good. If you've reached a creative standstill, the best thing to do is direct your attention away from the block and all the horrible things that might happen if you're stuck forever. You're not stuck forever; you're just stuck now, and now is the time to concentrate on other things. Here are a few "other things" that you may want to try when writer's block strikes:

✔ **Do something else.** Sometimes, you just need a break from the computer or from your notepad, even if it's just for an hour. The best ideas always find me in the shower or in the car. So take a drive, go play golf, have lunch with a friend, take a long walk, or indulge in a nap. Trick your mind into thinking that you just don't care about that script. Answers often arrive when you least expect them.

✔ **Switch projects.** John Logan, writer of **Gladiator** and **Any Given Sunday,** likes to juggle several projects at once. Why would anyone do that? First, doing so diverts your mind from the creative impasse and keeps you writing at the same time. Also, what you learn on one project may clarify a problem in another. If you try this strategy, make sure that the projects are at different stages of development. If you're in the first draft of script one, for example, script two should be in development or revisions. Otherwise, you risk ending up with not one, but two cases of writer's block.

✔ **Outline the script.** You probably outlined your script before you began writing, but it never hurts to do it again. Outline what you've already written first and then move on to what you intend to include later. If your story has changed, the outline will show you how. Tracing the steps leading to the block may lead to the next scene. You might also try writing a synopsis of the story. As you try to convey the plot in prose form, you may discover holes in the story that are keeping you from moving forward.

✔ **Read, read, read.** Other artists offer techniques, dramatic examples, and inspiration. You don't need to limit yourself to screenplays; read literature, poetry, and nonfiction, too. Read newspapers or old letters. Read anything that ropes you into a world other than your own or the one that you're creating.

✔ **Return to research.** In Chapter 4, I detail the creative process. Part of that process involves the *saturation stage,* where a writer seeks creative input of all kinds that may inform her script. Return to that stage now. Visit museums, collect photographs, listen to music, eavesdrop on conversations, and record what you hear. You've written part of the story, so your imagination knows what to look for now. You may discover details that you missed the first time around.

✔ **Try alternate forms of writing.** By alternate, I mean try writing something other than a screenplay. Write a letter, send an e-mail, start a diary, or give yourself an assignment and write for an hour. Like switching projects, this strategy also redirects your concentration while keeping your imagination alert.

✔ **Sleep on it.** If you've been tackling a block for a while, you're probably tense and exhausted. Go to bed. Your mind still works while your body sleeps. You'll definitely wake up refreshed. You may even wake up with an answer.

You'll discover many more avenues through creative standstills as you go. Do what works for you — just don't give up. The worst thing that you can do is push the script aside completely. You're almost always abandoning something worth keeping, and more writer's block is waiting for you ahead. If you don't overcome it now, how will you survive It the next time?

Reevaluating Your Routine

A solid work regime helps writers coast through creative blocks with their sanity intact. It also cuts the frequency of the encounters in half. If you think that your routine can stand a change, try one or all of the following suggestions:

✔ **Write at the same time every day.** As I say in Chapter 4, the more habitual your writing routine is, the better. If your schedule allows you to write from 9 a.m. to noon every day, your imagination will adjust accordingly. Pretty soon, you'll be in working mode by the time you sit down, and if the muse is looking for you, she'll know where to go and when.

✔ **Set aside preparation time.** Preparation time includes anything and everything you do to prepare yourself to write. I keep a Later list near me at all times. This list reminds me of the parts of the script that I intend to write later. It includes character details, events, pieces of conversation, or images that occur unexpectedly. This way, I always have something I can work on when the current scene eludes me. Some writers spend an hour each day dreaming up tomorrow's scenes. Doing so leaves them ready for the next day, but more importantly, it leaves them excited to begin again.

✔ **Keep a notepad handy.** You never know when inspiration will strike. My ideas arrive while I'm driving or in the shower. Many writers find ideas bubble up right before they fall asleep. Make sure that you have a way to catch those ideas as they strike you. Don't make the mistake of thinking you'll remember them later. Trust me, you won't.

✔ **Set clear goals.** Some writers try to finish a certain number of pages each day; some writers set aside a certain amount of time. When three hours are done, so are they. You may find it easier to work through choice moments, completing a scene or a monologue, for example. The specific goal is entirely up to you, but do try to achieve it. You'll always feel better if you end each day with some sort of success.

✔ **Devise an opening ritual.** Sometimes, the imagination takes a while to warm up. Find a way to help it out and start each day with that procedure. Some people write three to five pages of stream-of-consciousness thought each morning. Writing letters or rereading past work also prepares the imagination to begin. The opening ritual is yet another way to make the writing process habitual. Also, your ritual may not involve writing. A nice long walk may be just what your system needs to kick itself into high gear.

✔ **Keep a writing journal.** Writing journals are different from diaries. Everything in a diary is personal; it grants writers an outlet for pent-up anger, joy, and pain. Keeping a diary is a form of therapy. Writing journals is reserved for your work. Give yourself an assignment and record it here. Stuck on a scene? Write it in prose form in your journal. If you're a pen writer (as opposed to a computer writer), maybe your whole first draft belongs here. In this way, you separate unwanted emotion and personal judgment from dramatic writing.

✔ **Stop when you know what comes next.** Here's a piece of advice from Ernest Hemingway. He used to tell young writers to stop writing when they could envision what the next moment in the story would be. That way, they'd always have a place to begin.

These techniques won't stop writer's block entirely, but they'll help to make it less frequent. They represent the personal side of the process, measures that you take on your own. If you plan on writing professionally, you may also want to seek the help of others.

Seeking Outside Help

Writing is often a lonely endeavor. It requires a great deal of time away from family, friends, and the outside world in general, which can be disconcerting for all involved. However, you don't need to cut yourself off entirely while completing a script. Writer's block is the perfect opportunity to enlist support. Here are several ways that your colleagues and loved ones can become involved in the process:

✔ **Share your schedule.** Alerting other people of your writing schedule is advantageous in two ways. If people know when you work, they're less likely to interrupt while you're working. Also, if they know your goals in advance, they may be able to help you accomplish them. Not all writers make a living at their craft, and the encouragement of friends and family often takes the place of financial support.

✔ **Write with others.** Do you know any writers? Meet them for a few hours and write together. If you arrange the meeting, you'll most likely show up, which means that work will probably get done. If a script problem arises, there's someone across from you to help. Watch out though — you may have to enforce strict "no gabbing" rules to ensure that work gets done.

✔ **Join a writing group.** Writing groups usually meet once a week or once a month, and they can be a wonderful place to workshop new scripts as well as to make connections. Every writing group is structured differently. Some groups simply present and discuss new work. Other groups include writing projects for participants to try in between sessions. Some are mediated by an instructor and may charge a joining fee; others are more informal. I encourage you to try several before committing to one. These groups should act like support groups. They remind you that you're not alone in this crazy creative endeavor. Writing groups often post information on how to join at local libraries, universities, and frequently in writing journals or magazines. If you can't find one, you can always start a group yourself.

✔ **Talk it out.** I'm of two minds on this method. I suggest waiting to talk about a story until the idea's fleshed out, and you have at least one outline in place. In the early stages, you really can't talk about an idea until the desire and the immediate need to write it disappear. Wait until you're developing scenes and then seek advice. A new ear picks up details that you've long since forgotten, and remember, other people don't know the story yet. Their questions and reactions will quickly reveal any confusing or inconsistent moments. You may also consider this discussion to be your first pitch. How can you sell the story from the start?

✔ **Plan group readings.** Do you know any actors? Do you have any dramatic friends or family members? Invite them to read a few scenes out loud. Assign someone to read the description as well. There's no substitute for hearing your words out loud. If they flop in your living room, they'll likely flop with actors. But if they fly now, they'll likely fly onscreen.

A strong support group may help you end the period of writer's block more quickly. Having the support certainly makes the process bearable at the very least. So the next time you're in a creative rut, don't rant and rave in private. Rant and rave with others.

All in all, the best advice I've ever gotten about writer's block was from an old colleague who said, "Don't let it eat you alive; use it to sharpen your teeth." Writer's block isn't an end; it's a beginning. Use the break to reflect on your story and sharpen your skill. If it's true that human beings grow the most during times of struggle, you'll be infinitely wiser by the time your script is complete. Each draft of your script will reflect that new wisdom.

Knocking your block off

Here's a project that I use when a student gets stuck. It's a timed writing. In this case, you'll be writing for two minutes, and you'll be using a *tag line,* which is the first phrase you write and the phrase you return to if you can think of nothing else to write.

The rules of the timed writing are simple:

- ✔ Keep your hand moving on the page. If you can't think of anything to say, continue to write the tag line until something occurs to you.

- ✔ There are no expected responses. You're recording your thoughts as you think them; go where they take you. And don't limit yourself creatively here. A response you think is crazy can be more helpful to you than the more commonplace options.

- ✔ Pay no attention to grammar or spelling. They're entirely unimportant in this exercise.

- ✔ Stop writing when the time is over, even if you're mid-sentence.

So, those are the rules. Here are two tag lines. Write for a minute and a half on each one. The tag lines are:

- ✔ "Today I am . . ."

- ✔ "Tomorrow I see . . ."

After you've written your responses, read them out loud. Circle any phrase or image that sparks your fancy. After you're done, you can choose tag lines that direct your energy toward a specific script. Here are three such tag lines to get you started:

- ✔ "I see someone who . . ."

- ✔ "If you listen closely, you'll hear . . ."

- ✔ "Soon I expect that . . ."

Chapter 15

Formatting Your Screenplay

Skim a few books on how to land a great job, and you'll notice at least one similarity: They all reserve a section, if not a chapter, on first impressions. If you walk into an interview looking like you just rolled out of a bed and proceed to speak in half sentences while tugging at a hole in your shoe, you're not leaving with the job. If you walk into the interview in a ball gown or a tux, singing your extensive credentials and qualifications, you're not leaving with the job. To land the position, you should look and sound like you mean business. You should be clear, confident, and concise. You have a first impression to make, so make it well.

In screenwriting, your format is your best shot at a good first impression. If your format looks professional, the readers will assume that you're a professional. Unlike plays and novels where the structure is fairly loose, screenplays are written within precise formatting guidelines. Our challenge as a screenwriter is to tell a unique story within those guidelines. Even if you're writing for the fun of it and have no intention of sending your script out, a screenplay isn't a screenplay without the format. It's merely a set of ideas with no vehicle.

This chapter guides you through the basic screenplay format to help lift your ideas from the outline stage to the printed page. It also highlights the tools that you need to make a good first impression.

How the Screenplay Looks on the Page

As a screenwriter, your job is to immerse the readers in your story. Those readers may be editors, agents, producers, studio execs, actors or directors — anyone you hope to interest in your piece. You want their eyes moving down one page and onto the next without having to stop or flip back in confusion. For that reason, the screenwriting format is designed to fade into the background. Once mastered, it allows a screenwriter to convey location, character, and action in a quick and efficient manner. It also enables a screenwriter to design the mood, angle, and pace of a scene without drawing attention to the mechanics involved.

Imagine a blank page. In the screenwriting format, six parts are all vying for space on that page. Those parts are

- ✔ **The description:** The description of the location, the characters, and any action indicated throughout the scene (The description is sometimes referred to as the *action* or *business* of the scene.)

- ✔ **The character name:** The person doing the talking

- ✔ **The character dialogue:** What that person says

- ✔ **Parenthetical directions:** How the person says a line. The general rule here is "less is more." Better to let the scene convey how a line should be delivered than to direct every line reading. Also, parentheticals should not be confused with action. They describe how a line is delivered, not what's going on at the time it's delivered.

- ✔ **Transitional directions:** Any camera information or indications of how the scene should be visualized and/or read

- ✔ **The page number:** Page numbers appear on the top right-hand side of every page except the title page, which is numberless. Scene numbers, however, are not necessary. Those are reserved for shooting scripts and will be added by studio personnel later.

Each component has its own placement on the page, and a reader should be able to distinguish one component from the other at a glance. Together, these components convey all the necessary information to an audience.

Setting your typeface and your margins

The proper typeface for your script is Courier font. Courier is the font most widely used in the industry, as it most closely resembles the font of a typewriter. In general, that means that there are approximately ten spaces to every inch of line. Why this rule? This type size ensures that, on average, one page of script reads at one minute — a detail helpful to directors trying to determine the running time of an individual scene or of the script as a whole. Once you've become successful in the industry, you may switch to a font that has equal proportions to Courier, but it's best to start with the industry standard.

After you set your typeface, program your computer to remember the following marginal guidelines for each formatting section.

- ✔ **Left margin**: 1½ inches

- ✔ **Right margin:** 1 inch

- ✔ **Top margin:** 1 inch

- ✔ **Bottom margin:** 1 inch

- ✔ **Scene headings (also known as slug lines):** Begin at the left margin

- ✔ **Description:** Runs the length of the page (after you've set your margins)

- ✔ **Character name:** 4 inches from the left-hand side of the page (2½ inches from the left margin)

- ✔ **Dialogue:** Begins 2½ inches from the left-hand side of the page (1 inch from the left margin) and ends at 6½ inches from the left-hand side of the page (5 inches from the left margin)

- ✔ **Parentheticals:** 3½ inches from the left-hand side of the page (2 inches from the left margin)

- ✔ **Page numbers:** ½ inch from the top of the page, ½ inch from the right-hand side of the page

Transitional directions (which mainly convey camera information) take several forms and have several placements on the page. I detail those forms later in the chapter in the section called "Camera concerns."

The method behind this margin madness is simple: Actors concentrate on dialogue; directors look for the composition and pace of each scene. If your format is correctly aligned, everyone's happy. You've created special compartments for each element. A glance down the left-hand side of the page reveals the primary locations and actions of each scene. A glance down the center provides the character list and accompanying dialogue. This structure lets a reader concentrate on one portion of the scene at a time. Again, this format is also the industry standard and has been for a long time. While it may feel restrictive at first attempt, it's best to get used to it now.

Spacing your script correctly

A screenplay is not a novel. A screenplay is comprised of quick visual clips. Your central images should be strong and easily accessible. If you lump three or four of them together in the same scene, they'll be neither strong nor accessible. Seeing blocks of text with little or no interruption can be very daunting to a reader. If I get tired just glancing at your script, I'll be unlikely to start reading it and even less likely to finish it. Your format is an invitation to read.

Here's how to space your screenplay to highlight each image in a visually inviting way:

Single space: Unless you've set your computer to double-space mode, it should automatically single space your work for you.

- All description
- All lines of dialogue
- All parentheticals
- All camera directions, sound cues, and visual effects
- Between the character name and the ensuing dialogue

Double space:

- Between paragraphs of lengthy description
- Between the end of a dialogue clip and a new speaker's name
- Between the end of a dialogue clip and a new description
- Between the *slug line* (see the "Key Formatting Elements" section, later in this chapter) and the description

Triple space:

- Before starting a new scene

After you become familiar with the formatting parameters, you have a choice to make. How do you want to move between them? You may set your tabs in advance and tab from one element to the next. However, this method makes editing cumbersome because any textual alteration disturbs the spacing. As an easier choice, most computers allow you to define new styles (dialogue, name, and parentheticals, for example) and assign them to a keystroke. One key takes you to the dialogue box, another to the name, and so on. On most computers this feature is found in the toolbar at the top of your page under Format. A quick scroll down the Format list should reveal the Styles component (Formatting and Styles in Microsoft computers). Click that option and follow the directions from there. Defining your styles makes editing easier as you rework each section individually. Or, as a final option, you may choose a program designed to format the script for you.

Making your computer work for you

Many screenwriters write with software, and I detail those options for you later in this chapter. However, it's important to know how to write without the software, if only to understand formatting basics. Screenwriting format is like a calculator. It will solve problems for you, it will simplify your efforts, but if you don't understand the principles behind it, you're losing a skill.

That said, I encourage you to create your own formatting template before relying on software. And while every computer differs slightly, there are ways to spacially structure your page on both MAC and PC. I will assume that you're working in Microsoft Word. If you don't own that program, go purchase it. Once you've got it, try setting your page up this way:

1. **Open a new Word document.**

2. **Set your margins.**

   If you're working on a PC, you find this option by choosing File⇨ Page Layout. If you're working on a MAC, choose Document⇨Format.

3. **Choose and set your font to Courier.**

4. **Type a character's name and space it in the appropriate margin on the page.**

5. **Highlight that name so that the computer recognizes it.**

6. **Choose Format⇨Styles.**

   The Styles command is also sometimes found under the Document menu where it is called Styles and Formatting. Either way, Styles is the key.

7. **In the Styles dialog box, click the New Style or Create New Style button.**

8. **After you choose that style, name it.**

   I suggest calling it Name or Character so that you can recognize it quickly.

9. **After you named your style, click the Format or Options button.**

   The Shortcut Key dialog box appears. The shortcut key is what you'll hit every time you want to write a character's name.

10. **Choose a shortcut that's easy to type quickly.**

    Shift+N or Shift+C are good, because you can remember them as Shift Name or Shift Character.

11. **Click Apply Changes.**

Screenwriting software: Let the computer do the formatting

Some writers find the screenwriting format to be overly complex and time consuming. After all, you want to spend your time concentrating on the story, not the look of the page. It's important to know the basic formatting rules, but once you have those down it may be time to purchase some screenwriting software. Software certainly allows writers to work more quickly without the hassle of individual tabulation or margin setting. It also produces scripts that look industry-ready right away. Screenwriting systems abound these days, so peruse your options carefully. The best packages do the following:

✔ Format and paginate your script as you write

✔ Provide templates for movie scripts, teleplays, and stage plays

✔ Offer direct Web links to screenwriting sites

✔ Organize your notes for quick reference

✔ Help you register your scripts online with the Writer's Guild of America

✔ Provide troubleshooting advice from professionals on everything from character development to writer's block

✔ Breaks your script into sections and transfers those onto index cards, which is particularly helpful when you want to rearrange scenes or eliminate them altogether

✔ Help turn your script into a stage play or novel (should you want to)

I encourage you to investigate your software options online prior to purchasing anything. Some systems focus on story and/or character development; others, on formatting only. Of the systems available, the most common are Movie Magic Screenwriter) www.screenplay. com; 800-84-STORY) and Scriptware (www. scriptware.com).

All three of these systems are compatible with Macintosh and Microsoft Word, and all three offer a similar array of features. Final Draft and Movie Magic are the most common programs in the industry. Movie Magic includes free tech support (Final Draft charges) as well as a program with built in 3 x 5 note cards that you can rearrange and print. Scriptware is less expensive, but also less widely used in the industry. It also doesn't provide tech support.

Now you've created a Style for character names. If you want to jump to another character in dialogue, you simply type your shortcut. You should now make similar styles for description, dialogue, and parentheticals. This way, you can move between them with a strike of a key.

Creating a PDF

PDF means portable document file, and it's a quick and easy way to freeze your script in one format. You should create a PDF of your script before you print it or before you send it to any kind of reader via e-mail. That way, your format doesn't become confused in transfer.

Most MAC computers come with the option of turning a document into a PDF. You'll find that option when you try to print your script. Under the Print box (where it asks you how many pages and what printer) is a PDF button. Click that button instead of Print, and your computer will convert your document into a PDF.

Many PC computers come with this option as well. If yours doesn't, there are many free PDF program downloads available online. My personal favorites are

- ✓ **CutePDF writer:** www.cutepdf.com
- ✓ **Desk PDF:** www.docudesk.com
- ✓ **Primo PDF:** www.primopdf.com

It may also be advisable to purchase Adobe Acrobat. It not only creates PDF files, but it helps you read more unusual ones that may be sent to you. However, Acrobat is a bit pricey, so try the free downloads first.

 Once you've created a PDF version of your script, you won't be able to alter it in any way, nor will the people you send it to. Always date the PDF so that you can keep track of it. Also, always save the Word version of your script, as that is the copy you will revise. You'll probably create many PDF versions of your screenplay as time goes by. Many of those you should feel free to discard after they've served their purpose.

Key Formatting Elements

Here's a dilemma: You're an aspiring screenwriter struggling to format your script correctly. You have a lot to say and little time in which to say it. You can't be terse or verbose; you must land somewhere in between. To top these requirements off, you want the script to smack with a unique style and flair. Now, how are you going to do all that?

In a first draft, your primary objective is to get the information onto the page. You can trim, twist, and tweak it into a work of art later, but for now, craft one element at a time with an eye toward a story. What's happening, who's it happening to, why is it important, and how efficiently can you let an audience know these things? The format directs your information to its proper location on the page, and every location has a distinct set of tasks.

Character introductions

Always capitalize every letter of a character's name when she first appears in the script. This layout indicates a new figure on the protagonist's or audience's horizon and focuses the attention, however briefly, on a new energy in the script. From that point on, only capitalize every letter of the character's name prior to her dialogue.

When you introduce a character, give a brief but telling description, and then plunge her into the action. For example:

> MOLLY MALONE, a 30-something former beauty queen, strides confidently into the room.

I use all capital letters for Molly's full name this first time she's introduced, and then I type it normally throughout the ensuing text. If she first arrives as a mere figure or a silhouette, the initial description might read as follows:

> The FIGURE of a woman stands in the doorway. Moonlight silhouettes her ample form.

This is the first character description. When Molly moves into the scene, the description then reads:

> The figure steps firmly into the room. It is MOLLY MALONE, a 30-something former beauty queen with the confidence of a bobcat and the claws to match.

I've capitalized both introductions, first the figure, and then Molly Malone, emphasizing the transition from the suggestion of a character to the full character herself.

Here are a few more details to keep in mind when crafting character introductions:

✔ **Use full names for the character's initial introduction and one part of the name thereafter.** My character's full name is Molly Malone. I let the reader know this as soon as she enters, but thereafter, I refer to her as either "Molly" or "Malone" in both description and in dialogue. If your character's full name is Mr. Nelson, refer to him as "Nelson" for the rest of the text.

✔ **Allow incidental characters to remain incidental characters.** Your script may call for a waitress, a busboy, a nurse, a ticket agent, a clerk, and so on. These characters are functional roles and will return in your story sparingly. Therefore, their introduction need only be minimal. For example:

> The WAITRESS, clearly a veteran server, brings him his coffee and winks in passing.

> Two ARMED GUARDS barrel past, shoving people out of their way as they charge after him.

> The HOTEL CLERK checks the bill and glares at him before disappearing into the back room.

More description than this is distracting. It diverts attention from your main character and the scene's action. Capitalize incidental characters' titles, suggest an age or distinguishing characteristic if necessary, but don't linger on them. They're meant to fulfill a functional role and disappear.

✔ **Avoid using names of real actors.** You may imagine your main character as an Al Pacino–type or a Meryl Streep–knockout. You may imagine as much, but don't include those details in your description. Actors reading your script want to imagine themselves (who else?) in the role. They'll be discouraged at best and insulted at worst to see someone else's name on the part.

✔ **Avoid detailed description of age or physical characteristics unless pertinent to the story.** Consider this character description:

Sarah Smith, a 29-year-old, 5-foot-10-inch strawberry blonde, strolls into the office.

No look says 29 years old, so unless the script centers around her fear of growing older, you'd do better to say "late 20s" or "pushing 30" here.

You're trying to capture the character's essence. I want a suggestion of age and type, yes, but more importantly, I want a peek at her fundamental nature. If her vital statistics — hair, eyes, height, weight, exact age, and so on — help suggest that nature, include them. It's important, for example, that Erin Brockovich wears tight, revealing clothing. Her physique becomes an asset to her in the quest for information. However, if these details are unimportant to the story, including them simply limits you to actors with a certain build and hair color. Why alienate talent unnecessarily?

Finally, avoid overly brief and overly long character descriptions. Here are two examples of awkward introductions:

Too brief:

Leslie Bell, a typist in her mid-20s, jogs through Central Park.

What does a typist look like, exactly? I'm not sure. This description provides information but fails to suggest a picture of the person in question.

Too long:

Leslie Bell, a short, skinny powerhouse in her mid-20s, with dimples and a persistent twinkle in her green eyes, sprints through Central Park in her purple Adidas sportswear with a water bottle in one hand and her Sony Walkman in the other. She stares ahead, her gaze fixed on some unseen finish line, her brow is furrowed in determination.

This moment provides more details than a reader can absorb. Character descriptions should be short, no longer than two sentences if possible. Adjectives and adverbs are the enemies of clear writing. Does the running suit absolutely have to be purple, or does the Walkman need to be a Sony? Probably not. When in doubt, cut it out.

Here's a possible reworked version of the description:

> Leslie Bell, a powerhouse of a woman in her mid-20s, sprints through Central Park, her eyes fixed ahead. A quick glance at her shoes reveals that the soles are worn thin.

This rewrite may even be too long for some tastes. However, I've consolidated it to include the most telling details, those that suggest a person behind the physique.

A capable introduction of a minor character offers the necessary information without detracting attention from more important players in the scene. On the other hand, a compelling main-character introduction shouts, "Here I am! Watch me!" and follows the character into action.

Cinematic description

Screenwriting is a visual art, so visual description makes up more than half of every strong script. Screenplay description includes

- The slug line
- A description of each location
- The choreography of characters in a scene
- Any and all ensuing action

Slug lines

The first line of every scene is called a *slug line*. Slug lines break the script into individual scenes, guiding readers through changes in time and locale.

Master slug lines are informative tags that appear at the beginning of every scene. They provide the following information:

- Whether a scene takes place inside or outside (INT./EXT.)
- The scene's location
- Whether it's day or night

Subsidiary slug lines, also known as abbreviated slug lines, indicate that the action has switched to a different area of the same general location. Because time also remains consistent, subsidiary slug lines include only the new location. They may also be used to call attention to one important object in the scene. In this case, the line consists of the object alone. Because slug lines are important, they're always capitalized. They run from the left-hand margin to the right and are generally one line in length. If they run longer, break the line at a logical point and continue writing immediately below the first line without skipping a space.

A typical master slug line looks like this:

INT. AIRPORT TERMINAL — NIGHT

Notice that I'm not including scene or act numbers here. Scene and act numbers arc used only in outlines should the writer wish to organize the scenes prior to writing the draft. Never include them in a working draft, as they distract a reader from your story. The director and cinematographer will number scenes for the shooting script in production.

Slug lines should be as standardized as possible. They're designed to quickly establish the general location and time of each shot. For this reason, *interior* and *exterior* are always abbreviated (INT. and EXT.). You skip a space and provide a more detailed description after the slug line. For example:

INT. AIRPORT TERMINAL — NIGHT

The terminal is all but deserted. An elderly MAN and a teenage GIRL slump on chairs at opposite ends of the space. He is asleep. She is not.

If your action then switches to the check-in counter, you might follow this description with a subsidiary slug line.

THE CHECK-IN COUNTER

Two AGENTS wearily type information into the computer. One looks up, gives the girl the once-over, then returns to his work.

If he notices that she has a tattoo, an alternate subsidiary slug line may read

One looks up and gives the girl the once-over. His eyes linger on her shoulder and

HER TATTOO

of a dragon with a sword in its mouth. He then returns to his work.

This line suggests that the camera lingers on the image of that dragon. Perhaps it will be important later. Generally, slug lines require no more information than in the preceding slug line. The following exceptions to this rule are called *extensions* and should be used sparingly.

- **An establishing shot.** Establishing shots are designed to orient a reader to a new location. If my film begins during a poetry lecture in a high-school classroom and then jumps to the dining room of an obviously wealthy estate, my audience will have no idea where that dining room is in relation to the school. To solve this problem, I add an establishing shot of the outside of the estate and then move to the dining room. In this sort of a slug line, the word ESTABLISHING follows the DAY or NIGHT direction.

    EXT. GEORGIAN MANSION — DAY — ESTABLISHING

- **A stock shot.** Stock shots are images that will be pulled from previously filmed footage. They're clips from other movies, newsreels, documentaries, and so on that are now "in stock" at a film library, waiting to be reused. Skylines and historical landmarks are prime stock material, as are beach, woodland, or generic neighborhood shots. You format stock shots in the following way:

    EXT. THE CHICAGO SKYLINE — DAY (STOCK)

- **An indication of specific time, time passing, or season.** If your film takes place in 1776, the date is an important detail to include in the slug line. If the film bounces between time frames, doing so becomes even more important. If your action spans several seasons, you may add that detail as well.

    EXT. THE CHICAGO SKYLINE — DAY (WINTER)

    EXT. PARIS — DAY (1885)

    EXT. TIIMES SQUARE — DAY (13 YEARS EARLIER)

A reader will read these distinctions, but a movie audience knows only what it sees. Always follow a slug line with some description of the location that indicates how an audience might know that it's winter or 1885.

Sound and special effects

Detail both sounds and special effects in the description of a scene, and format them with capital letters. With sound cues, capitalize the sound of the effect — for example, the WHISTLE of a train, or the KNOCKING on a door. The capitalization is reserved for sounds made by outside forces or off-camera. Sounds made by characters in scene are not written using all capital letters.

Special effects are sometimes abbreviated FX or SPFX, but this term is generally reserved for shooting scripts. If you envision special effects in a scene, describe them so that director can envision them, too. For example:

EXT. PARKING LOT — DAY

Without warning, the station wagon EXPLODES, spewing flames and smoke onto nearby cars.

Location, choreography, and action

Most cinematic description is composed of single-spaced prose paragraphs that run from the left-hand margin to the right. They're generally no more than three or four sentences in length, if that. Readers like to see as much white space as text, so reserve a separate paragraph for each shot. Double-space between these paragraphs. Doing so divides the action clearly on the page. For example:

INT. FAMILY ROOM — DAY

Two small GIRLS press their faces to the window and exhale. They giggle at the prints they've left on the glass. One draws a heart in the print, then slashes at it with her finger.

A WOMAN tiptoes up behind them, ready to pounce. The oldest girl spins around seconds before her hand reaches their shoulders.

When describing location, avoid including too many physical details. Close your eyes, envision the setting, and then describe any essentials that the camera will pick up. If the shot is of two children in their play room, I might need to see a trail of crayons leading from the door to where they sit, but I probably don't need to know exactly what color those crayons are.

The other type of description appears in the parenthetical portion of the script. Parentheticals are typed in lowercase letters and are offset by parentheses. They generally depict how a line should be said. For example:

SANDY
(softly — after a moment)
I don't think that's going to happen.

These descriptions are only necessary if nothing else in the scene suggests how a line should be read. Strong actors often discover the intent naturally.

All description follows the same basic rules as character introduction: Be clear, be compelling, and be concise.

Camera concerns

You're a writer; your job is to tell the story. The director and cinematographer will rewrite that story in a language designed for the camera. Therefore, your concern isn't the camera or its terminology. In fact, technical jargon will distance a reader from the world of your story.

The script that you're crafting is known as a *presentation script,* or the *reader's script,* which is the version designed to seduce a reader into seeing the film. Any technical encumbrances, such as camera angles and scene numbers, are removed to let the story emerge.

The *production script,* or the *shooting script,* is the director and/or cinematographer's script. A much later draft, it includes technical notations, such as camera angles, special effects, and editing requirements.

That said, you may find it helpful to understand the camera and its associated terms so that you can visualize the scene and emphasize the details of your film. You can write a scene to suggest an angle, without employing the technical term. If you know what a close-up is and you want to use it in a shot, you can rework your description to suggest it.

For example, if Henry proposes to Sarah in the scene and you want a close-up of the diamond ring, you might write the scene in one of two ways:

> Henry pulls a box from his coat pocket. He opens it to reveal a large
>
> DIAMOND RING
>
> He takes Sarah's hand and slips the ring on her finger.

Or:

> Henry pulls a box from his coat pocket and opens the lid. Inside the box is a large diamond ring. It sparkles in the light.
>
> He takes Sarah's hand and slips the ring on her finger.

In both cases, the description suggests that a close-up is needed, without jarring the reader with terminology. A director would have to linger for a second on the diamond ring itself, prior to the shot where Henry slips the ring on her finger. Without the close-up indication, the description would read

> Henry pulls a box from his coat pocket and opens the lid. He removes a ring from the box and slips it on Sarah's finger.

Whenever possible, imply the necessary camera angle. Doing so not only keeps a reader locked into your story but also hones your writing skills.

The following sections cover some basic camera directions, but be warned: I include these terms only as an overview of possible shots. I strongly advise you not to include the technical jargon in the reader's script. It distracts a reader's attention away from your story and annoys directors and cinematographers who may envision a shot differently than you do. So if you're interested in utilizing one or several of these effects, craft description that conveys the effect without calling attention to the camera itself.

Intercut

This direction indicates that two scenes are occurring simultaneously in separate locations. This term appears in all caps as the slug line or in the description. See the following examples:

INTERCUTTING:

Sarah shops in preparation for the date, Henry dresses in front of his mirror.

Or:

INTERCUT: SARAH AND HENRY

The scene INTERCUTS between Sarah shopping for the date and Henry dressing in front of his mirror.

The writer then describes individual moments of each scene without using a subsidiary slug line to bounce between then.

Insert

A writer uses this direction when he wants to highlight an object in the scene or include a detail that's outside the scene but important to it. To complete an insert, do one of three things: Return to the dialogue, switch locations with a new slug line, or type BACK TO SCENE at the end.

INSERT — PHOTOGRAPH

Small scissors remove a woman from the image.

BACK TO SCENE:

Series of shots

This technique serves as a way to abridge action sequences into a number of short moments involving the main character, usually without dialogue. The format is as follows:

Type SERIES OF SHOTS in place of a slug line, skip a space, and then list a short description of each shot. Skip a space between each description. You may assign a letter to each shot, but many screenwriters opt not to. End the series by typing END SERIES OF SHOTS.

SERIES OF SHOTS

A) Sarah and Henry notice each other across a dance floor.

B) Sarah and Henry dance together at their wedding.

C) Sarah lies in a hospital bed, watching Henry hold their newborn baby.

END SERIES OF SHOTS

A series of shots has a distinct beginning, middle, and end, and is often used to dramatize a passage of time. A series of shots can also be scripted traditionally, as individual scenes with slug lines. Writers generally choose this method to suggest a certain pace. A series of shots is different from (but often confused with) a montage.

Montage

A *montage* is the dissolving of two or more shots into each other to create a desired effect, usually an association of ideas. These shots need not include the main character, and they don't have a beginning, middle, and end. They're formatted in the same way as a series of shots.

MONTAGE:

A) Hands shuffle a deck of cards.

B) A screen door SLAMS shut.

C) An unshaven face leers in the darkness.

D) The cards scatter across a table.

END MONTAGE

A montage is often used in dream or nightmare sequences. Because of the surreal feeling it evokes, your best bet it to use it sparingly, if at all.

Close-up

A *close-up* is a shot that emphasizes a detail in a scene. It's often abbreviated to CU in shooting scripts, as follows:

CU — IMMENSE DIAMOND RING

Angle on

This shot suggests another view of a previous shot. Here's an example:

ANGLE ON Sarah staring down at the ring.

POV

Shorthand for *point of view,* this direction implies that the scene is being viewed from another character's perspective. You must identify whose point of view it is and what exactly he sees. If the POV alternates within a scene, employ the term REVERSE POV.

SARAH'S POV — HENRY

He stares at her across the table, then pushes the letter her way.

HENRY

He wants you to have this.

REVERSE POV

Sarah takes the letter and rips it in half.

SARAH

As usual, we want different things.

For strong examples of POVs, watch horror films. They're commonly used when a killer is following his victim.

Split screen

This shot indicates two subjects in different locations on-screen simultaneously. **When Harry Met Sally** uses this shot when the protagonists share a phone conversation from separate bedrooms.

Sally dials Harry's number.

SPLIT SCREEN

Harry and Sally lie in their beds watching the same film on TV.

The split screen shot conveys a distinct film style and is rarely used.

Super

Shorthand for *superimpose,* this term is used if another element is being superimposed over the action of a scene. A super is often used to show dates, locations, or translation texts.

The yacht barrels toward the shore. The mainland looms ahead.

SUPER — MARSEILLES 1921

Terms that defy categorization

A few formatting details don't fit into a particular category. I tentatively label them *transitional directions*. These terms help readers follow your action, and they tell them how to read the script.

Fade in

Screenplays usually begin with these words. They suggest the movement from darkness to an image on the screen. They're typed in all caps at the left-hand margin followed by a double space and the first slug line.

> FADE IN:
>
> EXT. COLLEGE LIBRARY — DAY

Fade out

These words usually end a screenplay. They're typed two spaces below the final line of the script, flush to the right margin. After FADE OUT, writers generally space down six lines and type THE END in the center of the page.

> Henry and Sarah link arms and walk into the sunset.
>
> FADE OUT.
>
> THE END

V.O.

VO is shorthand for voice-over. This direction is used when the audience hears a character speak who's not in the scene. It's often used to underscore a scene with narration.

> EXT. SUBURBAN HOUSE — DAY
>
> The ranch-style house is in desperate need of attention. Weeds obscure the front path, and the remaining shutters threaten passersby.
>
> HENRY (VO) or (V.O.)
>
> I've always thought my neighbor's house would look better as a parking lot or a strip mall.

O.S.

Shorthand for off-screen, this abbreviation is used when a character speaks outside the camera's view, or when the audience hears a sound but doesn't see where it's coming from.

A door SLAMS OS then FOOTSTEPS hurry toward him.

Or:

SARAH (OS) or (O.S.)

As usual, we want different things.

Remember, both V.O. and O.S. are abbreviations to be placed after a character's name. Use the whole phrase (off-screen and voice-over) when utilizing them in description.

Cut to

This term was used to cut quickly between scenes, but it's rarely used anymore. It appears at the bottom of a scene, to the right-hand side.

Henry pulls Sarah close, and they begin to waltz.

CUT TO:

Dissolve to

This direction is used in place of the CUT TO when you want to suggest a slow transition from one scene to the next. You may dissolve to suggest the passage of time between one shot and another, or because you want the effect of one image fading into the next.

Continuation

When a scene or a speech is interrupted by a page break, type MORE in parentheses at the end of the last line on the first page and then type CONT'D after the character's name on the next page.

Many of the preceding considerations are automatically formatted for you with screenwriting software. While it's helpful to know how they're useful and where they belong on your page, it will certainly save you time to allow a computer to place them there for you. I overview several software options in the first part of this chapter.

HENRY

I wish you'd thought of this sooner. It would have

(MORE)

——————page break——————

HENRY (CONT'D)

Saved us so much time if you had.

When a speaker is interrupted by an action, use a dash to suggest the interruption, type the action, and then type "continuing" in a parenthetical after the character's name when he starts speaking again.

HENRY

I do wish you'd thought of this sooner. It —

Sarah hands him the plane tickets and her purse.

HENRY

(continuing)

Would have saved us so much time.

You can also script that last line as:

HENRY (CONT'D)

Would have saved us so much time.

As with all creative elements, formatting takes time. Screenwriting is an art, and as every artist differs, so will every format a little. Notice I say "a little here," though. Clear screenwriting format is vital to being taken seriously in the industry. The key rule to remember with presentation is this: If it doesn't look right, it's probably not right.

A Sample Scene

The format becomes clear when you see it on the page. I've included a small sample in Figure 15-1 to help clarify both the spacing and several key formatting components. You can also find screenplays online or at your local library or bookstore. The more you read, the more ingrained the format will become.

                          "A DIME A DOZEN"

FADE IN:

EXT. A COUNTRY ROAD - DAY

The road is empty. Fields of corn stretch for miles along
either side. Nothing but green and gold.

                         ELLEN (V.O.)
                I used to think there were places that time
                didn't touch. Places too small to consider.

An abandoned tractor lies by the side of the road. A scarecrow
leans awkwardly in one of the fields.

                         ELLEN - (V.O.)
                Where people do as they've always done and
                days go on and on and... on. Places like
                my home town.

The sound of a car ENGINE RUMBLING farther off. It grows louder
over the following speech.

                         ELLEN - (V.O.)
                Now though, I wonder if time's just waiting.
                Waiting for its moment to pull everything apart.

A sleek black car barrels down the road spinning dust in its
wake.

EXT. A ROAD-SIDE FRUIT STAND - DAY

DARRYL HOPKINS, the 75 year old owner of the stand helps RUTH
MADSON, 60, load bags into her vehicle.

The black car streaks past them. Pebbles fly up around its
tires. A few of them slam into Ruth's shoes.

Darryl spins around fast enough to catch the

LICENSE PLATE

which reads PUMA 30.

                              DARRYL
                    Puma.

Figure 15-1:
A sample
scene.

RUTH
(quietly)

You know what that means.

DARRYL
Trouble with six cylinders.

RUTH
Car like that? Going that fast? More like
eight, Darryl. Eight and some change.

They exchange a glance, then peer down the now empty road.

EXT. SIDE OF THE ROAD - MOMENTS LATER

Wide-eyed ABBEY REYNOLDS, 8, and her friend ELLEN KURTZ, 13,
walk home from school. Abbey carries a pinwheel.

ELLEN
Hurry up, Abbey, we're going to be late. Not that
it matters.

ABBEY
If it don't matter, why're we hurrying?

ELLEN
'Cause I'm not getting in trouble over something
that don't even matter,understand?

An ENGINE ROARS behind them. The black car streaks past.
Abbey's pinwheel twirls furiously in her hand.

ABBEY
Whoa.

ELLEN
Double whoa.

ABBEY
Think that's him?

ELLEN
Maybe. But I sorta hope not.

The girls exchange a glance, then take off down the road. The
top of Abbey's pinwheel twirls off its handle, and as she runs
it falls to the ground.

Figure 15-1:
(continued)

Chapter 16

Putting It Together: Structuring Your First Draft

- -

In This Chapter

▶ Crafting a dynamite first image

▶ Establishing your story's world

▶ Structuring your action

▶ Working toward a resolution

▶ Structuring your subplots

- -

*E*very writer reaches a point where the cup of possibilities runneth over. The head spins with evocative locations, fleeting conversations, feats of strength and daring, impossible odds, side-splitting witticisms, moments of grief and agony, and, above all, hope. You can't possibly absorb any more. And what do you have to show for it? An outline, a treatment, maybe a pile of notes.

At this stage of the writing process, you're like a field guide. You have a destination in mind and a troupe of individuals (otherwise known as your audience) behind you, ready to follow your every move. You have a sense of what you'll encounter along the way, and you know why it's important that you try to make it out with everyone intact. You're looking for the roadmap. In screenwriting terms, you're looking for the *structure*. I talk about several different structures in Chapter 11, but in this chapter, I concentrate on one in particular — the three-act structure. It is the oldest, the most common, and therefore, the most useful structure — designed to help you and your travelmates reach your ultimate destinations.

Navigating the Three-Act Structure

Every great story is composed of three principal segments: a beginning, middle, and ending. In screenwriting, those segments are known as Act I, Act II, and Act III. Without a strong opening, no one wants to watch your film. Without a strong middle, the audience will lose interest partway through it.

Without a strong ending, well, that's like the radio cutting out on the last line of your favorite song. The audience leaves unresolved — confused at best, angry at worst — and wondering what it just saw.

The lengths of each act may differ film to film. As movies are getting longer, so are their acts. But traditionally, feature films run from 90 to 120 pages in length, which is roughly two hours of screen time. Each act in a 120-page script is broken down into the following number of pages:

- ✔ **Act I:** pages 1–30 (pages 1–23 in a 95-page script)
- ✔ **Act II:** pages 31–90 (pages 24–70 in a 95-page script)
- ✔ **Act III:** pages 91–120 (pages 71–95 in a 95-page script)

How important are these divisions? There are variations to be sure, but if you're a new writer, you should try to stick to industry standards the first few times you craft a script. Why? The most important reason is perhaps only obvious after you complete a first draft. The three-act structure is a strong organization of text. Stories seem to fall into it naturally, and they were falling into it well before Aristotle publicly analyzed the structure's worth in 320 B.C. (more on Aristotle's *Poetics* in Chapter 5). Like any craft, if you understand the basic rules, you'll be better equipped to alter them, when necessary, later on.

Also, many agencies and film companies give new scripts what's known as the *five-and-dime treatment*. They read the first five pages of your script and the last ten and determine its worth from there. If you've followed the three-act structure, which calls for a bang-up opening and a swift conclusion, you may just make the cut. If a producer notices that your script is less than 90 pages long, he may assume that your story doesn't have enough punch to make a feature film. If he notices that it's more than 120 pages, he may doubt your ability to streamline action. Your best bet is to fall somewhere in between until he knows and trusts your work.

The three-act structure isn't a formula; it's a guide. It won't write your film for you or hinder your creativity, but it does provide a solid foundation on which to build. Each act traditionally contains several landmark moments. By *landmark,* I mean scenes that help structure the action or pivotal moments in your story. Again, these landmarks are simply suggestions for how to structure your piece. They're not meant to provide a formula.

Act 1: Introductions

Every act in the three-act structure has a set of tasks to accomplish. The first act serves as your audience's introduction to the entire world of the script — people, places, time frame. Remember that your audience members begin in darkness. In their advance toward some new awareness, they're not unlike visitors in a foreign country. You need to orient them fairly quickly to the story that's about to unfold. So, the first act is all about setup.

Your opening moments

If I could offer you one piece of advice concerning your first act, it would be this: Begin with an image. Stories that begin with anything else, voices in darkness or immediate dialogue, for example, are often difficult to absorb. A strong opening image can convey backdrop, character, and theme in seconds. *Kill Bill* opens with a bride, badly beaten, clawing her way across the chapel full of dead wedding guests. This image and the film's title pit good against evil from the start.

The eye picks up details much more quickly than the ear, and nothing's more disconcerting than staring at talking heads. In a way, you haven't earned the right to open verbally. As someone in the audience, I don't yet know the people speaking; I haven't decided whether they're interesting enough to pursue. Let me watch them for a bit and make some initial assumptions before you let them talk my ear off. Doing so keeps me actively involved in guessing what your story will be.

Also, everything that happens in the first moments of a film is important. If you provide vital information verbally, I'm likely to miss it in my quest to appraise the environment visually. People come to the movies to see pictures in motion. Why begin with anything else?

The first ten pages

If your opening image grabs my attention, you have roughly ten pages after that opening to convince me that your film is worth watching. Don't believe me? The next time you go to a movie, ask yourself how you feel about it after the first ten minutes. If you're bored or confused, you'll likely deem it a failure. If you're riveted, odds are that you'll consider it a success.

The first ten pages provide an initial criterion on which to judge the ensuing story. They should provide just enough information to establish a clear world without giving too much of the eventual plot away, and they should create enough mystery to keep me wondering what's in store. Your first ten pages should accomplish the following tasks:

- Introduce the main characters
- Establish the primary environments
- Convey a distinct mood or atmosphere
- Establish the time period

✔ Illustrate a routine or way of life

✔ Provide any relevant *backstory* (events which transpired before the film began)

✔ Introduce the antagonist

If you haven't already settled on an ending to your script, now is the time to do so. If you don't know where the script is going, how will you determine which pieces of information to highlight at the beginning?

Everything that happens now is a setup for what comes next. So you need to know what comes next.

Some films reveal the villain right away. The opening scenes of *No Country For Old Men* reveal the character Anton Chigurh to be a ruthless sociopath. By contrast, the murderer in *Ghost* seems to be a nice guy until well after the protagonist is killed. When you reveal the antagonist is up to you; you don't have to do so in the first ten pages. However, if you wait much longer, you risk a restless audience.

The inciting incident

The *inciting incident,* also known as the *catalyst,* marks the film's first turning point. It tilts the story from order to chaos, from complacency to combat. It's the point of no return. In this moment, you answer three questions:

✔ What do your characters want?

✔ Why do they want it now?

✔ What might prevent them from getting it?

Together, these queries make up the film's *premise,* or what it's ultimately about. In *Lord of the Rings,* one hobbit wants to rid Middle Earth of an evil force. The Dark Lord and human greed stand in his way. In both *Ordinary People* and *Good Will Hunting,* young men struggle to forgive and forget their tortuous past. Personal demons and unsympathetic adults stand in their way. A strong premise clearly defines a need, a reason for that need, and an impediment. As soon as an audience senses these details, you can pose the central question:

Will your protagonist(s) succeed?

If the answer is yes, you may have a happy ending; if it's no, a tragedy is in the works. Your inciting incident isn't complete until you pose this question. Until then, audiences wait. They wait for action; they wait for intent; they wait to be told what they're waiting for.

An inciting incident generally occurs in one of the following ways:

- An action plunges the characters into conflict.
- A piece of critical information arrives.
- A sequence of small events prepares an audience for the story.

In *Pulp Fiction,* a young couple robs a diner. In *Stand By Me,* four kids receive word that a body's been found in the woods across town. That newsflash launches their journey together. The film *Zorro* is an example of the third technique. Two brothers witness Zorro attempting to thwart an execution. They save his life in the process, and he rewards them with a silver medallion. Government troops then invade Zorro's house, kill his wife, abduct his child, and throw him in jail. Years pass before he escapes. Meanwhile, the brothers, now grown up, also flee government soldiers. When one of them is killed, the other would risk his life avenging the death, if he wasn't first intercepted by (who else?) Zorro. These events prepare an audience for the real story, which involves the training of a new masked hero. This preparation takes longer than ten pages, but the result is the same.

Plot point one

Plot point one is the first big turning point in your script. It occurs at the end of the first act, approximately 30 pages into the action, and propels an audience into Act II. It must do the following things:

- Push the action in a new direction
- Force the protagonist to make a choice and take a risk
- Raise the central question for the first or second time
- Raise the stakes

Pivotal events, like plot point one, are usually surprises. Audiences know that something grand will happen eventually. They might even know what the result of that event will be. But don't allow them to guess the details of the event itself, or you'll spoil the surprise. *Star Wars* audiences know that Luke Skywalker will eventually be called away from the safety of his family and into training. They may also guess that, as a result, he will have to fight Darth Vader, but they don't know exactly how these proceedings will transpire. Stories that hint too thoroughly at upcoming events become predictable and less exciting to watch.

In *Zorro,* the young hero meets his future mentor. He must choose to fight the villain now or follow this instructor and heed his advice to wait. His decision tilts the plot toward the true story — the training of a legend. The first plot point may be as shocking as the death of a loved one or as gentle as the touch of a hand. Both actions have the power to launch a great story.

Act II: Salting the Wound

If Act I ends by asking, "What does your protagonist want?" Act II continually begs the question, "What will she do to get it?" In many cases, Act II tests not only what your character will do, but also what your character will *endure*. Act II is like a video game with life or death odds. Each level pits the protagonist against stronger resistance, be it outside forces or internal turmoil. The protagonist must defeat them all in order to succeed. Traditionally, these conflicts arrive more frequently as the story progresses, with the most difficult obstacle lying in wait until the end.

Don't put the toughest obstacle first, or you'll have nowhere to go but down. The audience might as well go home. Instead, script your obstacles to escalate in difficulty as the story unfolds.

Your job in Act II is to create a snowball effect with your action. One moment adds to the next and the next until the action barrels toward some culminating event. Harnessing the momentum so that you can steer it without slowing it down is a constant challenge. Because Act II is twice as long as the first and final acts, writers commonly bemoan "second-act problems" as the task of keeping track of the various characters, their conflicts, and their goals becomes unwieldy. Here are a few checkpoints to help you manage the second-act madness:

- Make the conflict personal.
- Let the protagonist fail more than once.
- Allow the antagonist to succeed, perhaps several times.
- Teach the protagonist a new skill.
- Test the protagonist's current abilities and/or expertise.
- Further explore the subplot.

Think about how each of those points affects the action. First, your protagonist needs a personal stake in the conflict, or she might jump ship halfway through. Zorro and his apprentice, for example, desire revenge for the murder of their loved ones. Theirs is a highly personal fight.

Next, the failures of your protagonist create extraordinary odds, especially if the antagonist thrives during this time. Audiences can't be sure that the protagonist will prevail; they can only hope she will. Both Zorro and his apprentice fail to protect their loved ones. They err in other ways throughout the film, but these initial failures prove them capable of personal defeat.

Finally, human beings are not perfect; neither is your protagonist. A protagonist who learns from her mistakes and who acquires new skills to help her succeed is that much more human. If she triumphs despite startling odds, using abilities she's newly acquired, you've crafted an inspiring tale that audiences can relate to. Zorro's apprentice doesn't become the masked avenger until he's undergone rigorous training. He has natural talents that help guide him, but he must also acquire new skills before he can succeed.

The second act is often dedicated to raising the stakes in one or all of these ways. These points strengthen your script's conflict and make the protagonist's success that much more important.

Know where the action is

Even if your second act boasts all the items I list in the preceding section, its structure still may elude you. Here's where the formula for action comes in handy: Actions cause other actions to occur. Notice that I'm not saying that action causes reaction. It might, of course. If a son does something to make his mother cry, then his action has caused a reaction. However, her crying may not lead to anything else. If that's the case, it's a logical but inactive choice. If his mother's tears cause the son to become further enraged and do something reckless, then the choice to have the mother cry becomes an action. Try structuring your plot with the following techniques in mind.

Create scenes that result in other scenes

When you're overwhelmed with the multiple plotlines of Act II, it may help to strictly follow the rules of action. That means structuring each action so that it causes not only a future scene but the next scene. Here's a sequence from the second act of *The Untouchables.*

1. Ness successfully raids Capone's illegal liquor warehouse.

2. Capone sends him a bribe to stop the raids.

3. Ness publicly refuses the bribe.

4. Capone's thugs threaten Ness's family.

5. Ness relocates his family and retaliates with another successful raid.

6. In this raid, he confiscates Capone's financial records.

7. His accountant pursues Capone for income-tax evasion.

8. Capone has the accountant killed.

The action in this second act is tight; every scene sparks the next. The cause and effect relationship holds the act together, refusing to let it stray into unimportant events. You can do this as well. The trick is to create action that's so poignant, so shocking, so revealing that it demands a quick response.

Create strong impediments

An *impediment,* or a *roadblock,* is an unforeseeable event that forces the protagonist to switch tactics or formulate another plan. Suppose that your main character spends his entire journey searching for one corner of a treasure map. If he finds the person with the map but that person doesn't speak English, that's an impediment. If that person swallows the map in the protagonist's struggle to obtain it, that's another impediment. In the first example, the hero needs a new tactic. In the second, he needs a new plan.

Tactics refer to the specific methods that a character employs to reach a desired end. In other words, they're "the plan." Seduction, bribery, bartering, guilt, pleas, tricks, and threats are among the most common.

Impediments or "roadblocks" force the character to make a different choice and act upon it, often immediately. By seeing what choice the character makes, the audience gets an opportunity to glimpse his true nature. What lengths will he go to, how quickly does he think, what skills can he muster?

Here's a tip: Be sure to let him find the answer and choose the new route himself. Don't let him become a victim in the action or contrive an easy answer for him. If your character's running from an army of opponents, let him hunt, dig, or swing himself out of harm's way. You may simply toss him a hiding place, but where's the fun in that?

Plant future conflicts

Plants are conflicts that you foreshadow in an early scene and bring to fruition later. The audience anticipates that they'll be a problem eventually, and your job is to make that moment arrive. If your character boasts of skills that he doesn't have, he should be called to use those nonexistent skills. If your character hates spiders as Jeff Daniels does in ***Arachnophobia,*** he'll have to battle one eventually. Indiana Jones makes his fear of snakes known early on, yet later he must confront what? You guessed it. A cave full of snakes.

If you plant the potential for these conflicts in the first act, let them payoff in the second. Or, plant them early in Act II and let them pay off at the end. If your audience watches for them, you've created dramatic tension. If it forgets about them, they're in for a satisfactory reminder.

The about-face

Much like the military command, an *about-face* is an abrupt and complete turnaround in the action. The turnaround, also known as a *reversal,* may be physical or emotional in nature. If your characters hate each other, as they do initially in **When Harry Met Sally,** they'll love each other by the end. If your character struggles to maintain a solid job, as Lester Burnham does in **American Beauty,** he'll switch to an opposing career or abandon work completely. The about-face is as exciting as a breakthrough. Both moments propel the characters into a new understanding and an opposite path.

Use this technique sparingly so that it doesn't loose its punch, but when the opportunity to use the about-face arises, take it. Audiences love the surprise.

The midpoint: A halfway house

One more thing may help structure the action of Act II — the creation of a *midpoint.* Can you guess where this turning point lands? If you said halfway through the script (around page 60 in a 120-page screenplay, 47 in a 95-page screenplay), you guessed correctly. More importantly, this event divides the second act in half, providing much-needed structure in a portion of your story that's so immense.

In **When Harry Met Sally,** for example, the protagonists sleep together. They don't mean to; it just happens, and the action reverses from there.

Not every script has a midpoint; some stories don't require one. How do you know if yours does? If you're looking for a landmark to steer the first 30 pages of your second act toward the last 30 pages, a strong midpoint is it. Otherwise, build your action consistently toward the next major plot point at the end of Act II.

Plot point two

Plot point two occurs at the end of the second act, roughly around page 80 in a 120-page script and page 70 in a 95-page script. It mimics the tasks of the first plot point: It broaches the central question again, propels the action in a new direction, raises the stakes, and forces a risk and a choice. However, at its conclusion, you will do two things:

- Remind the audience of a ticking clock
- And either lift the protagonist's spirits *or* crush the protagonist's will

In **Speed,** the villain reminds the protagonists (and therefore the audience) that their time on the bus is running out. In **American Beauty,** Lester Burnham decides to sleep with his daughter's best friend at the end of Act II. His eventual refusal to go through with the act brings him closer to his estranged wife and daughter. He ends the second act content for the first time in ages.

Act III: The Final Frontier

Act III begins around page 90 in a 120-page script (page 70 in a 95-page script) and runs for 20 to 30, although because of its fast pace, it often seems like less. At this point, you've raised the central question, "Will my protagonist succeed?" several times. Why? Your entire film revolves around the quest for an answer. Act III provides that answer.

At the beginning of Act III, your protagonist either faces the upward hike or the downward sprint to the most gripping moment in the script. To push him toward this last lap, one of the following things generally happens:

- **The protagonist abandons hope and must be inspired back to action.** In **Juno,** a young girl watches the couple she's chosen to raise her baby dissolve their marriage. She has to re-imagine the future she planned for her child before she's prepared to bring it into the world.

- **The protagonist makes a breakthrough discovery.** The kids in **Goonies** discover the pirate ship and a way to get out of the cave.

- **The protagonist acquires a final necessary skill.** Ralph Macchio's character gains the life lessons necessary to encourage his newfound karate skills in **The Karate Kid.**

- **The villain forces the hero into combat.** In **Rear Window,** the villain discovers that he's being watched and brings the fight to Jimmy Steward's front door.

- **The protagonist overcomes an internal obstacle that enables him to fight a physical antagonist.** In **Erin Brockovich,** the heroine harnesses her temper and uses it to her advantage.

Shortly after Act III begins, the protagonist has to make the choice to continue forward. It may be a reluctant choice, but it nevertheless pushes him to pursue one last chance for success.

The climax

The *climax* is your script's final battlefield. It represents the most intense and, generally, the grandest scene of the film in which the protagonist makes one last attempt at achieving his or her goal.

There's a subtle irony surrounding your story's climax. Your entire plot moves toward this point in one sense or another. It's the most shocking, devastating, hysterical, or frightening scene in the film. And how long does it last? A few minutes at most. The climax, which begins around page 110 (or 85 in a shorter script) usually lasts about five to ten pages and is followed by an even faster resolution. Why build 100 pages to such a short burst of action? There's a saying, "Life's a journey, not a destination." That saying's true of film life as well. *You've* had your eye on this final battle, but your film is really about how you got there.

Keep these points in mind when crafting your climax:

- ✔ Your character should be an active participant.
- ✔ Your villain should be equally formidable.
- ✔ Something personal is now at stake.
- ✔ There should be little time to think.
- ✔ Something unexpected should occur.
- ✔ Your character should use some acquired skill in his attempt to succeed.
- ✔ You should answer the central question, which for most stories is, "Will your protagonist succeed in achieving his goal?"

Don't let life happen to your protagonist; let her happen to life. Keep the pace fast, create a few surprises, impediments, or miscalculations — anything to force the characters to think on their feet. And please, answer the central question. If your character succeeds, marvelous. If she fails, so be it. But give an audience its well-deserved conclusion.

The resolution

The key words for the final one to five pages are fast, fast, and fast. You've illustrated the most dramatic scene, and your character has solved the problem or been defeated by it. Don't linger too long thereafter. A slick resolution offers just enough time for an audience to absorb the final outcome. In those few pages, the action may

- ✔ Suggest a future life for the protagonist
- ✔ Illustrate the repercussions of the climax
- ✔ Establish any changes in the protagonist
- ✔ Suggest a just or an unjust world

The resolution tackles the question, "So what?" What sort of world have you led your audience to, and was it worth the journey? Find a way for the final answer to be yes, it was well worth the journey.

A Note on Subplots

Often, writers will pitch an idea based on some theme that they're enamored with only to realize that there's little in the idea to generate an action-based plot. In fact, themes don't make great foundations for a story; they tend to produce theoretical discussions in place of goal-oriented interaction. Yet every story needs one. For this reason, most screenwriters rely on subplots to carry their theme.

Subplots are plots involving secondary characters included to provide depth and dimension. Movies without them tend to be dull and self-indulgent. Secondary characters provide new outlooks, differing opinions and advice, and alternate ways of life. They often bolster the main character's confidence, provide necessary tutelage, or sharpen his personal beliefs by downright disagreeing with him. In some cases, subplots arise between protagonists.

In crafting your subplot, follow the three-act structure of the main storyline. In the following list, I provide a series of questions for you to answer, and I use the subplot from **When Harry Met Sally** as an example of each:

✔ **What setup does your subplot require?** In **When Harry Met Sally,** the audience needs to meet the protagonists' respective best friends and assess their personal views on relationships.

✔ **What is your subplot's central question?** In this case, the subplot shares a central question with the main plot: Will the characters find a love that they can sustain?

✔ **What is the inciting incident that starts the action?** Sally is set up with Harry's best friend, and Harry is set up with Sally's best friend on an awkward double date. The two best friends end up having more in common with each other than with Harry or Sally, and they leave the evening as a couple.

✔ **What obstacles do the subplot characters endure?** The new couple moves in together, surviving fights over decor and living arrangements. They also continue to counsel their still-single best friends.

✔ **How do they answer the central question?** This is a romantic comedy, so they get married, of course.

Structuring a fairy tale

Because restructuring an existing story is less intimidating than structuring your own, I include a project here that lets you do just that. See whether you can pinpoint the three-act elements in some of your favorite fairy tales. The following elements lie somewhere between "once upon a time" and "happily ever after": the setup, the inciting incident, the central question, plot point one, the midpoint, plot point two, the climax, and the resolution.

I've broken down *Jack and the Beanstalk* as an example.

Act I

The setup: Jack and his mother are so poor that she instructs him to sell their last cow for money or food.

The inciting incident: Jack meets a man who claims he has magic beans, and Jack trades the cow for those beans instead of money or food.

The central question: Will Jack find a way to provide for his family?

Plot point one: Enraged that Jack has returned empty-handed, his mother tosses the beans out the window. They grow into a beanstalk overnight.

Act II

Midpoint: After climbing the beanstalk and discovering the giant's castle, Jack successfully steals the giant's golden egg. This success emboldens Jack to return to the castle after a bag of gold.

Plot point two: Jack tries to steal a magic harp, but it sings a warning, and the giant wakes up.

Act III

The climax: The giant chases Jack down the beanstalk. Jack chops the beanstalk down with an ax.

The resolution: The giant perishes in the fall. Jack and his mother live a prosperous life thereafter, and (hopefully) Jack has learned a life lesson about theft.

Now, you try it with a fairy tale you're familiar with. I recommend *Hansel and Gretel, Rumpelstiltskin,* or *The Princess and the Pea,* but if you don't know these stories well, just pick whatever fairy tale you like best.

However you craft your subplots, make sure that they do the following:

- ✔ Require their own setup, turning points, climax, and resolution
- ✔ Offer the protagonists a chance to breathe, confess, love, rage, dream, and so on
- ✔ Criss-cross the main plotline at pivotal moments
- ✔ Express the story's theme
- ✔ Offer opportunities to witness changes in the protagonist

Allow the subcharacters to be as strong and vibrant as possible, but make sure that the protagonists match that vitality in some way.

Finally, remember that your secondary characters don't know that they're part of a subplot — and it's a good thing they don't. Craft them as if they were main characters and allow them to be unwilling, skeptical, and unkind should the situation call for it. Otherwise, they become pawns, fulfilling a role that you've contrived for them. They become punching bags or sounding boards for the main characters, both of which are dull and unrealistic options. They're an integral part of the story. Let them be cruel or supportive, but above all, let them be complete.

Chapter 17

Take Two: Rewriting Your Script

. . . .

In This Chapter

▶ Completing a technical revision

▶ Tracking character arcs

▶ Reworking problematic scenes

▶ Appraising critical feedback

. . . .

Ernest Hemingway once said that the first draft of anything is garbage. His language was more colorful than that, but the sentiment remains the same. Everyone's first draft requires a revision or two, or ten. If your first draft is perfect, stop reading; you don't need this book. And don't tell any writers. Trust me: They don't want to know. For most people, the second draft is where the real writing gets done.

Writers have two modes in which they work: the right-brain mode and the left-brain mode. Consider them the wild animal and the rider, or the creator and the critic. However you envision them, one mode colors outside the lines while the other erases until a recognizable form appears. The right brain dreams, and the left brain outlines. The right brain produces the first draft, and the left brain manages the revision. This chapter concentrates on the latter: revision.

Downshifting between Drafts

Many writers tackle the first draft at a feverish pitch, churning it out in record time. Why so fast? They know that the first draft is about immersion, about pinning down the story without thought to spelling, grammar, and possibly even format. The first draft is the story-only draft. If you worry about perfection, you'll lose time, momentum, you may even drop the project before completing a draft at all. Perfection isn't possible yet. You don't know what the story's about, not really. At the pace you're going, you won't know where you've been until you get to the finish line and look back.

When you throw the door open and stride into the room exhausted and flushed, with a stack of pages in one hand and a glass of champagne in the other — then and only then can you worry about perfection. And even then, you'll hold off because the first thing that you're going to do is rest.

How to work when you're not working

How long should you stay away from your work? It's up to you, but I advise a two-week hiatus at the very least. If you're on a deadline, two weeks may be all you get, but if not, take more. Lock the manuscript away somewhere or save it on your computer and forget about it. You have other things to do.

Some writers can't abide the thought of leaving their work. After all, it consumes your life for anywhere from two months to a year. And now I'm telling you to forget about it? Yes. You really do need to ignore that voice screaming at you to rework the draft right away. Here's why:

- ✔ Your imagination needs time to replenish itself.

- ✔ You need time to absorb the story's conclusion.

- ✔ You're going to slash it eventually. The less consumed you are with the project, the less personal it will seem when you do.

- ✔ Now's your chance to return to visual research.

Writing an original piece is like raising a child. By the time you complete a draft, you know it intimately, you respect what it has become, and you're likely to protect it at all costs. You need that sensitivity to fade. It's difficult to protect a work and tear it apart at the same time.

What do you do in the interim? You continue working, of course. But you work minus the computer, the late nights, and the aching wrists — minus everything but the awareness. You're going to be visually employed now. Here are a few suggestions for keeping your mind on your story while you're keeping your hands off:

- ✔ **Immerse yourself in the time frame.** Now's the time to revisit past research. Read novels written at the time in which your film takes place; find newspaper clippings, classified ads, and obituaries. Peruse the poetry and music of the era. Do anything to keep the views and language of the time frame alive. If your story takes place in a futuristic or fabricated era, see whether you can dig up stories that suggest what you envision. Other writers and filmmakers have presented fictional worlds — are they similar or different from your own?

- ✔ **Return to other visual mediums.** Photographs, paintings, sculptures — these mediums helped craft your backstory, so return to them now. Different images will catch your eye, or you'll discover new details in an illustration you previously visited. Playwrights surround themselves with images that convey details in a play. What happens if you do the same? You immersed yourself in your writing; now, immerse yourself in art. You'll be surprised what catches your eye after completing a first draft.

✔ **Visit appropriate locations.** Does much of your script take place in an office? Find one and spend some time there. With this kind of research, you're seeking out an environmental rhythm. The pace, the sounds, and the patterns of movement in Grand Central Station, for example, are considerably different from those in Central Park. If you can't visit a similar location, if your settings are obscure or fictitious, find places with a similar essence. Perhaps I can't visit a circus or an amusement park with ease, but I can sit at a McDonald's play area for a while or drive past a grade school at recess.

✔ **Observe human behavior.** Does your protagonist fall in love? Is he cynical on a regular basis? What does that mood look like? Observe a few people who share tendencies with your main characters. Which exact set of gestures, postures, and activities seem to match? Watch duos or groups of people and search for status. This search is about perception. If you perceive that the woman in the park controls her romantic relationship, for all intents and purposes, she does. You made that assumption for a reason. Think about why you perceived that woman's status as you did and how you might translate that status to the page.

✔ **See lots and lots of films.** Other films may help you clarify and further define your sense of structure. Strong films can provide positive examples, but even weak films do their part. Hopefully, you'll be able to pinpoint what you believe makes a stronger and a weaker script for when you finally revisit your own story.

✔ **Read books on the craft (or re-read them).** The first read is about trying to find techniques to complete a draft. The second go-around is to compare what you're reading to the draft you now have.

Generally, I advise writers to avoid films with premises comparable to their own. If the other film's great, you'll worry that your own doesn't match up. If it's wretched, you'll worry that your own premise is too. Either way, you worry. And who needs that when you're trying to write?

So, when *will* you revisit your story and get started on the revision process? That depends, of course, but I generally suggest that you're prepared to rewrite when one of the following three things occurs:

✔ You feel you're refreshed enough to return to the work.

✔ You consider or begin another project.

✔ You stop worrying about your script every day.

✔ You've forgotten exact details of character or plot development.

✔ Your deadline approaches.

Your first time back: Read-through #1

Your first glance through a beginning draft may feel like a punch in the gut. You may find so many awkward paragraphs and glaring improbabilities that you decide to leave the writing profession altogether. However, if you've allowed yourself enough time away from the piece, and if you prepare yourself for the encounter in advance, revisiting your first draft needn't be traumatic. It may actually feel like coming home.

Reserve a stretch of time for this first read. In order to assess the story as a whole, you need to be able to read the entire story in one sitting. If you absolutely must divide up the reading time, I suggest skimming the first act, stopping, and then skimming the second and third acts together. The second act is traditionally where your problems arise, so it's important to read that as a unit. Oh, and before you do, unplug the phone and close the door.

The first thing that you'll need is a pen of some distinguishing color. If you prefer to revise on the computer itself, use the revision marks feature or change the color of the type so that you can see your edits. I advise printing a hard copy, though. Flipping between pages is less cumbersome than scrolling through the screen. You may want to rearrange the order of scenes or read scenes side by side, and you're going to hand the draft to another reader fairly soon. How are you going to do all that without a hard copy?

After you've chosen a pen, consider how you're going to use it. Every writer devises a set of revision symbols, those chicken scratches in the margins that scream, "Hey you! Come back to this section later." This first read is technical, so the symbols that you choose will delineate the following details:

- ✔ Misspellings
- ✔ Grammatical errors
- ✔ Formatting trouble
- ✔ Awkward description or exposition
- ✔ Unanswered plot questions
- ✔ Character inconsistencies
- ✔ Implausibility
- ✔ Excessive dialogue, or dialogue that is too "on the nose" or direct

Of that list, misspellings, grammar, and formatting are the easiest to correct. If you can fix them quickly as you go, be my guest. The last four items on the list require a rewrite, and I advise you to simply mark those sections and move on. This first read is your chance to sense the story as a complete entity, to determine where it picks up momentum and where it falls flat. Pausing that process to rework a scene defeats the purpose. You'll have time for that later.

Some writers keep lists as they read. When they stumble upon clumsy dialogue or a bland character voice, they mark the page number on one list. On another list, they keep track of pivotal questions the draft raises and double-check later to see whether those questions find answers. And the final list is reserved for consistency and plausibility concerns.

When you realize that your main character spends the first act afraid of heights and the second act leaping across the tops of buildings, you have a consistency problem. If the protagonist runs into the barn crawling with spiders in *Arachnophobia* right away, this action would be inconsistent with his fear of those insects. When your main character, who's never left her house, drives the getaway car in scene five, you have a scene implausibility.

Here's a quick way to determine the difference between consistency and plausibility problems:

- ✔ If your character *would* never do something that she does, you have a consistency problem.
- ✔ If your character *could* never do something that she does, you have a plausibility problem.

The final symbol is for clear, well-written drama. Even the worst drafts harbor cinematic gems. Odds are that you've done something right. Circle it, star it, flag the page, whatever. If there's something that you want to keep, find a way to remind yourself later, or you're likely to rewrite it along with everything else. You'll enjoy the comfort that those triumphs provide when you're wading through all the other not-quite-so-brilliant scenes ahead.

A second glance: Read-through #2

You probably don't know this (we've never met, after all), but I have Aristotle's *Poetics* taped to my computer screen. They're that important to my writing. I outline Aristotle's *Poetics* in Chapter 5. You can refer to that chapter to get the full scoop, but in a nutshell, they're the building blocks of a story. Aristotle's *Poetics* can help you devise backstory, prioritize exposition, generate action, and, yes, even help you revise. I list each Poetic here as well, so you copy them down and carry them with you, too. They are plot, character, thought, spectacle, diction, and music.

In the rewriting process, each element on the *Poetics* list becomes a lens through which to view the draft. One lens enables you to isolate action, another lens highlights character shifts, still another focuses your attention on language, and so on. The first revision is technical and should move quickly. The second revision takes longer. In this stage, you trace the movement of each dramatic component through the entire text. In medical terms, these are preliminary tests you run before offering a diagnosis.

Deconstructing plot

Most first drafts suffer from flashes of plot frailty. I say flashes of frailty, not frailty in general, and therein lies the problem. If your entire plot is weak, the solution is simple — start over. But chances are your whole plot isn't weak; moments of it are. Certain actions feel unsubstantiated. Something's missing from the final scene. You can feel the story falter, but do you know *why* it falters? Can you locate the source of the trouble?

You can't fix a script unless you know what's broken. For this reason, I usually begin my second round of revisions by tracking the action. Remember that plot is a series of actions, and actions spark other actions. That cause and effect relationship can be traced, and more often than not, the resulting outline reveals over half of what needs to be changed. Here's how you begin:

1. **Number your scenes.**

    Don't bother adding these numbers to your format; a director will do that in a later draft. Number them in pencil for revision purposes.

2. **Move from beginning to end, hunting for actions.**

3. **Jot each action down under the appropriate scene number.**

4. **Find the result of each action in ensuing scenes; record those results below the original action.**

5. **Also below the action, write the number of the scene where its result occurs.**

For example, suppose that your main character robs a business in scene one. This robbery results in the closing of that store, the death of its owner, and another robbery years later. Your outline for that action will look like this:

Scene 1

Action: Dennis robs the local five-and-dime. A boy witnesses the crime.

Result: The store is forced to close. (Scene 3)
The owner passes away. (Scene 6)
The boy robs a bank years later. (Scene 22)

These results will probably spur further actions. When that happens, rerecord them in the same way. If Dennis realizes that he's responsible for the second robbery and decides to end his wicked ways, that action will look like this:

Scene 22

Action: The young boy robs a bank.

Result: Dennis realizes that this robbery is partially his fault, and he seeks out a job in law enforcement. (Scene 24)

This process may seem tedious, but after a few scenes, it moves quickly. And take the time you need; it's important to be precise. If you plant an action that never pays off, this outline can tell you that. If your plot has a hole, this outline can tell you where. You may know what the result of an action should be but find that the payoff scene never occurs. The action outline is invaluable. It's like the red arrow on the map that says, "You are here," and then proceeds to mark all locations that you need to hit before you leave. The outline is your revision roadmap.

Character makeovers

Dull or inconsistent characters are the next most common script ailment. In the first-draft dash to capture the plot of a story, many writers neglect the players. That's to be expected. Fix them now. Here's how:

1. **List your main characters on a separate sheet of paper.**

2. **Reread the first act and the third act, assessing each character.**

3. **Make a list of each character's physical and emotional qualities prior to Plot Point I.**

4. **Make a list of each character's physical and emotional qualities after Plot Point II.**

5. **Compare the lists.**

These inventories represent the beginning and the end of your character's *arc,* or her transformation. Act II takes her from one point to the other. If you compare the lists and find that your character changes in a plausible way, congratulations. That's one less rewrite. However, most writers discover one of the following complications:

✔ The character doesn't change.

✔ The character changes completely.

✔ The character's change is not plausible or inconsistent.

✔ The character hasn't learned anything new.

✔ The character is inconsistent.

Your action outline may troubleshoot some of these character complications. Characters often seem inconsistent because scenes supporting their transformation are missing. The fact that the protagonist in ***Arachnophobia*** is afraid of spiders in Act I but battles a barn full of them in Act III seems inconsistent. However, scenes in Act II justify the change. Characters are only inconsistent if they change without explanation. In other words, I have to see it to believe it. Use the outline to check Act II for those crucial transition scenes. If your character doesn't change at all, restructure her arc. Something about her should flourish, and something should fade.

Alas, an action outline can't fix everything. You know the phrase "Some things don't change"? That's true of characters. People don't reshape their entire lives; it's unrealistic. A timid person may perform a courageous act, but he's probably not ready to become the next superhero. The traits that a character most wants to change in herself are often what make her unique. In *Kissing Jessica Stein*, Jessica becomes more open-minded and approachable after dating women, but she's still stubborn, overly organized, and neurotic. These traits make her Jessica Stein. Character changes are essential, but don't kill the good stuff in your quest to revamp the bad.

Here are some final techniques for identifying character rewrites.

- **Revisit your backstory.** Backstory refers to details and events you imagine took place prior to your first scene. Backstory includes all the research that made it possible to write your story. Although revealing all these details to an audience isn't necessary, they often add flavor and dimension to your characters. For example, the fact that Captain Quint in *Jaws* has hundreds of shark jaws hanging in his shop is an exciting but unnecessary detail. The writers include it to further illustrate his obsession with the hunt. You may have such details in your backstory that are waiting to be incorporated into the action. Now is a good time to revisit the information that you came up with prior to writing a draft.

- **Trace your character's skills and opportunities.** Two things commonly result in contrived action. First, a character suddenly exhibits skills that just happen to push the plot forward. Second, a character's original skills just happen to solve every conflict that she encounters. Notice the repetition of the phrase "just happen to"? When things "just happen to" work out in a script, the conflict slips away. It's too convenient, it's unrealistic, and it's too darn easy. Here's how you fix it:

  - Create a conflict that requires a new skill or a new plan.

  - Make sure that your character begins the journey with a reasonable list of skills. (They may be superhero skills, but limit the list.)

  - Create scenes that require the skills of another individual.

  Try not to give your character talents simply to solve a problem. Real people in real trouble — that's your goal.

- **Strengthen your antagonist.** If your character feels flat or simplistic, reinvestigate what she's up against. In theory, the obstacles that a character faces should exceed her ability to overcome them. Audiences want your character to survive in spite of the odds against her. If your villain is too easily defeated, your action will seem unimportant.

- **Mix and match your characters.** Look at your cast of characters. Have you placed each character together in scene? Introducing your villain to your protagonist's best friend may not make sense, but then again, maybe it does. Even if you decide against a pairing, it never hurts to consider it.

Giving it a thought

Thought is the theme or the argument of your script. What are you trying to communicate? Why did you write this story in place of others? Many films are thoughtless, and I don't mean inconsiderate. Action-adventures are often written for entertainment purposes alone. The **Mission Impossible** films are fast-paced and fun, but what do they really communicate? Many of the James Bond movies are written to raise the collective pulse of an audience and little else. Comedies often fall into this category as well. Look at **Airplane** and the **Naked Gun** series. What's the point? Entertainment is the point.

Nothing's wrong with this type of movie, but most first-time screenwriters have a point, thank goodness. They have an opinion, a belief, and, most importantly, a question that they want to explore on the screen. If you want your movie to have a purpose, glance through your draft with the following questions in mind:

- ✔ Which characters share your beliefs?
- ✔ Which characters oppose your beliefs?
- ✔ Have you given them opportunities to actively share their views?
- ✔ Are their arguments clear?
- ✔ Have you portrayed both sides of the argument?

Every smart lawyer knows that, in order to win a case, you have to understand the opposing counsel's argument. The same is true with thematic structure. You have something you want to say — fantastic. You have something you fervently believe — better yet. However, a script shouldn't become a vehicle to brainwash an audience into agreeing with you. A script lets you craft scenes in such a way that an audience understands your point of view. Whether they believe it or not is up to them. Great drama doesn't preach — it persuades, it seduces, it explores, and most importantly, it asks. Controversy works in film. Nobody likes to be told what to think.

If you want to write about substance abuse, you should understand substance abusers. If you despise politicians, you still have to understand the crazy world of politics. In other words, you have to know the opposing arguments in order to refute them. Check your work. Are you asking a question or pushing a belief? Have you crafted people who believe differently than yourself and, more importantly, have you crafted them with equal vigor? If you don't at least hint at a choice between points of view, you're not crafting drama. You're writing a public service announcement.

Re-envisioning your visuals

Spectacle refers to the images in your piece that elicit a palpable response from your audience. They shock, they arouse, they frighten, they delight, and the strongest examples help an audience to better understand the story. Because all cinematic scenes rely on moving pictures, you can easily forget that some images are more compelling than others. As you revise, look for the two kinds of spectacles that may enhance your action:

- **One-time spectacle:** These images crop up once in a film to liven it up, to cap an action, or to provide work for the special effects department. The helicopter chase in *Outbreak,* the first kiss in *When Harry Met Sally,* the fires in *Gone with the Wind* — these are prime examples of one-time spectacle. They catch your eye and then your breath.

- **Recurring spectacle:** These images crop up periodically as reminders of some theme. The film *Chocolat* is about two people who move from town to town, leaving when the winds return. When they finally settle into a home, the writers craft images to remind them of life on the road. A band of gypsies comes to town in a boat that's always ready to leave port. The winds return periodically. Shots of the woman's suitcase suggests that she could leave any minute. These images vary in form and dramatic weight, but they serve as reminders of theme.

Recomposing the score

Music and diction problems generally result in awkward dialogue, flat character voice, and generic locations. The good news is that they're easy to find and fun to fix. A few simple tests reveal the moments that need help.

- **Compare the length and look of character dialogue.** If you glance through a scene and discover that every character speaks in three-line sentences, you've got a problem. If every character ends sentences with an exclamation point, you've got a problem. If I can't identify the speaker by the words that he uses, you've got a problem. These are indications that your characters suffer from similar voice. Rework their diction so that they sound distinct.

- **Reconsider location.** Scenic location shouldn't be an arbitrary choice; it's too important. A location affects the way a character speaks and behaves, as well as how the audience views that character's actions. Suppose that your character is incredibly crude. Imagine that character in a church or a library. Your scene suddenly becomes awkward or funny. If someone tells a character to grow up while standing in the middle of a kindergarten classroom, the scene is suddenly ironic. Make sure that you've chosen all your locations for a reason and then double-check that they affect how the characters behave.

- **Consider intent and emotion.** Sometimes, dialogue falters because the characters forget their goals. Characters base their tactics on what they want from the other person. Those tactics, in turn, affect dialogue and behavior. Consider how your character feels about the situation she's in. Those emotions might also underscore the action. If your character is frightened, make sure that the rhythm of the scene (dialogue included) suggests this fright.

The best writers aren't necessarily those who craft the finest first drafts. They're the writers who know instinctively what to rewrite. They've adapted an ear for awkward and an eye for excess. The more you write, the better you become at sensing which portions of your first draft require attention and how you might administer help. For now, consider the preceding revision tips as places to begin when you don't know where to begin.

Back in the Saddle Again: Rewrites

You've read through your script once, twice, perhaps many times over, and you have a list of things to fix. What's that? You have an entire scroll of things to fix? That's all right. Think of this time as an opportunity to make your script better. Yeah, that's it. It's an *opportunity.*

Rewrites are daunting — that's all there is to it. You have to be critical, you have to be cruel, and you have to memorize phrases like "It's for the good of the script" because the first thing you have to do is cut. If you have more than 120 pages of script, cut one-fourth of it. That means cutting 30 pages or so. If you have fewer than 120 pages, cut 10 percent. Be strict about this cutting; 30 pages is 30 pages. You can reach that goal by cutting lines here and there, or you can eliminate entire scenes. It's up to you. While you're script should ultimately run between 90–120 pages, cutting these pages now forces you to discover what's truly important to your story. You can always reinstate material later, but cut it for now.

Cutting poorly written text is a breeze; you'll hum as you push delete. However, you'll also encounter magnificent speeches, witty repartee, and dazzling images. And guess what? You're going to have to cut some of them, too, or put them aside for a future script. Good isn't the same as necessary.

How do you know what should stay and what should go? Ask yourself why you want to keep it. The following arguments are *not* convincing:

- ✔ I like it.
- ✔ It sounds good.
- ✔ My friends like it.
- ✔ It worked in that other film.

If any or all of these excuses serve as your only reasoning, the section should probably go. However, the next arguments may suggest otherwise:

- ✔ It sets up crucial information.
- ✔ It expresses character.
- ✔ It supports another scene.
- ✔ I know that it means something.

If these arguments apply to the section in question, consider before you hit delete, especially the last phrase. Your first instinct on a rewrite is often correct. If you know that a section means something, don't cut it just because you can't verbalize what that something is. Live with it until you know.

After you cut, tackle the problems that you discovered in your first and second read-throughs. Generally, writers move scene by scene, so I include a final list of questions that can help guide you through those revisions.

- Where did the characters just come from? Where are they going next?
- How much time has elapsed since the last scene? What's happened in that time, and how does an audience know?
- What do your characters want in the scene? Is that goal clear?
- What tactics do they use to achieve that goal?
- What's the obstacle in the scene?
- What is your character's relationship to other people in the scene?
- Who's in control of the scene? When does that change?
- Could this scene really occur this way?
- What changes occur over the course of the scene?
- What happens as a result of this scene?
- If you had to cut one element, what would it be?
- What's your argument for keeping that element in?
- Can you combine this scene with another one and get the same effect?

Hopefully, one or two of these questions can help you. You may discover that you have several scenes left to write. If you've cut the necessary pages prior to the revision, you'll have room to accommodate those new scenes. Rewrites have no time frame. Some writers locate all the problematic text and rewrite quickly thereafter. Others move chronologically, revising each scene as a unit before moving on to the next. How you do it is up to you. Take the time that you need to get it right because the next step is out of your hands.

Finding a Reader

Some writers write with a specific reader in mind. This reader is your first target audience. You want that person to laugh, cry, or gasp in certain spots, so you craft scenes that (hopefully) elicit that response. This system is a smart one, and it tends to produce reliable drama because it keeps you focused on an audience. If you have such a person in mind, great. Hand her a copy of your script right now. If you don't, start searching for a reader.

Honesty is your top priority in this search. Your readers must care enough about you and/or your script to give you an honest critique. Therefore, try to avoid the following readers:

- Anyone who's afraid of hurting your feelings
- Anyone who believes that you can do no wrong
- Anyone whom you consider to be direct competition
- Anyone whom you indiscreetly based a character on

These people have a bias that may get in the way of an honest read. You can show it to them after you've crafted a polished draft. The following people, however, make excellent second-draft readers:

- **Someone who's supportive of your craft:** Family members and friends make strong readers if — and this is a big if — they are capable of mixing criticism with compliments. Also, family members are notorious for recognizing themselves in the work. If you're even slightly worried that this may be the case, hand the script to someone else.

- **Someone who's brutally honest:** The truth is often hard to take, but truth couched in false praise is worse. Find someone who will tell you what he thinks about your script without pause or ornamentation. Then, force yourself to listen.

- **The perfect target audience:** Film companies poll their target audiences by screening the film prior to the final cut. If you find a reader who exemplifies your target audience, you can do the same thing in advance.

- **The antithesis of your target audience:** Find someone who you think would never go see your film. Your instinct may be right; that person may hate it. But that person also may surprise you. And her commentary may prepare you for future reviews.

- **A film virgin:** People who know nothing about movies let alone the writing craft are the best readers. They'll be the first to tell you when something doesn't make sense, and they'll pick up on details directing their attention away from the story. If you know someone like this, enlist them at all costs.

- **A film buff:** Film aficionados are fun readers. They'll tell you if your film's already been made, and they're familiar with your lingo and your form. Better yet, they have high expectations. If your film doesn't match up, they'll be sure to tell you why.

As you can see, the credentials of these readers vary, and so, therefore, will their feedback. It's important to enlist several readers at once, so print three or four copies of your new draft and pick up the phone.

Your Critique: Surviving the Aftermath

The jury is back, and the verdict is in. As you listen to your reader's feedback, at some point, you'll want to scream. You may also want to run, crawl under the couch, or melt into the floor. Don't do any of these things. Nod and smile and listen. Remember, this critique hurts, but it will help you develop a critical tool — the writer's filter.

Every writer needs an internal filter to help sift through all the criticism that she receives. The filter works in two ways: It listens for criticism that seems to make sense for one reason or another, and it filters out the rest. How does it know what to take seriously? It uses the following criteria.

It remembers

- Any criticism that it hears more than once
- Anything deemed confusing or unclear
- Anything that you suspected was problematic prior to the reading
- Anything that elicited a surprising or unintentional response
- Anything that supports your original intention

It forgets

- Anything deemed "bad" or "good" without explanation
- Any comments that differ among the majority of readers
- Pretty much everything else

The best criticism reflects the script back to you. Sometimes, the comments "I liked it" or "I hated it" are important, but they rarely help you revise. You need to know what the reader saw, what he heard, what he took away from the script in as much detail as he can muster. Those comments help you determine what to change completely and what to bolster. Remember that you're the one sitting at a computer or a notebook every day. You sit with these characters for hours at a stretch. You're the only person who really knows the script and what it wants to explore. Although criticism is usually given with the best intentions, that doesn't mean that it's all worthwhile.

Chapter 18

Adaptation and Collaboration: Two Alternate Ways to Work

So you've found a story; it just landed in your lap. It has well-developed characters, plot twists galore, style, wit, emotion, and a theme to pull them all together. You only have one problem: Your story already exists in a different form. It's a novel, a stage play, a poem, an article, a song; the point is, it's not your story, and it's not your form. Or is it?

If you're at this crossroads, now is the time to consider *adaptation*. By adaptation, I mean taking that story from its original medium and transforming it into a film. Some writers find this process exhilarating and infinitely simpler than devising a script from the ground up. However, adaptation requires a knowledge of and a respect for many different kinds of writing, and this sensibility often takes years to develop. For this reason, many people choose to collaborate with a writing partner, dividing the tasks and bouncing ideas back and forth. This chapter illustrates the challenges and advantages of the adaptation process and provides tips for how to proceed after you've found the story of your dreams. It also offers suggestions for writing with another artist, should the need or the desire arise.

Acquiring Rights to Primary Material

Before you go to all the trouble of *adapting* any original material into a film, you'll want to secure the rights to it. Trust me, there's nothing more heartbreaking than spending months writing a draft only to discover that you're not allowed to market the film because someone else owns the original story. And it's safe to assume that someone does or did own the original story, so the following sections take a look at how you might garner permission to use it.

Understanding copyrights

Even if you've never written anything to conclusion, my guess is you're familiar with copyrights. The symbol © shows up in most literary works, and it means that property is owned by the author or the author's estate. Once you determine which work you'd like to adapt, that copyright date is the first thing to look for. The date is how you'll know if the material is something you must purchase, or if it's in the public domain.

The term *public domain* refers to materials with expired copyrights or those ineligible for copyrights. These materials, also sometimes called *intellectual property,* aren't owned or controlled by anyone. Screenwriters can therefore adapt those stories in any way they see fit without fear of arbitration. Jane Austen and Charles Dickens are examples of writers who's work is in the public domain and often adapted into film.

Copyright laws change periodically, so it's always best to do some research of your own. However, the public domain dates currently follow this logic:

- ✔ **Works published prior to 1923:** These works are in the public domain

- ✔ **Works published between 1923–1978:** The writers (or their estates) own these works for 28 years past the publication date. They may renew that copyright for up to 67 years, or the works fall into the public domain.

- ✔ **Works published between 1978–1989:** The writers (or their estates) own these works for 95 years past the publication date.

- ✔ **Works published after 1989:** The writers (or their estates) own these works while the writer is alive, and for 70 years thereafter.

To find out whether a copyright has been renewed, you'll need to do a record search at the U.S. Copyright office. Often, you can do this search online at www.copyright.gov.

Obtaining permission

Should the work you're after not fall into the public domain, you'll need to obtain the rights. Here are some things to consider before doing so:

- ✔ How much of the primary material do you anticipate using?

- ✔ How long do you think it will take you to adapt?

- ✔ How much money are you willing to spend up front and in general?

If you're simply inspired by an idea or plot point from the original work, you may not need rights at all. Ideas are not copyrightable, nor are individual events.

If you're planning on adapting the plot structure or the characters, however, you'll want to contact your selection's owner. I suggest approaching the author first, if possible. Authors tend to fancy the idea of their work as a film, and they may be more open to contract terms and financing. If it's not possible to approach the author, try the publisher instead. Start by visiting the publisher's Web site. Some publishers provide online permission forms, which may give you a sense of what kind of negotiation you're in for.

The final steps include contracts and financing. If you have an agent, this sort of haggling is his job. If you don't have an agent, you should speak to a lawyer prior to negotiation. The general contract for rights acquisition is called a *Literary Property Agreement.* This contract delineates whether you're buying the material outright, in which case you pay one sum for control of the piece indefinitely, or whether you're optioning the material.

In an *optioning agreement,* a writer purchases the right to consider the primary material for a specified amount of time. If the writer fails to pay the remaining fee in the time allotted, all rights revert back to the original owner of the material. This agreement is temporary; it allows the writer time to attempt an adaptation before final purchase, as well as time to raise enough money for the full rights. It's a little like putting a book on hold at the library, except you're paying for the right to do so. Optioning agreements generally last from 6 months to 2 years.

There's no way to predict how much you'll be spending in either scenario, and acquiring rights can be a long and arduous process. However, adapting the material into a film may also be a long and arduous process.

Your primary concern when acquiring rights of any kind is to acquire them from the right person. Authors may not own the rights to their own stories — sometimes those rights belong to the publisher. If the writer is no longer living, an estate may control that work. After you identify who owns the material, work with an attorney to draft a contract that states as much. That contract is the only legal way to be certain all the rights to the material are being turned over to you, temporarily or otherwise.

Determining how much to adapt

Screenwriters rarely adapt their entire source material for the screen. Usually, they drop whole plotlines and characters. Sometimes all that remains of the source material when it reaches the screen is the mood it inspired in the writer. After you've acquired rights, it's yours to do with as you please. Consider which of the following types of adaptations you expect to pen:

✔ **Based on:** This type is the most thorough. The film follows the original characters and most, if not all, of the original plot. The art of such an adaptation lies in converting the story into moving pictures. The *Lord of the Rings* trilogy and *Cold Mountain* are examples of films that are *based on* fiction. These scripts adhere very closely to the original stories.

✔ **Adapted from:** In this type of adaptation, the source material is recognizable, but liberties (sometimes grand ones) have been taken. *Cider House Rules,* for example, was adapted by John Irving who also wrote the novel. In translating that book to screen, Irving rearranged and dropped large sections of it, including the primary female role. *No Country For Old Men* was adapted from the Cormack McCarthy novel, and while the plot is recognizable, the film drops most of the dialogue and condenses the third-person narrative to a few lines here and there.

✔ **Inspired by:** Films that are *inspired by* a source material are under little to no obligation to adhere to it. *The Cat In The Hat,* for example, is a movie based on the short story by Doctor Seuss. The characters are lifted from that book and the style, but the events are mostly made up. You may see the term inspired by next to films that draw from real-life events. Both *Texas Chainsaw Massacre* and *Psycho* were inspired by the same real-life serial killer, Ed Gein, who murdered several people in the 1950s. However, Gein did not use a chainsaw, and he did not run a hotel. The writer of *Texas Chainsaw Massacre* lifted the location and description of Gein's house. The writers of *Psycho* lifted Gein's obsession with his dead mother. The rest of those films are entirely original.

Again, unless it's so stipulated in your rights agreement, you're under no obligation to use the primary material if you don't want to. If you feel strongly about its content, then perhaps the first form of adaptation is for you. If you're struck by one image or line, perhaps the last form is what you're after. That material is simply there as a springboard for your film.

Navigating between Forms

I'm a firm believer that stories seek the form that best expresses their narrative content. In other words, if *The Cider House Rules* had wanted to be a film first, it would've been a film first. It didn't. It wanted to be a novel by John Irving. Does that mean that crafting a screenplay from a work of fiction is wrong? No. It means that you'll have to change that work of fiction into a different kind of story, a kind of story that's best expressed cinematically. Let me repeat that first bit — you'll have to *change* the work.

Every literary form is structurally unique and has its own advantages and limitations. Fiction and poetry invite scenic description where plays and film invite physical action, for example. In order to write the film version of a poem then, you have to know what makes a poem structurally different from a film and change the story accordingly. (For details on the specific elements of different and artistic forms, refer to Chapter 2.) Now's the time to consider how the structure of the original source might mold your eventual screenplay.

From fiction to film

Fiction is the medium most often adapted into film. *The Cider House Rules, Gone with the Wind, Jaws, Lord of the Rings, Silence of the Lambs,* and every John Grisham piece are just a few examples of adapted novels. Several writers have successfully converted short stories as well. The movie **Stand By Me,** for example, is based on a piece by Stephen King called "The Body."

With such a long list, you may think that jumping between these forms is simple, and it can be. After all, characters, events, and dialogue are already in place for you to utilize. However, more often than not, the success of a film adaptation is a result of how the writer chooses to work around cinematically troubling aspects of the original form. The following sections describe techniques specific to fiction along with potential ways to approach them in film.

Description

Novelists describe everything in detail, from the location to the characters' physical conditions to their thoughts. Henry James spends more than 20 pages depicting Isabel Archer's daydream in *Portrait of a Lady,* for goodness sake. The sheer amount of physical and psychological detail can be both a benefit and a boon to the screenwriter, who must capture the essence of important description through image, dialogue, or action. I include the pros and cons of fictional description to further prepare you for the adaptation process.

Pros: Description clearly conveys

- ✔ A detailed sense of location, atmosphere, and person.
- ✔ A complete *backstory* (everything that you imagine takes place prior to your story's beginning).
- ✔ The composition of key images.
- ✔ Metaphors and allegories that link scenes together.

Cons: Description may be challenging because

- ✔ What occurs in a chapter can take seconds of screen time.
- ✔ What fiction depicts in a sentence may require several scenes on-screen.
- ✔ Details in abundance may quickly become overwhelming.

Adapt description on-screen by

- ✔ Condensing several characters into one.
- ✔ Condensing several events into one scene.
- ✔ Choosing one or two protagonists to follow, eliminating characters that don't support their journey.
- ✔ Suggesting metaphor by revisiting an image several times.

Internal and external worlds

Novels move between physical and psychological action in a sentence or two. In other words, fiction takes place inside and outside a character's mind. Fiction writers call this technique *narrative movement,* and again, it can both help and a hinder a screenwriter. Because cinema relies on what a writer can translate into image and action, narrative movement poses the following pros and cons to the world of screenwriting:

Pros: Narrative movement provides

- ✔ A complete psychological and physical profile of each character.
- ✔ Each character's opinion or take on what they witness.
- ✔ A sense of how, when, and why characters move into and out of thought.

Cons: Narrative movement may be challenging because

- ✔ Films primarily dwell in the external world of action.
- ✔ The number of memories and daydreams may become overwhelming.
- ✔ Characters usually harbor thoughts and beliefs that they wouldn't readily discuss with another character or the audience.

Adapt narrative movement on-screen by

- ✔ Condensing and eliminating reveries.
- ✔ Creating active scenes that suggest a character's thoughts and fears.
- ✔ Dramatizing key moments in the backstory that suggest what a character might be feeling in the present.
- ✔ Creating a pace between scenes that mimics the pace between internal and external worlds in the novel.

Narrative voice

Fiction relies as much on the story's speaker as it does on the characters themselves. The narrator may or may not have a personal investment in the events. He may be omniscient or restricted to certain knowledge. He may be trustworthy or unreliable. The narrator sometimes changes from section to section, as different people tell the same story. Unless a screenwriter allows a character to directly address the audience, as in ***Ferris Bueller's Day Off,*** she'll have to find alternate ways to convey the narrative voice.

Pros: Narrative voice provides

- An opinion or judgment of specific events.
- A suggestion of events in the future.
- A context and/or reason for telling the story.

Cons: Narrative voice may be problematic because

- The narrator's information may be difficult to dramatize.
- Without a narrator, the tone of the piece may be lost.
- The narrative voice provides texture that general scenes may not.

Adapt narrative voice on-screen by

- Eliminating the narrator altogether.
- Distributing the voice among other characters.
- Creating a new character to embody that voice.
- Transferring the sense of the narrator to the film's style.

From stage to screen

Marvin's Room, Steel Magnolias, On Golden Pond, Glengarry Glen Ross, and ***Who's Afraid of Virginia Woolf?*** are just a few stage plays to make it onto the big screen. In film adaptation, stage plays present their own set of benefits and complications. The following list touches upon a few of each.

Dialogue

In the past, stage plays relied on dialogue to convey everything from backstory to character to mood. Nowadays, plays are becoming more physical in nature, but they still place great importance on language. Screenwriters may transfer some of the dialogue directly into their scripts, but many of the dramatist's words must become moving pictures. How do you know which words to keep and which to transform? Consider these dialogue suggestions.

Pros: Stage dialogue provides

- Strong sense of character voice.
- Rhythm for each character and the piece overall.
- Suggested backstory and theme.

Cons: Stage dialogue often

- ✔ Impedes the screenwriter's ability to concentrate on image.
- ✔ Suggests too many or too few events to convey on film.

Adapt stage dialogue by

- ✔ Turning references of past events into visual scenes.
- ✔ Transferring the character's vocal pattern into a physical pattern.
- ✔ Restructuring events so that they take place in a new chronology.
- ✔ Maintaining key dialogue moments and crafting images around them.

Character and location limitations

Unlike film, which jumps between any number of places and eras, most plays concentrate on a handful of locations, if not on one alone. The same rule applies to the number of characters in each medium. Films use extras to create the most realistic environment possible; plays rely on lights, sound, and their main characters to provide that environment. These limitations sometimes stem from budgetary concerns, but they tend to have artistic reasons as well. In film, location is usually a backdrop. In theater, it's a competing force. And more characters in a play means less time spent on any one journey. The detailed locations of a play will certainly help a screenwriter, but the limited number will not. While you'll need to condense the material in fiction, in stage plays you generally need to expand. Consider the following suggestions when transferring locations from stage to screen.

Pros: Location and character restrictions provide

- ✔ A strong sense of protagonist and the protagonist's journey.
- ✔ Clearly defined goals for all the characters involved.
- ✔ Enough time to detail an environment and its ensuing mood.

Cons: Location and character restrictions

- ✔ Do not often suggest the realistic setting a screenwriter desires.
- ✔ Limit the number of settings, which can become static on-screen.
- ✔ Limit the drama to the scope of a few characters.

Adapt these limitations to film by

- ✔ Discovering other places and/or times for the scenes to occur.
- ✔ Considering all characters referenced in the play as possible characters to dramatize on-screen.

✔ Creating characters that aren't suggested but might exist in this world.

✔ Exploring parts of the primary locations referenced in a play but never shown — script scenes in all rooms of the main house, for example.

Poetry and music

If poetry and music share anything in common with film, it's a fondness for image and mood. Poetry is condensed into several strong pictures that drive the rest of the piece. Music creates a sensual world through rhythm and melody. While these mediums rarely inspire an entire plot, they can easily become a source of inspiration for a filmmaker. Cinematic strengths and weaknesses for these forms include the following.

Pros: Music and poetry provide

✔ A set of clearly composed images to work from.

✔ Universal metaphors that may speak to a film's theme.

✔ A suggested rhythm and style for the eventual piece.

Cons: Music and poetry are

✔ Fleeting in nature.

✔ Often highly allegorical and, therefore, subjective.

✔ Driven by emotion instead of event.

Adapt music and poetry to film by

✔ Finding possible narratives hidden within the piece and work from there.

✔ Uncovering the historical background of the piece and dramatizing it.

✔ Using the mood of each piece as a backdrop for a different film.

✔ Using one or two choice phrases as a starting point for an entire film.

In any adaptation, you're searching for the essence of the original form. Remaining true to every aspect of the source is not necessary. In fact, screenplays that try to maintain every aspect of a story tend to fail. Why? You're not re-creating a primary source — you're creating a film, which is a new story with a language of its own. What caught your fancy? What about the story is unique? What aspects of the piece are vital to understanding the narrative? If you can answer those questions, you're ready to begin.

The Process of Adaptation

I often tell students that adapting a work is like a different kind of magic with roughly the same spell. You're creating an original piece — this one just happens to be based on something else. The work you're adapting may suggest a setting, characters, or a theme; it may give you a blueprint for the action. But it's still just a source.

How to approach an original work

With any adaptation, writers are scanning the original piece for two things: character and plot. Occasionally, a theme becomes the backbone of your film, but generally, the *who* and the *what* take precedence. You can move from one medium to another in three primary ways:

✔ **Follow the form.** Take everything that you can from the original piece — character transformations, locations, tone. Turn them into action or image and begin.

✔ **Work from key scenes.** The scenes that strike your fancy may or may not be pivotal moments in the text. Pinpoint the moments that speak to you, rearrange them as necessary, and write what comes in between.

✔ **Use the story as a launching point.** Often, a single character, line, or action jumps out at you. Spin your drama upon that one piece.

If you enjoy complete creative freedom, you'll probably choose the third method. If you crave structure, the first one will be a better match. However, don't be surprised if the original source suggests a way to work.

After you determine which method to follow, the creation process is similar to that of an original piece. I encourage you to continue dreaming and researching and demanding more of the work. Don't assume that the information you start with is all you need. It's really only a beginning.

Here's a basic set of steps to follow in order to proceed with your adaptation:

1. **Read the original piece *at least* three times.**

   You first encounter a work in a state of naiveté. Everything is new; nothing is certain. You're left with a series of impressions and a general sense of the piece. You notice structure on a second read, and by the third read, you should know what you'd like to keep and what you could do without. By the third read, the original piece is in your bones.

2. Write an outline of pivotal scenes and actions.

Outline all key moments from the source, even if you're certain that you won't use them. You're searching for a base structure from which to work. Pay particular attention to where this story begins and ends. You may want to transfer these scenes to index cards. This process allows you to quickly rearrange, add, or remove key events as you go.

3. Make a list of all the characters.

Again, list all the characters, whether or not you intend to use them. You may need to layer their attributes onto someone else later on. Take special note of which characters are primary, secondary, and incidental. This process is particularly helpful when you want to condense several smaller characters into one larger role.

4. Reduce the story to a three- or four-line premise.

How would you pitch this story? What's the main storyline? What makes this piece exciting? If you can reduce the story to a nutshell description, you'll discover what the story is ultimately about.

5. Determine the question, concept, or point of view.

Why was this story written? What does it demand of a reader? Asking these questions helps maintain the integrity of the original piece.

6. Find the holes.

What is not dramatized is often as important as what is dramatized. You may discover that the story not told is the one worth pursuing. Imagine around the original piece; you may be surprised at what you discover.

7. Choose several key moments, put them in order, and fill in the gaps.

Now's the time to choose which elements to use and arrange them in some chronology that makes sense to your film. After you have two or three key moments in place, build scenes that bridge them together.

Films are primarily concerned with image, not dialogue. As you sift through your material and identify which moments to adapt, try to convert as many of those moments as possible into moving pictures. In other words, show viewers what's important instead of telling them.

By the time you start writing, the characters may seem different from the ones that you discovered in that first read. Your plot may hinge on events that were merely suggested in the first piece. If this is the case, congratulations. You've hit upon the balance between someone else's work and your own. Best of all, if you become frustrated along the way, you can always return to the source.

What to do when you're stuck

Adaptation is a challenging and often cumbersome process. You have to strike a balance between remaining true to a source and writing your own piece. If you find yourself leaning too heavily on one side, try one or all of the following suggestions:

✔ **Imagine the story in a different time period or location.** Sometimes, viewing the action out of context helps to clarify what it's really about. What adjustments would you have to make if *Gone with the Wind,* for example, took place in 1950s Manhattan instead of in the Civil War–torn South?

✔ **Imagine the work from a different point of view.** The original piece may clearly delineate a main character, but what if you chose someone else to lead the story? What if the new protagonist was the rarely seen neighbor or the protagonist's arch rival?

✔ **Eliminate flashbacks or memories.** Flashbacks aren't forward moving; they pause the action in order to recall an event. Fiction is riddled with flashbacks. If you find yourself unsure of how to include them, try reorganizing the plot sequence so that the events occur in sequence. You may also allude to them in a scene or eliminate them entirely.

✔ **Condense and expand.** This may be your grandest challenge. If your original source is 500 pages, you're going to have to pick and choose your events, because you only have two to three hours of screen time in which to tell this story. Similarly, if you're taken with one paragraph, you'll have to imagine around it.

✔ **Determine your main characters and their goals.** Primary source material often has more characters than you know what to do with. Choose one or two protagonists and give them very specific goals. The rest of the action should revolve around helping or hindering those people in achieving their goals. In order to do so, you may have to cut secondary characters or condense several smaller roles into one.

The Art of Collaboration

Screenwriting, like playwriting, relies on collaboration. If you continue working in the field, you'll most likely collaborate with agents who sell your work, producers who buy it, and directors and actors who give voice to it on the screen. Screenwriters collaborate with everyone, including other screenwriters. Collaboration is a marriage of talent and imagination, and you should approach it with the seriousness that a marriage requires.

Writers collaborate for various reasons, but it usually begins when someone decides that it takes more than one person to write a particular story. That person then goes in search of another writer whose talents complement her own, whose knowledge and skill seem appropriate to the project, and whose schedule and connections will help the work to get done. Finding someone who fits this description is easier said than done, though.

What to look for in a writing partner

Searching for a writing partner is almost exactly like searching for a spouse. Here are a few things to look for:

- ✔ **Someone responsible whom you can trust:** Both you and your partner have your work cut out for you. Find someone who will keep her deadlines, pull her weight, and keep the project between the two of you.

- ✔ **Someone who respects your work, and someone whose work you respect:** If you don't know what your partner has written, how will you know if he's right for the project? Make sure that both of you are comfortable with the other one's interests, style, and vision.

- ✔ **Someone who has a similar concept of the project, if different reasons for pursuing it.** Eventually, you and your partner will have to agree upon a premise and a purpose for the work. Start that conversation now. If your thoughts of the work differ greatly, you may end up with two films instead of one.

- ✔ **Someone who complements your writing style and who brings different skills to the table than you provide.** It's important to share a concept of the project and to be equally invested in its creation, but you don't always have to agree. In fact, finding someone who will challenge your artistic opinions may be the best way to ensure a complex and well-developed script.

Discuss this list with your potential partner early on. You may feel bad if that person doesn't care to work with you, but you'll feel worse if you discover it halfway through the first draft.

How to approach collaboration

After you find someone to work with, the two of you need to have two discussions right off the bat. One involves the work itself, and one involves the writing process. I also strongly advise you to create a written agreement for each other before you begin writing. This agreement becomes your contract, which not only further clarifies your individual roles in the process, but is a document that you can alter and refer to as you work.

Sharing the work: Part 1

Ask and answer the following questions with your partner: What interests you about the project? What does not? Who do you believe the script is about? What do those characters want? What is the general premise of the piece? Why does this piece have to be written?

This discussion forms the foundation upon which you can write the screenplay. I ask students to pound out a mission statement of sorts, depicting what the project wants to achieve. Should egos arise later on — and they *will* arise later on — the writers have something to return to.

After you've spoken for a bit, take a stab at character biographies. Write them together or on your own and then compare. Do the same with an outline for the piece. The beginning, middle, and end may change as you write, but at least you're starting from a point of agreement. After an outline and a premise are in place, you're ready to discuss process.

Sharing the work: Part 11

You've spoken about the work as a story. Now talk about the work as work. In other words, discuss the division of labor. Within any writer's job are several tasks: research, interviews, outlines, draft work, typing, revision, the pitch, and so on. Who's going to take on what task? Be clear and divide the tasks according to your strengths and your interests. After you determine who's doing what and when, consider the following suggestions:

✓ **Decide on a schedule.** When do you like to write? When will you write on your own, and when will you write as a team? Give yourselves assignments and goals for each meeting. Finding a schedule that works for both of you will take at least a week, maybe longer.

✓ **Kill the ego.** This project is not about you. It's about the piece. When you feel the ego taking over, when you or your partner becomes overly sensitive, return to that mission statement.

✓ **Divide the work evenly.** When one person takes the lead, bitterness and resentment often follow. If one person wants the dominant role, discuss what dominant entails and devise some kind of an agreement. Remember that there was a reason you chose to collaborate in the first place.

✓ **Discuss problems as they arise.** Most creative problems occur because one partner forgets to communicate with the other.

If you've had these discussions, you're ready to start writing. As with any process, this one presents unique challenges. You and your partner *will* make mistakes. Acknowledge them and move on. You *will* become angry at each other. Talk about it and move on. You *will* reach a point where you'll want to write the script yourself. Return to your mission statement and move on. The key is to keep talking and keep working. The challenges don't stop, but the eventual rewards make it all worthwhile.

Learning from the Masters

With all this talk about the challenges of finding the right collaborative partner, I thought you might like proof that it is possible to find one. The following two duos have been collaborating successfully for years. Hopefully, you'll find inspiration in their examples.

Alexander Payne and Jim Taylor

This creative pair has made a career adapting fiction to film, and there's no indication they'll stop anytime soon. While Alexander Payne and Jim Taylor admit they don't often know their scripts' conclusions in advance, they have a writing routine that helps keep them on track. A typical writing day begins at 10 or 11 a.m. and lasts six hours. They spend much of that time talking through scenes and taking turns scripting them onto the page. They've coined the phrase "Who's driving" for the person doing the typing, and they're known for plugging two keyboards into one computer so that they can add to a scene as inspired.

Payne has said that their first drafts are generally three drafts: one draft to get all the ideas on the page, one draft to further develop those ideas, and one draft to edit and refine. Once you've written those three drafts, they maintain, you've actually completed your first. Their advice to screenwriters? Avoid writing the movie version of your story. Consider the circumstances you've set up for the characters, and then consider how a person would honestly react under those circumstances. Write from a place of what's true, not what's cinematic. Looking at their following body of work, it seems that may be good (and lucrative) advice.

- ✔ *I Now Pronounce You Chuck & Larry* (2007)
- ✔ *Sideways* (2004)
- ✔ *About Schmidt* (2002)
- ✔ *Election* (1999)
- ✔ *Citizen Ruth* (1996)

Joel and Ethan Coen

Perhaps no two collaborators are as well known as the Coen brothers. Since their critically acclaimed film *Raising Arizona* in 1987, the Coens have produced one hit after another, they're most recent success being *No Country for Old Men,* which picked up the Oscar for best film of 2007–08.

The Coen brothers are actually much more than screenwriting partners — they're *cinematic auteurs,* which means they're partners in virtually every aspect of the film's production and direction as well. They've written original screenplays (***The Big Lebowski***), adapted contemporary fiction (***No Country for Old Men***), and adapted classics like The Odyssey (***Oh Brother Where Art Thou***). They produce and direct their pictures as well.

So what's their recipe for success? First, they suggest choosing challenging material, even material that seems too difficult at the onset. This challenge helps a writer avoid becoming complacent and overly predictable. They've also said it helps to take a break from one film by concentrating on another. Their film ***Barton Fink*** was written in just three weeks while the brothers were on creative hiatus from the plot-centric ***Miller's Crossing.***

They've called their writing process fairly arbitrary and laid-back. They spend hours dreaming out loud while one person types those dreams onto the page. They often storyboard their films while writing, or upon completion of a first draft. This process helps them find the look of the film which, in turn, contributes to the language of it.

Finally, they've been known to envision actors for the roles as they write them. Perhaps this explains why they tend to work with the same people film after film. It certainly explains why their characters are so specifically rendered.

Film collaborations include

- ✐ ***Burn After Reading*** (2008)
- ✐ ***No Country for Old Men*** (2007)
- ✐ ***The Ladykillers*** (2004)
- ✐ ***The Man Who Wasn't There*** (2001)
- ✐ ***Oh Brother, Where Art Thou?*** (2000)
- ✐ ***The Big Lebowski*** (1998)
- ✐ ***Fargo*** (1996)
- ✐ ***The Hudsucker Proxy*** (1994)
- ✐ ***Barton Fink*** (1991)
- ✐ ***Miller's Crossing*** (1990)
- ✐ ***Raising Arizona*** (1987)

Part IV
Selling Your Script to Show Business

The 5th Wave — By Rich Tennant

"The margins on your script are sooo even, Ms. Holly, and the type so black and crisp. I'm sure whatever the story's about is also good, but with centered headlines and flush left columns like this, we'd be fools not to put it into production."

In this part . . .

Ah, Hollywood. The producers, the directors, the agents, the studios, the stars and, well, you. Placing yourself in the show business scene is a juggling act unto itself, and making an entrance is no small feat. This part is all about equipping yourself for the market — how to assemble a network, what to prepare in advance, and how to package the product of you. Armed with that information, you should be able to launch yourself into the industry full speed ahead. And when you get there? No worries. The last half of the part details what to do when you arrive.

Chapter 19

Before You Send It: Premarketing Considerations

Completing a revised draft is cause for celebration. Take a vacation, do something mindless, and by all means, spend as much time away from your office as possible. After all, your work is half done.

Wait a second, did I just say "half done"? But you've survived research, interviews, plot development, treatments, months of writing and revisions — is that really just *half* of the journey? Possibly. If you wrote the script for yourself, to enjoy the craft for craft's sake, you're finished right now. However, if you wrote the screenplay for an audience, then yes, you're only half done. The second half of the journey involves getting your screenplay ready for that audience, be it reader, agent, or studio executive. The time's come to consider the business.

Unlike creative work, which may begin haphazardly and fly you down several paths on your way to an idea, the next stage of the game involves immediate and thorough preparation. One of the worst things that a writer can do — to her career, to her script, and to her self-esteem — is to enter the market prematurely. In Hollywood, time is always of the essence — meetings are brief, openings limited, and attention spans short. Show business is not a business to approach ill-equipped. This chapter helps make the marketing process less intimidating and arms you with information and organizational skills for the crazy road ahead.

Understanding the "Biz" in Showbiz

You only have to glance at the opening and closing credits of any film to appreciate the number of people that it takes to complete a project. You have literary agents and their assistants, directors and assistant directors, actors, their agents, their managers, producers, production companies, and studios heads. The list reads like an Oscar acceptance speech. How on earth will you navigate between all these roles? Well, you probably won't until you know what each person is responsible for and what each person wants. So for starters, familiarize yourself with the players.

Getting to know the players: The Hollywood hierarchy

Many people in Hollywood do various jobs at various times. Actors own production companies, actors are also directors, producers may be directors, and so on. That information changes on a yearly, if not monthly, basis. So keep your eye out for new developments. The following list is designed as an overview of the kinds of roles you'll run into when selling a script:

- **Producers — the wallet:** Producers manage and financially back the production elements of your work. They oversee everything from marketing and publicity to hiring a staff for the project. Some producers fund the project themselves (executive producers); others (independent producers) may be looking for a studio to provide financial support. Producers are looking for two things from a writer: the strength of your finished screenplay and your ability to write for other projects they have in mind.

- **Directors — the eye:** Directors are in charge of completing the screenplay. By completing, I mean bringing it to life on the screen and giving it dimension. Directors make the script camera-ready, breaking each scene into specific shots with the aid of a cinematographer. They also work with the actors, sound designers, camera crew, and so on to create a unified vision for the piece. The draft of the script crafted by the director and cinematographer is called a *shooting script.* It includes storyboard notations and camera directions. Please note that these notations are the director's job, not the writer's job.

- **Actors — the true players:** These are obviously the people who star in the films. However, many actors also own production companies and may seek out new work, most often scripts with large roles for them. Though showing an actor your work is often difficult, attaching an actor to your project is always a good thing. At best, that actor pitches it for you, and it gets made; at worst, the script gains recognition.

✔ **Agents/Managers — your ticket in:** These men and women represent new talent. They send scripts to various executives, seek writing assignments for their clients, arrange the meetings, and negotiate contracts on the writer's behalf. They may act as final reader for the piece and step in should legal problems arise. They're looking for writers with talent, a good attitude, innovative ideas, and staying power. What's the difference? *Agents* work primarily with writers trying to sell and market their work. *Managers* work with writers, actors, directors, studios, producers and marketing teams to pull together entire projects. They take a higher percentage of the writer's paycheck as a result.

✔ **Studios — the big guns:** Studios, such as Warner Brothers, DreamWorks, Paramount, and so on, finance projects and provide production space and materials. In many cases, they attach producers and directors to projects they've purchased. They're interested in a worthwhile investment and scripts that fit their audience. They keep a close eye on the budget proposal and marketability of each film they consider.

This list extends far beyond the five roles that I mention here. To name just a few more, *cinematographers* help design and shoot each scene, *editors* cut the film for pace, and *sound designers* do exactly what their title suggests — design your sound. But you won't meet these people until well after the script has been purchased. People in the first five roles are the ones who may help get you in the door.

Getting to know the buyers: The studio hierarchy

When you decide it's time to sell your screenplay, studios are the companies you or your agent will be courting. However, it's a good idea to know who the main players are in advance; find out what sort of work they're producing, and how many scripts they purchase a year.

There are currently six major film production companies in Hollywood, and between them, they own most of the smaller studios. While this list will, no doubt, change as the years go on, the following companies have been around long enough to merit citation:

✔ **Paramount Motion Pictures:** Paramount is owned by Viacom and has produced such recent films as *Vanilla Sky, Mean Girls, Elizabethtown, Babel, Transformers, Cloverfield,* and the soon-to-be-released *Indiana Jones* film. The following smaller studios fall under its domain:

• Paramount Vantage (formerly Paramount Classics)

• DreamWorks SKG (co-owned by Stephen Spielberg, Jeffrey Katzenberg, and Brad Gray)

- MTV Networks (which includes MTV Films, Nickelodeon Movies, and Comedy Central Films)

✔ **Sony Pictures Entertainment:** Sony Pictures is owned by (who else?) Sony and has recently produced such films as *Marie Antoinette, Vantage Point, The Pursuit of Happyness, Monster House, Casino Royale,* and *Capote.* Sony Pictures also controls the following studios:

  - Columbia Pictures
  - TriStar Pictures
  - Sony Pictures Animation
  - MGM Studios
  - United Artists
  - Samuel Goldwyn Company

✔ **Fox Entertainment Group:** Fox Entertainment has been owned by News Corporation since 2005 when the media conglomerate purchased all the Fox Stock. Since then, the studio has produced such films as *Horton Hears a Who, The Illusionist, The Simpson Movie, Waitress, Once,* and *Little Miss Sunshine*. They also own

  - 20th Century Fox
  - Fox Searchlight

✔ **NBC Universal:** This studio is owned by General Electric's NBC and Vivendi Universal Entertainment. In recent years, it's produced *The Bourne Identity, Love Actually, King Kong, United 93, Knocked Up,* and *Charlie Wilson's War.* It also owns the following studios:

  - Universal Studios
  - Focus Features

✔ **Time Warner:** Also known as Warner Brothers Entertainment, this studio is one of the largest, and the list of movies produced could extend for pages. A few recent highlights include *The Harry Potter Movies, August Rush, I Am Legend, Michael Clayton, V for Vendetta,* and *Oceans 11, 12,* and *13.* They also own the following smaller studios:

  - Castle Rock Entertainment
  - Warner Bros Animation
  - New Line Cinema
  - HBO/HBO Films

✔ **Buena Vista Motion Pictures Group:** Perhaps you've heard of this studio. It's also known as the Walt Disney Company. While this studio is perhaps best-known for its animation, it produces mainstream films as well. The more recent include *The Sixth Sense, National Treasure, Remember the Titans,* and the *Pirates of the Caribbean* series, to name just a few. The Group also controls the following studios:

- Walt Disney Pictures (which owns Pixar Animation and Walt Disney Animation)
- Touchstone Pictures
- Miramax Films
- Hollywood Pictures

It's impossible to say any one of these studios specializes in any one sort of film. Yes, Pixar is known for its animation, and Miramax often specializes in films that sweep festivals like Sundance. However, studios are primarily interested in making money and garnering audience.

So how can this list help you? My suggestion is you look at the smaller studios on this list and watch for trends. See what films they're purchasing in any given year, and predict which studio your screenplay seems to match. By doing so, you'll also get a sense of which executives work in which studio, and whether a movie like yours has come out recently. Again, trends change, but the more you know about this side of the business, the better equipped you'll be to sell your screenplay when the time comes.

Getting a "grip": Hollywood jargon

Do you know what a *grip* is? How about a *dolly* or a *super* or a *wipe* or a *pan?* It's okay if you don't; that's the biz talking. The credo "walk the walk and talk the talk" may hold true in Hollywood, but talking the talk is often more difficult than it sounds. Business jargon or *lingo* changes annually, and it would be difficult to record every new phrase out there. So instead, I've compiled a list of terms that predominantly affect writers. Some you'll hear quite often, some are reserved for production, and some are just plain fun.

- ✔ **ADR:** This term, which stands for *additional dialogue replacement,* refers to any material added to a film after production. It may be atmosphere additions, such as crowd noises or responses to action sequences, or it may be phrases that were simply replaced.

- ✔ **The buzz:** The buzz is the "hype" around a project, or what people are saying about it. The buzz is usually a positive expression, signifying excitement over the work.

- ✔ **Coverage:** The report that a professional reader gives a new screenplay is referred to as coverage. It includes the vital stats as well as a synopsis and/or commentary on the work. It rates the strength of dialogue, characterization, plot structure, and so on. Coverage also provides a Pass or Consider rating so that the agent can quickly determine which scripts are worth a read. I cover coverage more thoroughly in the next few sections of this chapter.

- **The hook:** I've mentioned this one before, but it's so important that it bears repeating. The hook is that unique aspect of your story that immediately grabs a reader's attention. You use your hook with producers, agents, in query letters, and in marketing. It may be the major selling point of your story.

- **On-the-nose:** This phrase describes dialogue that too plainly reveals the characters' or the author's intentions. On-the-nose dialogue tells audiences what the story is about instead of allowing them to discover it.

- **Pinks:** Printing shooting-script changes on multicolored paper is a common practice. Those pages are traditionally pink, blue, and yellow — generally in that order. Pinks refers to those rewrites, as in "It was switched in the pinks." You'll probably hear them referred to as "the pinks" regardless of what color the rewrites really are.

- **The pitch:** The pitch is a concise story synopsis that you verbally sell to agents and producers. Like a movie trailer, it grabs attention, suggests a tone, and provides enough character and plot information to indicate a feature film. For more on how to pitch, see Chapter 20.

- **The polish:** A highly revised draft of your script is called the polish. It's been through several readers, workshops, and/or script analysts. It's tight, efficient, and ready for you to send out.

- **Script doctor:** A script doctor (also known as a script consultant) is someone who's hired to revise part or all of an existing screenplay. These jobs often pay well, though you may not get credit for them. These writers are also commonly referred to as *ghost writers,* as their contribution generally goes unmentioned.

- **Second-act curtain:** In a three-act screenplay, this is the moment of greatest conflict. It generally precedes or becomes the script's climax.

- **A sleeper:** A sleeper is surprise box office success. No one expects it to do as well as it does, despite a strong story or interesting concept. ***My Big Fat Greek Wedding, The Blair Witch Project,*** and ***The Sixth Sense*** are recent examples of sleeper hits.

- **Spec script:** This term refers to a script you write on your own, without being paid or asked to do so by a studio — in other words, scripts you write on the hopeful speculation that someone will purchase them later. These scripts don't include camera directions or personal commentary. Those items are reserved for a *shooting script,* which is generally composed by the director and cinematographer before production. The spec script is the script that sells you as a writer, if not the script for production.

Preparing Yourself for the Biz

Writing a screenplay involves concentrating all your efforts on the story. How do events transpire? Are you accurately depicting the characters? Is the situation plausible and clear? These questions consume countless days.

With all the attention on product, you may assume that your foremost goal in Hollywood is to sell that particular script. Luckily, that assumption's incorrect. Selling the screenplay is always an objective, but your first priority is selling yourself as a competent writer. You are the commodity here. The script may not sell for reasons that defy explanation — the story has too many characters, it's not the "right time" for a screwball comedy, another studio just purchased a talking donkey film. You can't foresee everything. But if studio executives like your work, they'll hire you for other projects. Who knows? They may even ask for a second script. Because you're the commodity, you need to prepare yourself for the market now.

Putting on a happy face: The art of attitude

Regardless of how you behave in your private life, you're going to have to don a few traits to get through the Hollywood maze. Here are a few characteristics to foster in yourself as you proceed:

- **A professional air:** There's a fine line between confident and cocky. Master the art of presenting your work with poise and assurance while remaining open to critique.

- **Enthusiasm:** You love this project, and you love this profession. Even when it drives you insane, you love it. If this isn't the case, find a way to convince yourself that it is. Enthusiasm is contagious, and nothing's more enticing than someone passionate about his work. Find a way to communicate that zeal to others.

- **Intelligence:** Knowledge is power. The more you know about your script, about the business, and about the world, the more willing people will be to hire you. You may be a novice in the business, but you certainly don't have to sound like one.

- **Patience:** Every writer wants to be read and read now. It usually takes a long time to introduce your script, let alone your name, to Hollywood and its various agents. Now may not be the right time to pitch your script, either. Frustration is understandable, but don't let it affect the quality of your work or your work ethic.

✔ **Persistence:** Rejection is a given in this profession. Disregard it and keep working. Many mediocre writers are produced because of persistence. Screenwriters build up an immunity to rejection. Don't let it stop you. Eventually, you'll catch a break.

Producers, like agents, are looking for a team player. Before you approach them, make a list of your strengths as a writer and as a person. Be specific. If you write historical dramas, call yourself a historian and list which eras you're familiar with. If you're opinionated, find a positive way to phrase that. You have a unique vision of the world or a different spin on politics, for example. Don't underestimate punctuality and organization; studios look for both. And a sense of humor never hurts, either.

You might think that maintaining a positive attitude is the easy part of the process. However, after a dozen or so rejections, even the most confident people start to doubt their abilities. Should you experience this dejection, repeat the following facts diligently to yourself. They're inspirational and better yet — they're true.

✔ Every writer begins without an agent.

✔ Every writer works for little or no pay at some point.

✔ There's a lot of bad writing out there; there's a need for great material.

✔ Only you can tell your stories.

Everything worth anything in life involves risk, fear, and struggle. This is where persistence comes in. Keep writing; success can strike at any time.

Organizing your records

Do you know which studios are looking for romantic comedies or which agent represents your favorite writer? Do you know how many thrillers were purchased last year, and, of those, how many made it into production? Do you know who to contact about submitting work to independent producers? By the time you're through with this chapter, you should be keeping several lists. Those lists serve as your network in written form and as a marketing progress report, so keep the following records updated and close by.

Your contact list

Everyone in your life is a potential contact. Don't be picky when you begin this list. You never know when someone's expertise will prove invaluable. Think about who you already know. Record the person's name, her relationship to you, any pertinent details you want to include, and her contact information. You might divide this list into two sections — those contacts who work in the film industry and those who do not. You'll consult the first section when you need help revising, marketing, or selling your script. Contacts in the second list may help you generate ideas or research a project.

The marketing list

This list includes studios, producers, directors, agents, actors, the companies they work for, and what kind of movies they purchase or accept. When you discover who represents your favorite screenwriters, include that information here. When Matt Damon and Ben Affleck request submissions for their next new film contest, include that information here. When producers switch studios or actors launch their own companies, include that information here. Consider this list to be your screenwriter's sourcebook. Each new entry should include the following:

- The person's name and position (if applicable)
- The organization he works for or represents
- Previous projects he has commissioned or purchased
- The kind of work he's recently requested
- The contact information (if you have it)

Everyone acquires this information in a variety of ways. However, the Hollywood Creative Directory (www.hcdonline.com) is a good place to start. This directory provides up-to-date Hollywood agent, manager, studio, and attorney contact information. After maintaining this list for a while, patterns begin to emerge. You'll notice what sort of story sells quickly, which screenwriters generate interest, and which genre might be ripe for revival. After all you can't join the market without first knowing how it works.

Meetings and phone calls

This list begins the moment that you start calling people for information help. Anyone whom you speak to regarding your story, in an official capacity or otherwise, should be logged in your records. This log might include

- Anyone who helped you with initial research
- Anyone whom you've interviewed as part of the process
- Anyone reading and/or critiquing your work
- Any calls you make or replies you send
- The agencies copyrighting and/or registering your work (and the date of official copyright)
- Anyone in the business whom you meet with or speak to on the phone, and the outcome of that exchange

This log tracks your history with various studios and individuals. It offers a quick summation of meetings, should you need to recall people quickly. It also reminds you to follow up with anyone kind enough to inquire about your work. Finally, the list can actually protect you against copyright infringement. If you have a log of the individuals you've spoken to about your story, you'll be better able to prove the material was yours first, should someone try to steal the idea. The list should include the person's or agency's name, the date of the meeting or submission, a brief description of what transpired, and a notation of any impending exchange.

Transfer anyone on this record to your contact list as well.

Submissions and results

Some people include this information in the previous list, but I find it helpful to keep a separate record for submissions and results. After all, meeting with someone is a different process than submitting your work. You may wait months to hear from a studio, and you'll want a place to keep rejections or positive feedback.

Writers usually send scripts to several places at once. It's not uncommon for a writer to circulate one script to several agencies or contests at the same time, and if you have more than one polished script, you might market both simultaneously, albeit to different venues. Multiple submissions can become confusing. So when you submit a work, record the following:

- The title of the script
- The organization or person you sent it to
- Their contact information
- The date it was sent
- A line about the nature of the submission — a request, a referral, something else

Leave room below each item to add follow-up reports later. You should *always* send a thank-you note to anyone interested in your work, so log that information below the submission date to make sure that you've sent one. This list ensures that you don't submit the same work to a studio twice, and after a while, it reveals patterns. If no one is interested in a script, the time may have come to launch a new one. If a script generates mass curiosity but doesn't sell, a rewrite might be necessary. If the script sparks a meeting or a phone call, well, you have a whole other list for that info, don't you?

Acquiring the right information

When you first enter the business, your contact list may be short, your marketing list limited, and the other two records may be nonexistent. That's okay. Everyone starts somewhere. Luckily, a variety of resources are available to help expand that network.

The media

An array of publications report on the Hollywood marketing scene. The trade publications (also known simply as the *trades*), which include *Daily Variety* (www.variety.com) and *The Hollywood Reporter* (www.hollywood reporter.com), announce which screenplays are bought and sold, what their premises are, who's doing the purchasing, when they're slated for production, and when to expect a release. Articles and weekly focus sections include studio progress reports, information on promotions and position shifts within organizations, and updates on television programming and acquisitions. The trades are available in daily and weekly editions.

Other publications include *Script* (www.scriptmag.com), a magazine focusing on writing and marketing scripts of all kinds; *Premiere* (www.premiere.com) and *Entertainment Weekly* (www.ew.com), which focus on the players, their bios, and up-and-coming projects; *The Hollywood Scriptwriter* (www.hollywoodscriptwriter.com), another trade publication with an emphasis on feature films; and *The New York Screenwriter* (www.nyscreenwriter.com) for writers positioned near the East Coast market.

An important set of directories for Hollywood is *The Hollywood Creative Directory* (www.hcdonline.com). These directories contain regularly updated booklets: for producers, distribution, agents, and so on. They are helpful when looking for sources to submit your screenplay to.

Finally, if you're Internet savvy, you might want to check out the Hollywood blogs. *Blogs* are a medium that have become popular in the past five years, and many of them contain extensive and sometimes inside information about the business.

A note of caution though: Bloggers aren't held to the same ethical standards as trade papers or magazines. Most blogs are opinion-based, and bloggers are not required to reveal the sources of quotes or surveys, so consider this information suspect until further searching. A few fairly reliable blogs are unitedhollywoodblogspot.com, www.portfolio.com, and www.riskybusinessblog.com, which is the Hollywood Reporter blog.

A quick computer search reveals many more publications that you may subscribe to, online and otherwise. I suggest subscribing to at least one trade paper and one magazine. You can follow the others as your budget allows. The updated information that you glean from them is invaluable.

Conferences and symposiums

Most metropolitan areas sponsor annual screenwriting conferences and symposiums. If your city doesn't, you can probably find one nearby. They range in price anywhere from $50 to $500, depending on who's attending and how long the forum lasts. Many are daylong or weekend events, but a few stretch into a week. What do these functions provide? Among other things, conferences offer

- ✔ A panel of established writers, directors, and studio executives
- ✔ Literary agents and script analysts
- ✔ Marketing tips and strategies
- ✔ Discounted books and software
- ✔ Possible contacts with other fledgling writers and established agencies

Longer symposiums may schedule workshops with writers or marketing gurus. Some may also have script analysts available to look over a treatment of your work (for an additional fee, of course). You can find complete listings of conferences online, as well as through advertisements in trade papers and Hollywood publications. Should one jump to your attention, do some research to see who might be attending. Surrounding yourself with professional or would-be professional writers may be the jumpstart that you need.

Courses and contests

Writing classes, workshops, and contests are other great ways to network. If you live near a university or an institution that provides continuing education, inquire about creative-writing courses. Some courses require that you pay on the spot to reserve a space in the class, but others allow you to sit in on a class before you decide to join. Artistic workshops are also advertised in writing publications or at your local library, so keep an eye out.

Workshops certainly aren't for everyone. Some writers fear that their ideas may be stolen by other participants, or that the criticism might affect their work. However, in addition to constant feedback, workshops provide contacts with writers who may succeed in the industry. You might learn the process through example, and any support group has its emotional advantages.

You can also research contests online. New competitions sprout up every day. If you're considering this route, pay attention to the following items:

- ✔ **The submission request:** What kind of material do they want? Are they looking for full-length features, short films, or adaptations? Do they support work by any writer, or do they specialize in films written by minorities? In other words, do you fit the bill?
- ✔ **The cost:** Most contests have a nonrefundable submission cost. They're often less than $50, but watch out — some cost more.
- ✔ **The deadline date:** Most contests are annual, but some are biannual and even monthly. Also, deadlines change every year, so make sure that your information is current.

✔ **The award:** Some contests award cash prizes, some introduce you to Hollywood executives, and some offer winners a one-on-one meeting with agencies and script analysts. Know what you're getting into in advance.

✔ **Past award winners:** Some contests publicize winners now working in the business. If the names are familiar, it may be a good contest to enter.

Send a SASE (self-addressed stamped envelope) unless the contest rules specifically state that scripts will not be returned. You might as well get that copy back, and sometimes the judges send comments to the runners-up.

Contests are also listed in periodicals. University callboards are another great source of information; local competitions may be posted there.

Setting personal expectations

Selling yourself as a writer is a big commitment that requires an immense amount of preparation, especially at the beginning. You can easily become overwhelmed with the sheer number of calls, records, and follow-up letters that fill up your week. Keeping a weekly list of goals is one way to manage the madness.

A typical weekly plan might include the following information:

✔ The dates of the week in question

✔ One primary goal for the week

✔ At least three secondary goals

✔ The amount of time you have available to tackle those goals

✔ A list of ways that you might achieve those goals

✔ A log of any phone calls, meetings, or follow-up responses

✔ A log of any information that you discover during the week

✔ A summation of what you accomplished, and what still needs to be done

Weekly plans clarify and prioritize the tasks so that you can manage them with greater ease. Better yet, you're putting those commitments in writing, which always makes them feel more official. You're making a silent but visible promise to continue forging ahead.

Polishing the Copy You Send

In Chapter 15, I mention the adage, "You never get another chance to make a first impression." If there was ever a time to take that phrase to heart, it's now, when you're considering sending work to producers and agents. Hollywood has thousands of writers, and many of them are newcomers. Organizations are looking for reasons to reject your script, and although a script's progress may not be hampered by one misspelling, why risk it?

A last-minute checklist

Agents and studios don't mind working with new writers, but they bolt at the thought of an amateur. If they see a clean, well-formatted script, they assume that the writing is strong. If the script looks messy and ill-prepared, they assume that the same holds true for the writer. The script's appearance is one thing that you have control over, so take the time you need to get it right.

Here are a few things to double-check before you submit work:

- **Spelling and grammatical errors:** If you're not strong in these areas, consider having a friend who is look over your script one last time. While it's a good idea to run your script through the computer spell-check, don't rely on it. Only a pair of human eyes can determine whether you've chosen the correct word.

- **Word usage:** Are you using the correct version of a word? For example, "you're" or "your," "tale" or "tail," "desert" or "dessert," "meat" or "meet," "it's" or "its," and so on.

- **Margins:** Don't make margins smaller in an attempt to cram the story in. Keep the margins at the desired width (see Chapter 15).

- **Dangling names:** Space the text so that a name never hangs at the bottom of a page while the ensuing dialogue floats at the top of the next. Scriptwriting software will automatically do this for you, but it's a good idea to double-check anyway.

- **All your writing is meant to be seen:** Make sure that your script is free of editorials or personal reminders.

- **Page numbers are accurate and in order:** Many producers give a script the *five-and-dime treatment,* meaning that they read the first five pages and the last ten to assess the story. They're primarily looking for scripts that are between 90 and 120 pages. If your page numbers are incorrect, they may assume that your story is longer or shorter than it really is.

✔ **No missing pages:** You want your readers immersed in your story. Imagine their frustration if part of that story is missing.

✔ **No quote marks around dialogue:** Dialogue is only quoted in your treatment, never in a script. It has its own placement on the page that makes quotes unnecessary. The only exception to this rule would be if the character is quoting someone within the dialogue. (See Chapter 15 for formatting details.)

✔ **No camera angles:** Camera angles fall into the director and cinematographer's domains. They will include them in the shooting script, which is the production version of your screenplay. They also clutter up your page and distract a reader from your story.

✔ **Scenes are not numbered:** A director will number your scenes later, in a shooting draft of the script. This is your story draft; numbers and technical notations quickly become distracting.

✔ **Font is 12-point Courier:** This is the standard screenwriting font utilized for timing purposes. In Courier, each page of script equates to around a minute of screen time.

✔ **No treatments or synopsis included unless requested:** If they've requested your script, send your script. You want them reading the whole story if possible, so don't send a synopsis, or they're likely to read that instead.

✔ **Work is undated or recently dated (unless registered with a copyright office):** It's always a good idea to offer the illusion that your story is a new one. If executives see that your script was written ten years ago, they may assume that it has been rejected for ten years and will shy away from purchasing it themselves. So if you have a date on your cover page, make sure that it's a recent one.

✔ **No use of bold print or italics:** Bold print tends to distract a reader, and italics are barely discernable in Courier. If you want to emphasize a certain line, write the scene that suggests that emphasis or direct the reader with a line of description. The only exception to this rule would be if a character is quoting someone or singing lyrics to a song. In those cases, you can use italics or quotes around the material.

After you scan through the script twice yourself, I suggest handing the script to at least two other people. One might read for form and spelling; the other for content. Paying a script analyst to read your work is another option. In addition to proofreading, script analysts often provide commentary on the strength of your story and its components. Fees can range from $75 to $200 or more, but the feedback may be well worth the cost. However, make sure that the analyst you choose comes recommended from another writer or editor who you trust. The Writer's Guild of America and the Hollywood Creative Directory may provide suggestions for legitimate script analysts as well.

Front-page news

Your script's appearance should scream that it's professional and direct, and nothing conveys that more clearly than the title page. The number-one rule here is no cover art, please. Draw attention to your ability as a writer, not as an illustrator. The title page includes your working title, centered and spaced one-fourth of the way down. Some writers put the title in quotes. Just below that, include your name. Put your contact information in the bottom-right corner. Include your address, phone number, and e-mail, if desired. Agencies should be able to reach you if they like your script. Scripts without return addresses are generally thrown out. If you have an agent, she'll include her information on the cover as well. Only date your work if you've registered it with the copyright office and update that copyright as necessary. No agency wants to read a 7-year-old script, after all. You needn't include anything else on the title page. Figure 19-1 shows a sample page.

"A Sample Title"

by Laura Schellhardt

Laura Schellhardt
123 Success Ave.
Success, CA 12345
(123) 456-7890

Figure 19-1:
A sample
title page.

Screenplays are printed on 8.5 x 11–inch (standard letter size) white paper and then three-hole punched and bound with 1¼- to 1½-inch brass brads. You can purchase both the paper and the brads at any local office supply store, and if you're planning on writing a lot, I suggest buying in bulk. Brads traditionally go through the top and bottom holes, leaving the middle hole empty. That's the current trend, but it's not a requirement. I suggest buying them in bulk as well. Choosing a cover for your work is optional. I prefer the clear plastic covers, something to shield your work from the numerous hands that you hope it will pass through. It's not necessary, though, so if you do cover your work, make it simple.

Protecting Your Work

Eventually, after the script's been through readers, proofreaders, and revisions, you'll be ready to send it. The only thing left to do is to register it. Bear in mind that you can't protect everything. Titles, names, short phrases, slogans, historical data, ideas, concepts, and anything within public domain are up for grabs. You can and should protect your polished draft, though. Here are a few ways to do it.

The Library of Congress

The current law states that works are automatically copyrighted from the moment of conception. In other words, you own the material as you write it. The following procedure then involves *registering* that copyright, or making it official. The traditional way to register works is with the U.S. Copyright office. To do so, you need send only a completed application, a $45 payment; $35 online), and a copy of your script to the following address:

> The Library of Congress
> Copyright Office
> 101 Independence Ave., SE
> Washington, DC. 20559-6000

You may download an application from its Web site (`www.copyright.gov`), or you can ask it to mail you a form. You'll receive a notice of registration after four to five months. Under the law, your work is protected from the moment that it receives your application to 70 years after your death. The law used to state that after you'd registered a work with the Library of Congress, you were required to place the copyright date on the script. That's no longer the case, although it still recommends it. Because it can take so long to receive proof of copyright, however, I recommend that you send your script registered mail with return receipt so that you have proof of the sent date while you're waiting.

The Writer's Guild of America

Most established writers register their work with the *Writer's Guild of America* (WGA). There are two Guild offices, one on the East Coast and one on the West. Writers living east of the Mississippi River register with the New York office, and writers living west of the river register in Los Angeles. The addresses of both offices are as follows:

The Writer's Guild of America, West
7000 W. Third St.
Los Angeles, CA 90048
(323) 951-4000 (within S. California)
(800) 548-4532 (outside S. California)

The Writer's Guild of America, East
555 W. 57th St., Suite 1230
New York, NY 10019
(212) 767-7800

The current registration fee is $22, and it protects your script for five years. However prices change annually, so be sure to check its Web site at www. wga.org for updated information or to register your script online. The WGA offers other services to nonmembers as well. In addition to holding your script for five years, the WGA will

✔ Register treatments, outlines, and a synopsis.

✔ Provide a list of agencies that participate with the Guild.

✔ Provide a script library open for perusal.

✔ Arbitrate artistic disputes over credit and ownership.

✔ Provide standard contracts if your script is optioned by a studio or producer who participates with the Guild.

After five years' time, you may retrieve your work or register it again.

If you choose only one method of registering your copyright, I recommend this one. The contacts and aid that the Guild provides are more than helpful, especially for beginning writers in search of representation.

The "poor-man's copyright"

Writers have used this method as an initial protection against theft. After you have a draft, either mail one to yourself or visit the post office and ask it to stamp and register it for you there. Whatever you do, don't break the seal once it's registered. The idea is that if you suspect that your work has been stolen, you have a script postmarked on the date that you completed the work. I don't recommend this method as your primary protection, but it certainly doesn't hurt. Because you officially copyright only polished or published works, you might try this method with a first or second draft.

Whatever you do, register your material in some fashion prior to sending it. Although most of Hollywood is more interested in purchasing your story than stealing it, you can never be too careful.

Chapter 20

Getting Your Screenplay Noticed

. . . .

In This Chapter

▶ Creating the package deal

▶ Pitching your script like a pro

▶ Finding an agent

▶ Approaching production companies

▶ Knowing what happens after you get their attention

. . . .

Congratulations, you're ready to launch yourself into the industry. You have a polished script and a steadily growing contact log, and you're fairly market savvy. Now, all you need is what I call a "willing and able" — someone who's *willing* to read your script and *able* to generate work with it. This person may be an agent, a producer, a director, or a star — you don't know yet. But you're about to find out.

Steel yourself for a bumpy but enlightening ride. This part of the process involves risk and rejection. Behind every "yes" lies at least ten "nos," and not every "yes" will land you a job. However, you're also armed with a positive attitude and an unflagging determination, right? Make the promise to yourself now: You will do all that you can, and you will not give up.

This chapter helps you strengthen your marketing design and commercialize your product. It also guides you through the letters, phone calls, and meetings that stand between you and your "willing and able." Finally, this chapter touches upon what to expect when (not if) you do sell a script.

Designing Your Own Package

A film's package includes anything and everything that makes it commercially (which means financially) attractive to agents, producers, and the audience. Some of these elements may be

- A high-concept story with low-budget needs.
- Any director or actors already attached to the project.

- ✔ Star potential. (Does the film have great roles for Tom Hanks or Meryl Streep?)
- ✔ Possible advertising spin-offs. (What products might it inspire?)
- ✔ Universal appeal.
- ✔ Current Hollywood interest. (Is there a buzz on the project?)
- ✔ A resemblance to other financially successful films.

The producer usually assembles the package, but you should consider it as well. It will affect how you pitch your story to executives when you land a meeting, and if you can attach people to your project in advance, your story is more likely to sell right away. So consider whether you know of a specific director who might like the material. Perhaps you were writing with actors in mind — would they appeal to a mass audience? Can you come up with at least two other films that yours resembles? Answer these questions now before producers surprise you with them later. Selling your story is about predicting what the buyers are after and convincing them that you can provide it. Knowing the package is a step in that direction.

Before you begin the process — and this is important — you should be clear on what is sacred in your script. By *sacred,* I mean what components of your story do you hope to protect above all? The characters? The theme? The outcome? Film is a collaborative medium, and during collaboration, your script will undoubtedly change. Directors will add shots as necessary, editors will condense sequences, and actors may request dialogue changes. The time may come, heaven forbid, when they hire another writer to tweak the whole script. You're going to lose something along the way.

However, you can certainly highlight elements you want to preserve in your pitch, in your query letters, and in any synopsis you hand in. So know what's sacred now and plan your marketing strategies accordingly.

Highlighting the universal

Agents and studio executives want the same thing — a writer with universal appeal. You need to convince them that you're just such a writer. What does that mean? It means that your work will sell to a mass audience. It entices the college student *and* her parents. It speaks to the human condition. Executives look for that ability in your sales pitch and in your spec script, should they decide to read it. So glance through the script beforehand with the following thoughts in mind. Universal stories:

✔ Have a hero or heroes worth rooting for.

✔ Provide a goal or a dream for the hero to pursue.

✔ Evoke passions, such as fear, envy, joy, hatred, hope, lust, and so on.

✔ Include formidable obstacles and opponents.

✔ Offer something familiar: a location, a theme, character relationships.

✔ Suggest elements at risk or at stake.

Pay particular attention to that last item. You're likely to be asked what's at stake in your film, and that answer may very well be the selling point.

So what will be lost in your story if the protagonist doesn't succeed? It's most likely one or the following things:

✔ Someone's life (*Titanic*)

✔ Someone's reputation or integrity (*Unforgiven*)

✔ Another character's love or admiration (*When Harry Met Sally*)

✔ A sense of order or harmony (*Lord of the Rings*)

✔ Precious objects or information (*Raiders of the Lost Ark*)

Hopefully, your story combines several of these elements. They usually ensure you an audience larger than one socio-economic group of people.

When you discover and record the universal elements, you can then summarize them in a catchy phrase or two. This phrase may later become your pitch. Is your film

✔ A coming-of-age story?

✔ A family reunion?

✔ A fight to preserve integrity, reputation, or personal freedom?

✔ A story of revenge or betrayal?

✔ A quest for redemption?

✔ A story of love in the face of hate?

✔ A triumph of human will and ingenuity?

✔ A "from rags to riches" adventure?

If these phrases sound like clichés, it's because they are. Most films fit into one of these categories, so they're familiar to audiences. Yet each grouping includes hundreds of stories that differ in tone, content, and scope. *Billy Elliot* and *Back to the Future* are both triumphs of the human spirit. *West Side Story* and *Life is Beautiful* both champion love in the face of hate. Your film isn't less unique if it falls into one of these groups; it's marketable.

Gaining the competitive edge

In order to push ahead of the competition, you have to concentrate your efforts on portions of the market that your work seems to match. I'm speaking both about the public market and the industry market here. Imagine the ideal audience for your script. How old is he? What stories excite him? Does he like small- or large-scale films? What hasn't he seen in a long time? Where do his values seem to lie? How should you approach him?

If you give the public something that it wants, it'll advertise your work. If you give a producer something that he wants, he'll buy your work. Either way, you win.

At the same time you're choosing a market for your work, consider the competition therein. Other writers want the same job; other writers pitch to that market. What makes you unique? Is it your professional background? Former police officers and journalists intrigue studio executives, for example. These jobs require a person to track stories down, often from unlikely sources. So if you once held this kind of a position, executives assume that you can do the same on the page. Perhaps it's your cultural background. *My Big Fat Greek Wedding* is successful, in part, because the writer is able to poke fun at her own Greek heritage. Maybe it's who you know. Referrals are the number-one reason that new writers are read. Whatever it is, find something that distinguishes you from other writers in your market.

Another way to fine-tune your salesmanship is to imply both economical and emotional benefits. If your film has a great female role, make that a selling point. A great female role draws box-office revenue (an economical benefit for the company) and makes the film easier to market (an emotional benefit for the producer). The same strategy applies when courting an agent. A positive attitude means that you'll be more likely to work in the industry (an economical benefit for the agency), and you'll be easier to work with in general (an emotional benefit for the agent). If you advertise both qualities in yourself and the script, you're more likely to land the job.

Considering the reader

Very few agents or producers actually read the work that comes in. Most scripts are handed to professional readers who then type up a *coverage* (a brief synopsis and evaluation) of the story and pass that up for consideration. Coverage also includes a line for the reader to recommend your work or pass on it. If the story earns good coverage, the agent might read the first ten pages.

You can't control everything about how the reader receives your script. The reader may be in a bad mood when she reads it, or despise screwball comedies, or be writing a script of her own based on a similar premise. You can't do anything about that. However, knowing what readers are trained to look for in a script can be helpful. If you know what might make good coverage, you can work on emphasizing those elements in advance. Figure 20-1 presents the first page of a standard coverage form.

Other examples vary in format, but they generally include the same information.

The reader follows the front page of the form that's shown in Figure 20-1 with a detailed synopsis of the story and a commentary on the overall content.

Success Films
Coverage Sheet

Title: The Coverage Sheet   Form: Spec
Author: Jane Doe   Page: 110
Time: 1965   Draft/ Date: 1-11-01
Location: Rhode Island   Represented by:
                                   Submitted by:
Genre: Drama/Coming-of-age   Submitted to: John Doe
                                   Date Received: 2-2-02
                                   Date Covered: 3-3-02

Log Line: a young and rather high-strung screenwriter rises to stardom by slaughtering the competition, literally.

Comment Summary: An edge-of-your-seat thriller with a surprising turn of events. There might be a story here if the writer spends more time on character and less on gory detail.

	Excellent	Good	Fair	Poor
Concept				
Characterization				
Dialogue				
Cinematic Structure				
Story Line				
Setting/ Prod Values				

Pass for Features _____   Consider for Features ___X___

Figure 20-1:
The first page of a standard coverage form.

As a writer, your goal is to grab the reader's attention and give her a favorable impression of the story. In order to do that, your *logline* — that all-important one-line premise — should be exciting (or in this case gory), and the general elements of your story should be clear. You can see, though, that coverage forms are highly subjective. Readers are coached to put their personal preference aside, but this doesn't always happen. The response may hinge on a reader's taste in cinema. Nine times out of ten, the best and only defense is a strong script. The quality of the writing will impress a reader who might not otherwise favor the genre.

Preparing to Pitch

Pitching a script is an art form, and although it can be stressful, it's something every writer has to perfect before approaching executives or agents. So what is pitching exactly?

A *pitch* is an animated summation of a script with emphasis on the main characters, the conflict, and the genre. When pitching a script, you use this summation to persuade industry professionals to *option* the work (purchase it for consideration). Metaphorically speaking, you're pitching an agent your idea, in the hopes that they'll catch the pitch and pass it to production.

Pitches come in two forms: the two-minute pitch, also known as the *teaser,* and the *story pitch,* which is traditionally up to 10 minutes in length, though, the shorter the better. You absolutely must have both types of pitches prepared *before* you contact industry personnel. You never know when you'll be called upon to sell your story or how you'll be asked to sell it.

The teaser pitch

The teaser pitch is a short pitch, and when I say short, I mean *short.* Traditionally, you get three sentences to hook listeners into the premise, the genre, and the scope of your film. When crafting this pitch, pay particular attention to what you think they might be listening for. Producers probably want to know the following details:

- How the film might be cast
- How much it will cost to make
- How they'll market it
- What films it resembles

If you follow those requests, your first sentence introduces the characters, the next sentence illustrates their conflict, and the final sentence leaves listeners wanting more. The conflict generally suggests the film's genre, but if not, consider alluding to that in the final sentence as well.

Here are some examples:

> Europe, 1912. Jack Dawson and Rose DeWitt Bukater enjoy a secret and passionate romance after they meet on a ship chartered toward New York. That ships happens to be the *Titanic*.

> Jessica Stein has met and refused virtually every man in New York City. Maybe it's time she looked for a woman. (***Kissing Jessica Stein***)

> Northern England, 1984. Young Billy Elliot, the son of a poor local miner, decides to start training for a career. In ballet. (***Billy Elliot***)

These examples suggest the skeleton of a short pitch. It might entice listeners into asking for a more detailed description, but for now practice your pitch at home with a stopwatch. Never exceed two minutes — try to do it in one, if you can. If you maintain the three- to five-sentence limitation, timing shouldn't be a problem. If executives want to know more, they'll ask. Be animated, enthusiastic, and concise. Movie trailers are good examples of this kind of pitch; so are the blurbs on the back of video and DVD boxes.

Some writers craft a teaser pitch for stories that they haven't written yet, in case they're asked what other material they're working on. It never hurts to have two or three teasers on hand, in case you're asked to do the same.

The story pitch

The story pitch is much longer than the teaser pitch, but try to keep it under ten minutes, if possible. People in the industry keep long and frantic hours, which affects their attention spans. If you ramble on or get off-track, they're likely to start planning their next meeting before you're done. Some writers use note cards to help them through this pitch. That's perfectly acceptable, but don't rely on them. Reference the notes occasionally, but keep your focus on your listeners. If you practice pitching your story several times before the session, you should have it pretty well memorized, so keeping your eyes on your listeners and off your notes won't be hard.

The story pitch follows the basic pattern of a *treatment* (see Chapter 19). You start with your hook or your logline, and then you run down the rest of the story. Be sure to illustrate those universal elements — the heroes, their goals, the conflict, what's at risk and why they're fighting to save it, any pivotal events or emotional turning points, and the conclusion.

Because you're giving a longer pitch, you have more chances to go astray. Here are a few things to avoid right away:

- ✔ Don't compare your film to others too much. It used to be common practice to depict a script through a combination of two existing films. (It's **When Harry Met Sally** in **Waterworld,** or it's **Goonies** meets **The Field of Dreams.**) Know what your film shares with others, but keep the comparisons brief.

- ✔ Don't ever compare your script to box-office disasters. No one wants to make another **Ishtar.**

- ✔ Avoid listing action in order. Tell them a story instead.

- ✔ Avoid depicting too many subplots or details. Concentrate on two or three characters and pivotal events, or the pitch will become convoluted.

- ✔ Don't keep pitching if they express disinterest, and (on the bright side) don't keep pitching after they agree to consider it.

- ✔ Don't mention actors that you have in mind. Describe the characters so that your listeners will envision them.

- ✔ Never lie about the story or its hype. Producers discover false information quickly.

As with any sale, personality is paramount. If you're enthusiastic, they will be, too. If you're charming and witty, they'll remember you even if they don't accept the script. And never express desperation. There's always some other way to generate interest. Pitching scares some writers to death. If you're one of those frightened few, do something about it. Acting classes are a great way to build confidence in your presentation, as are courses in public speaking. Or, if you'd rather, practice in front of friends and family. See whether they'd want to purchase the script based on your description. While pitching is nerve-wracking and you may want to have someone pitch the idea for you, this is a skill you'll need to develop and deliver yourself. Should they accept your pitch, agencies and studios will be working with you. So in a pitch session you're selling the movie, yes, but you're also selling yourself.

After you've typed up both pitches and are comfortable delivering them, you're ready to search for an agent and/or a producer.

Finding an Agent

You've heard the contradiction: You can't find work without an agent, and you can't find an agent until you've worked. There's a grain of truth here. Unsolicited writers do have a hard time finding representation. It takes careful planning, meticulous organization, and luck — lots and lots of luck.

An *unsolicited* writer is one who doesn't yet have representation. Many studios and agents refuse to look at unsolicited work, fearing that it hasn't been through an initial screening process. As soon as you sell a script or find an agent, this dubious title disappears. You may also try submitting a script through an attorney. Arts attorneys will often write a cover letter on your behalf, which makes you appear more legitimate than the average pedestrian claiming to be a writer. They provide this service for a fee, of course.

So how does one go about finding an agent in the first place? The following list gives the four primary ways to track agencies down:

- ✔ **Your personal contacts:** Call anyone on your contact list who works in the business. Tell them about the script (maybe use that teaser pitch?) and ask whether they're willing to read it or whether they know any agencies that might. If they enjoy the piece, they might refer to it themselves. At the very least, you can use that person's name to help pave the way at whatever agency they recommend. Never underestimate the power of a referral.

- ✔ **The WGA:** For a nominal fee, the Writer's Guild of America (www.wga.org) can provide a list of agencies that work with them. It can also tell you who represents writers you admire, although it limits you to three answers per call. So make a list of movies that you adore, identify those writers, and find out who's representing them. If your work is similar, an agent might be more apt to consider you.

- ✔ **Trade papers:** If a deal's being made, *Daily Variety* or *The Hollywood Reporter* will announce it. They usually highlight the script that was bought, who wrote it, and who picked it up. If the agency's large enough, they might name the agent. If not, you have the writer's name, so get on the phone or online and find out who represents him.

- ✔ **Reference books:** Several reference books list literary agents and script analysts. *The Writer's Guide to Hollywood Producers, Directors & Screenwriter's Agents* is one of the most well known, but new ones crop up every year. Purchase one of these books only after trying one of the other methods, or as a supplement.

- ✔ **The Hollywood Representation Directory:** This directory is a comprehensive and frequently updated guide to Hollywood agents, casting directors, attorneys, publicity companies, and managers. It often provides e-mail addresses, Web sites, and phone and fax numbers. This is a great directory to use once you've created a short list of agents you might be interested in pursuing.

Scour through the resulting list of potential "hits." Highlight any agency that represents artists you admire, any you've heard good things about (or simply heard of), and a few smaller to midsize agencies as well. Don't bother prioritizing them. Writers never contact just one agent at a time; they'd be 90 years old before they made a sale. You're going to approach them all at once.

Approaching an Agent

Before pounding on doors, polishing off letters, or picking up the phone, you should know what an agent's looking for, and what you should be looking for in an agent.

An agent wants

- ✔ **Someone whose work they can sell.** Typically, agents make 10 percent of whatever sale or option they negotiate. If your works seems particularly marketable, they'll be more likely to take you on.

- ✔ **Someone who understands the business.** Yes, an agent's job is to find work for you. However, your work won't end when an agent accepts you. Most writers continue to hunt down work for themselves even after they find representation. So, if you're willing to work, your agent will be, too.

- ✔ **Someone pursuing a career.** Agents know that markets are fickle and that selling a script sometimes takes a long time. They need writers who will keep producing despite the dry spells. They need writers who are passionate about the craft and determined to maintain a career.

- ✔ **Someone who won't make his job more difficult.** Attitude is everything. If you seem like a high-maintenance writer who requires daily calls, agents will pass on your work regardless of its potential.

Take these items as silent requests on the part of each agent you approach. Try to be an agent's ideal writer. Doing so can separate you from hundreds of other less savvy petitioners.

On the flip side, you want

- ✔ **Someone who enjoys your work.** An agent may hate your work but recognize selling potential. If he is willing to take you on for that reason, so be it. However, you may find it difficult to accept criticism from someone who's uncomfortable with what you produce. Also, an agent's enthusiasm over a piece will wear off on whomever he calls about it, so it helps if he enjoys what you write.

- ✔ **Someone influential.** It helps immensely if your agent has connections all over the business. If she can't reach producers directly, she should know someone who *can.* Don't shy away from small agencies because you fear that they lack contacts. New agents have often worked for the most powerful people in the business.

- ✔ **Someone committed.** You want an agent dedicated to getting you work or selling your scripts. It helps if this commitment arises from interest in your writing and not simply financial gain, but really, either one will do.

✔ **Someone professional.** If you gain representation, you should expect to hear from your agent once a week while he's finding you work, and at least once a month while you're on a project. You should be updated on what's being done to help your career and what the response has been so far. He should return your phone calls within 48 hours or have a secretary tell you when to expect a call. He should, at the very least, respond to you in an e-mail, which takes little to no time at all. If your agent doesn't provide this service, you may need to look for more professional representation.

Let me say in advance that you don't need to have an agent to sell a script. There are at least three other ways to get your script through the Hollywood maze, and I detail those options later in this chapter. So don't despair if finding an agent doesn't work out in the first round. However, you go through the same process with anyone you approach, so make sure that you know what's required for agencies before you try something else.

Small versus large: Does size matter?

There are two types of agencies: literary agencies and packaging agencies. You may concentrate on one camp or approach both camps simultaneously, but it helps to know what you stand to gain either way.

✔ *Literary agencies* represent writers. Those writers may work in film, television, theater, or fiction or nonfiction. Literary agents predominantly sell their client's work, drum up outside writing assignments, negotiate contracts, help secure rights to material their clients may want to adapt, and oversee royalties and marketing strategies.

The benefit of literary agents is the individual attention they provide. While you're joining an agency, you're assigned to one person. The personal relationship and the attention they place on your scripts are the reasons many new writers choose this option first.

✔ *Packaging agencies* represent all sorts of industry personnel. Actors, writers, producers, directors — all are housed under one large roof. Packaging agencies find assignments for their clients and negotiate contracts, but they often attach stars and directors to the script before approaching studios. Then they charge a packaging fee for their efforts.

The benefit of a packaging agency is the connection it offers to actors and business executives. It's often easier and less time consuming for an agency to package your film in-house. However, your script may not remain the top priority of that package. While literary agents concentrate on selling your screenplay, packaging agencies concentrate on selling the film. If that means reshaping your script to appease a star, they might ask you to do that.

The query letter

Most writers approach agents through a query letter. You can also call or drop into an agency unannounced, but I don't recommend it. It tends to be awkward for both you and the agent (if you even get that far), and you'll be saying pretty much the same thing that you'd include in a letter.

A *query* is a pitch-in letter form. It's your attempt to convince a producer, agent, or star to take a look at your work or meet you in person.

Never submit a script without a request to do so. Agents will return it unopened or recycle it altogether. You can't afford to lose all that paper, so send a query first.

Taking your first step

First, call the agency and find out who to address the query to. **Always** be polite. The secretary can often get you in the door faster than the letter itself, and today's secretary may be tomorrow's agent. So be nice, explain what you need, and thank him profusely.

Putting the letter together

Now, construct the letter. Queries are no more than one page in length. Use plain white paper — no fancy letterhead, please. Single-space within each paragraph and double-space between them. Your layout should be clean, clear, and concise. You may remember from high school the mind-numbing effect that long blocks of uninterrupted prose can have on a reader.

On the top left-hand side of the page, type the date, the agent's name, the agency, and its address. Double-check the spelling of any name before you send the letter. The man you're calling "John Smith" might really be "Jon Smyth." If you spell an agent's name wrong, you're just asking him to not read your work.

Queries usually consist of three paragraphs. The first one may alter slightly, depending on who you're writing to; the second and third remain the same. In the first paragraph, introduce yourself and mention why you're writing. The first paragraph is where you should include any of the following information:

- A personal reference or mutual friend
- Writing programs or educational institutions you're affiliated with
- Previous work as a playwright or as a reporter, on television or radio (basically, past writing experience)
- Any contests you've placed in or writing awards you've received
- A compliment on one of the agent's deals or on a writer he represents (only include one if it's sincere)

The second paragraph introduces the title of the screenplay you're pitching and your teaser. Be sure to emphasize the hook, your protagonists, the conflict, and the genre in this section.

The third paragraph lets the person know how he can contact you should he wish to read the script or see other examples of your work. Let him how you want him to respond — if, for example, you've sent an SASE, tell him that here. If you don't live near the West Coast, you might tell the agent that you're interested in assignments and would be happy to travel as necessary.

Write "Sincerely" or however you prefer to sign off a business letter, sign your name, and print it below.

You may rearrange the order in which you provide this information, but I suggest starting with the three-paragraph method. It organizes your pitch and naturally restricts the length of correspondence.

You want to pitch the strong points of your package in a query. If your script has a great concept or hook, begin with that. If you were referred by someone with clout, by all means, say that up front. Agents are most interested in the work and in any detail that suggests you'd be someone they could generate work for. Give them what they want.

A sample query

Here's a generic version of what you might send to an agency. *Don't* send a script or an outline with this letter. Wait for someone to express interest.

2/2/02

Ms. Successful Agent
Success Agency
1234 Lucky Ave.
Prosperous Springs, CA 12345

Dear Ms. Agent,

I am currently seeking representation for my original film script, **Luck of the Draw.** The script won the New Screenplay Contest in Grandstand, New York, last year, and it has received two awards since then. The story originated during my stint as a journalist for the *Grandstand Times.*

In **Luck of the Draw,** energetic young reporter, Ace Dobson, finds evidence linking a prominent New Yorker to a string of bank robberies. It's a first-time journalist's dream come true, except for one minor detail. The thief in question happens to be his father. **Luck of the Draw** is a compelling look at one man's struggle to choose between family loyalty and justice.

I'd like to send the complete script for your review. I've enclosed a post-card for your reply, or you may call me at (123) 456-7890. Thank you for your time and consideration.

Sincerely,

(your signature here)

Jane Doe

Sending the letter

Try to send letters so that they'll arrive Tuesday through Thursday. Very few agents have time at the beginning or end of the week to look at new queries. Wait at least a week before your follow-up phone call. When you do phone, politely ask to speak with the agent. If the secretary asks what it's about, let him know that you want to make sure that the letter arrived and ask whether you should send a script. More often than not, you'll hear that the agency doesn't accept unsolicited work. If your salesmanship can't bypass this answer, don't fret. Tell them that you may try back again in a few months, thank them for their time, and move on to the next call.

Query aftermath: What to expect

The best news that you can get is a "Yes, send me a copy of the screenplay." If that occurs, type a brief cover letter reminding the agent of the phone call or written response, and include it with your script. Be sure to send an SASE (self-addressed stamped envelope) with the script as well. Follow up in a few days to make sure that the package arrived and wait at least a month to call again. You'll have other projects to keep you busy in the interim.

At the beginning, you're likely to receive three responses:

- ✔ The query is returned unopened.
- ✔ The query is rejected.
- ✔ You receive no correspondence at all.

As disheartening as these reactions are, try not to let it affect your work or your determination to succeed. Every writer goes through this at one point in his career. And remember that agents aren't the only way to sell a script in Hollywood. You have other options, which I discuss in the section, "Pitching Your Script without an Agent," later in this chapter.

Using rejection to your advantage:

It's a sad but true fact that some writers pursue agents for years to no avail. For every 10 query letters you send, you should be prepared to receive 8 or 9 rejections. If you receive 10 rejection letters, you may feel like throwing in the towel and going home. However, bear in mind two things:

✔ Most established writers have experienced rejection at some point.

✔ Rejection can point the way to future success.

That last point may seem far fetched, but when you get a rejection letter, consider the agent's response. Rejection comes in three tiers, and all of them can be useful to you in some way:

✔ **The standard rejection:** The first tier, and most common, is a simple rejection letter that thanks you for sending your work but says the agent can't represent you at this time. The key words here are "at this time." If you receive this letter, please note the agency in your records, note when the rejection was sent, follow up with a simple thank you, and remember to send that agent your next script when you have it.

✔ **The informed rejection:** This second tier of rejection is more personal. This letter suggests someone has actually read your script all the way through, and it will include details from your story or your characters that the reader responded to. If you're lucky, the letter will also suggest what the reader did *not* respond to. That information is often more important than the positive feedback, because it suggests possible revision and/or reader preference. Either way, send an immediate thank you and perhaps inquire if you might send them more work in the future.

✔ **The signed rejections:** This letter will be from the agent herself. It usually suggests that the agent enjoyed the read and will tell you directly why she can't accept you as a client at this time. In the best scenarios, the agent will ask you to send other work her way. Again, follow up with a thank you note, pitch another script if you have one, or promise to send further work as it comes. This agent would be the first person to send to on the next go-around.

No matter how you look at it, rejection isn't going to feel good. However, look at it as part of the learning curve. Rejection letters help direct you toward necessary revisions in your script, they suggest which agencies respond to which genre of work, and they should, if you're in the proper mindset, spur you toward perfecting your script and trying again. Generally, a strong script and perseverance win out eventually.

The "cold call" and the "drop in"

For those of you who are slightly more direct and/or brave, you may want to try calling an agency directly or dropping by. This approach saves time and money on postage, but it's also more nerve-wracking. After all, you have infinite time to compose a letter. When you're talking to someone directly, you have one shot to get it right.

Cold calls work in much the same way as a letter does. Ask for the agent directly; tell the secretary what the call is about. If he says that the agent is too busy to speak to you now (which is probably true), ask whether there's a better time to call back. He might let you leave contact information. If he says that they don't accept unsolicited work, tell him what the work is about and ask whether there's any place he might suggest calling instead. You never know what's going to work. Whatever the outcome, be courteous and kind.

If you do get an agent on the phone, go through the steps of a query letter. Tell her who you are, pitch the film, and ask the agent's permission to send it. If the agent asks where you're located, be sure to emphasize that you'd be happy to travel as necessary. If the agent says that she's not interested, ask whether she'd like to hear about the other film you're writing (if you have one). If she refuses the script, ask for suggestions on where else to send it and then thank her for her time. Do you see that pattern here? Always thank agents for their time. You may be calling them again later.

You may have heard success stories about writers who've stopped by an agency and convinced agents to glance at their scripts that day. Those stories are less and less common. Most big agencies have security, and you'll never see the office without an appointment, let alone the agent. You also run the risk of looking desperate, which will turn the agent off immediately. Query letters and phone calls are much more likely to curry you favor.

Pitching Your Script without an Agent

Waiting to hear from an agent doesn't mean that your career is on hold. Many scripts are sold without representation, so you should also be pursuing at least one of the following options:

- ✔ **Independent producers (Indies):** Independent producers run small companies of their own, work for larger studios on a project to project basis, or are able to find financial backers for projects that they option.

- ✔ **Actors or directors:** These individuals may read a script and shop it around for you, or they may have production companies of their own.

- ✔ **A private attorney:** Many companies will accept an attorney cover letter in place of an agent's. Legal representation suggests that you're serious about the script and its success, but you know the business better than some. Often, you pay the attorney up front for this service, but some attorneys will negotiate a larger fee should the script be purchased as a result of their help.

✔ **Private financiers:** This group includes grant committees, state commission departments, film festivals, and wealthy individuals who are willing to finance a film.

Executives in these groups are more likely to consider unsolicited scripts, though referrals never hurt. The primary difference between them lies in what they're after. Producers are looking for films to boost their production companies or writers who match projects they have in mind. Actors and directors want scripts that will boost their careers. Private financiers are looking for worthwhile projects and sound investments. Note these different needs in advance and plan your marketing strategies accordingly.

Here's what you need to pitch on your own:

✔ At least one polished feature-length script, preferably two or three.

✔ A teaser or story pitch for any script you have. You'll want copies of these taped to your phone in case you receive an impromptu call.

✔ Your nutshell synopsis (see Chapter 5) and a detailed treatment (Chapter 19). You may be asked to submit them in place of a script.

✔ A query letter tailored to the individual buyer. Mention other work the production company has done, and make sure that actors and directors know that you believe the project is well suited to their talents. This technique may feel phony, but you're approaching them for a reason. Let them know what it is.

✔ A standard release form that you feel comfortable signing.

What's a *release form?* Industry executives are wary of unsolicited material, in part, because they fear lawsuits. If you submit material and their company produces something later with a similar theme, you could sue them for theft. A release form, or a *submission agreement,* absolves them of responsibility should such a scenario occur. It's not the best agreement for a writer. If you sign an agreement and they do steal your work, there may be little you can do. However, few studios will even look at your work without a release, so more often than not, you'll have to comply. Most executives will accept a standard form that you draw up with an entertainment attorney, or they'll send you a copy of the release form they've drafted with theirs..

Avoid signing anything that asks you to agree on a selling price before they purchase the script. In fact, avoid signing anything without consulting an attorney. Some release forms ask you to agree not to sue them should an identical script crop up in this process. The pain it may save you later is well worth the cost of consultation.

After your paperwork's in order, you approach these backers in the same way that you approach an agent:

- ✔ Call or send a query letter.

- ✔ Send the script, outline, or synopsis when they request it.

- ✔ Make follow-up calls to make sure that your letter/script arrived, and after a month, call for a progress report.

- ✔ Send a written thank-you note to anyone who agrees to read your work.

Your script will probably go to a reader for coverage. If the backers want to meet you, you'll receive a call. If they can't use your material at the moment, you may or may not receive word back. Remember to still write during this process. Writing helps the wait and produces more material to shop around. Don't let rejection affect your work.

What to Do When They Say Yes

If you're persistent enough, eventually, you'll land a meeting with someone. Arrange a time with that person's secretary, thank her again, and celebrate. You're one step closer to a career in film. Meetings with agents vary slightly from meetings with executives. After all, these individuals want different things. Luckily, you'll be prepared for both.

Meeting with an agent

If an agent agrees to meet with you, she's already interested in something. It may be your current script, it may be your writing potential, and it may be something in your query letter. Either way, she'll need more information before signing you up. Be prepared to discuss the following items:

- ✔ **What else you're working on.** You should have one or two more pitches ready when this comes up.

- ✔ **What genres or markets interest you the most.** Are you drawn to thrillers or romantic comedies? Would you be interested in writing for sitcoms or cable television? Is there anything you're uncomfortable writing?

- ✔ **Your willingness to relocate.** You certainly don't have to move to L.A. to write, but an agent will ask. If you're willing to relocate for the perfect job, tell them that. If not, make sure that they know you'd be happy to commute.

- ✔ **Your career potential.** Why are you writing? How long have you been at it? What are your personal career goals and why? Who else do you know, and what is your business experience thus far?

✔ **How well you pitch.** You probably demonstrated this ability already, but you may be asked to do it again.

✔ **Your willingness to accept writing assignments.** Agents want to make money just like everybody else. One way they do that is by finding writing assignments for you while you're working on your own projects. They'll want to know if you're willing to accept outside jobs.

If you're lucky, the agent will also mention a contract. Most agents receive 10 percent of any sale they negotiate, and contracts are usually binding for at least 90 days. If your agent doesn't find you anything after 90 days, you can leave, although you'll probably want to give them more time than that at the beginning. If your agent is affiliated with the WGA, you'll receive a standard contract of some sort. If not, it never hurts to run the contract by an attorney.

Even though the desire to secure representation is overwhelming, never feel that you *have* to sign with an agency. You should make inquiries during this meeting as well. Two things that you might ask are

✔ Who else does the agent represent? What sales is she most proud of?

✔ What does the agent think of your work? (Don't be alarmed if she offers constructive criticism. She may be right.)

Always be honest. If your script has not generated any interest, that's fine. Tell the agent that you've just begun shopping it around. Let her know where you've submitted the work. Doing so saves her the embarrassment of pitching it to a studio that may have rejected it in the past. The agent will understand if you're unable to relocate or if you're hesitant about certain projects, although I wouldn't emphasize the negative. You're looking for someone you're comfortable with. The agent's looking for an enthusiastic and prolific new writer. Make sure that you both win in the deal.

Meeting with executives

You might find yourself pitching to producers for three reasons:

✔ Someone read your work and recommended a meeting.

✔ The query or script teaser caught their attention. They may or may not want to discuss the script, but something interests them about your work.

✔ Your agent submitted a spec script, and though they rejected the piece, they're interested in you as a rising talent.

These meetings are nerve-wracking, especially because more than one person may be involved. Dress comfortably, but look professional. You don't need to worry about wearing a fancy dress or even a business suit if doing so makes you feel out of place, but choose something with clean lines — nothing frumpy. On a first meeting, I'd avoid jeans and a T-shirt, for example, and opt instead for a skirt, dress pants, or khakis and a nice shirt or sweater.

Arrive at least 15 minutes early and sign in with the secretary. Let her know you have an appointment, but it's not for another ten minutes or so (in other words, let her know you're early). Be kind to whomever you meet out front; these people work hard and are often executives in training. Eventually, someone will lead you into the room.

The first portion of the meeting will most likely involve informal chit-chat. Keep your energy up and try to relax. Inquire after a project you know they're working on perhaps. If they ask you about yourself, be careful. They're not looking for your biography or even a short summation of your work thus far. They're just breaking the ice. Tell them something interesting, possibly make a joke, and keep whatever you say brief.

Eventually, they'll ask what projects you're working on. Pitch an idea; if possible, pitch two or three. If they like one of these ideas, they may offer you a deal to develop material. If not, they're most likely interested in your creative ability. Ask whether they're looking for any projects in particular and listen carefully to what they suggest. They probably have a writing assignment open. They may ask you to come up with a pitch for one of their ideas. Be aware that you aren't the only writer they've asked. Eventually, they'll sift through all the results and assign one writer to the project. However, the fact that they've even extended a request is a step in the right direction.

When the meeting is over, they'll thank you and say that they'll be in touch. Maybe you've landed a job, maybe not. Either way, send a thank-you note and congratulate yourself. You're moving up.

Looking Ahead: Upon Achieving Success

Success always has two parts — the financial and the personal. Your financial success will be based on acquiring one of the following deals:

- ✔ **The sale of a spec script.** This deal is rare, but fantastic when it occurs. If you have an agent, she'll contact as many potential buyers as she can. The ensuing auction may mean a six-figure check, more if your script is produced. Again, this event is rare, but you can always dream!

✔ **A development deal.** This deal occurs when a studio or producer likes a pitch and hires you to develop it. It might be a pitch you brought in or one they asked you to design. You agree on a purchase price and are paid in installments.

✔ **An option.** Here, the producer or studio options the rights to a script for a smaller sum and maintains them for a specified length of time. During that time, the producer or studio attempts to attach talent to the project and generate a buzz. At the end of the time, the producer or studio will either purchase the script or pass on the deal altogether.

✔ **Staff position.** This option is for writers interested in television. If a producer likes your work, he may hire you for the writing staff of a new show. This is steady pay, but the hours are long, and you may have to relocate to L.A. This position may or may not help your film career.

Should you be offered any of these deals, your agent will handle the contract negotiations. If you don't have an agent at the time, you can try to use the interest in your script to secure one. Otherwise, negotiate the contract through an entertainment attorney.

The Hollywood market is all about highs and lows, ups and downs. One moment, you'll be in a meeting, pitching like a pro; the next minute, you're back to sending query letters and collecting rejections. Yet throughout the roller coaster ride, one thing remains constant: You're still writing, which leads me to the second definition of success — artistic success. Because I consider your artistic success more important than financial success, I've crafted it into a final note to send you off.

A Final Note

If I have one final message for you, it's this: Writing is an ancient art form and a noble profession. When people ask what you do for a living, practice saying, "I'm an artist" or "I'm a writer," and leave it at that. Take pride in what you do. Write for reasons unconnected with development deals, options, or beachfront property. Write because you love the process. Write because there are things that you want to know. Write because you can't imagine life without writing. If you maintain this passion for the craft, the rest will fall into place.

Part V
The Part of Tens

"I don't have the attention span for a full screenplay, but I've written several rather exciting coming attractions."

In this part . . .

So who's writing all these great scripts? Who has been doing it for years and who, like yourself, is up-and-coming? What sort of films do those people write? And how much of what you've heard about the business is actually true? This part is a sampler of sorts. It details a few writers to watch, a few of their films to see, and a few screenwriting myths you may encounter and should feel free to ignore.

Chapter 21

Ten Screenwriters You Should Know

So who's behind all this writing for Hollywood? That's a good question — and one that's rarely asked outside the confines of studios. By the time a film comes out, the all-star cast is usually what's drawing the crowds, or perhaps the director's reputation is causing a stir. It may also be the film's premise, but ask movie-goers who came up with that premise. They're likely to cite the director or simply shake their heads and admit defeat. You can't really fault them for not knowing who wrote the epic adventure, piercing drama, or romantic comedy they're about to enjoy. Most writers spend their whole careers in general anonymity. And yet, without writers, where would we be?

This chapter celebrates ten artists and the words they've brought to the screen. I've chosen these ten writers because, together, they present an eclectic and diverse body of work. Some of them adapt fiction, some dabble in sci-fi, some in comedy, and many of them work in several genres. I also chose writers who arrived in Hollywood via different paths. Two sold spec scripts immediately, one worked in television first, and another began onstage. Some of these writers have been in the industry for years, and some are up-and-comers. So here's the question: You've probably seen their work, but do you know their names?

William Goldman

Occupations: screenwriter, novelist. Industry credits:

> ✔ *Masquerade* (1965)
> ✔ *Harper* (1966)

> - *Butch Cassidy and the Sundance Kid* (1969)
> - *The Hot Rock* (1972)
> - *The Stepford Wives* (1975)
> - *The Great Waldo Pepper* (1975)
> - *All the President's Men* (1976)
> - *The Princess Bride* (1987)
> - *Misery* (1990)
> - *Chaplin* (1992)
> - *Maverick* (1994)
> - *The General's Daughter* (1999)
> - *Hearts In Atlantis* (2001)
> - And many more . . .

William Goldman is a virtual icon in the screenwriting world. Born in Chicago, Illinois, in 1931, he spent much of his childhood watching movies in the Alcyon. This theater and his experiences therein may well have sparked his interest in storytelling. He started writing novels after the war, the second of which he adapted into a screenplay (*Soldier in the Rain*). Shortly thereafter, he wrote *Butch Cassidy and the Sundance Kid,* which won him an Oscar, a Golden Globe, and a WGA screen award. It also launched his career in film.

Over the years, Goldman has worked steadily with various studios and stars. He's known for his gift of dialogue, his tendency to approach difficult subjects with humor and humorous subjects with depth, and the ability to craft multifaceted characters in fast-paced plots. He's increasingly excited by the advances in film technology. He believes that now screenwriters will be able to see a finished product that may match the one in their heads. He also encourages any new writer to study his craft. In his book *Adventures in the Screen Trade,* Goldman muses that all people want is a well-told story, but there are fewer and fewer storytellers around. He suspects that many new writers become frustrated too easily, and he wants to rid them of the notion that professional screenwriters have some secret stash of information or technique. "They don't," he says. "We're all just tearing our hair out together."

Ruth Prawer Jhabvala

Occupations: screenwriter, novelist. Industry credits:

> - *The Householder* (1960)
> - *Bombay Talkie* (1970)

- ✔ *Autobiography of a Princess* (1975)
- ✔ *A Room With a View* (1985)
- ✔ *Mr. and Mrs. Bridge* (1990)
- ✔ *Howards End* (1992)
- ✔ *The Remains of the Day* (1993)
- ✔ *The Golden Bowl* (2000)
- ✔ *Divorce, Le* (2003)
- ✔ And many more . . .

Ruth Prawer Jhabvala (pronounced JAHB'-va-la) has been writing for more than 50 years, and her life reads like one of her Merchant-Ivory collaborations. Born in Berlin, Germany, in 1923, Jhabvala immigrated to England where she eventually received a degree in English Literature from London University. She moved to India in 1951 with her husband, and there, her writing career began. Like William Goldman (see preceding section), she began writing novels, and her work eventually caught the attention of producer Ismail Merchant and director James Ivory. They asked her to adapt her novel *The Householder* for the screen, and the collaboration of a lifetime began. Since that time, the three have produced more than a dozen films, with two of them receiving screenwriting Oscars (*A Room With a View, Howards End*) and one of them earning a nomination (*The Remains of the Day*). Not bad for a woman who wasn't particularly interested in film.

Jhabvala suggests writing fiction as a precursor to film. She believes that you can discover a lot by spending the concentrated time on a project that fiction writing demands. When adapting novels, she reads the source two or three times, writing a general synopsis of each scene. Then, she pushes the work aside and writes a first draft from those notes. Her scripts lack direction as a rule — she thinks that too much direction hampers actors and directors who need room to maneuver. Instead, she fills her work with prose that's full of possibility. She encourages writers never to select projects simply for financial gain. She believes that if you're true to the work and to yourself, you'll inspire the same sentiment in others.

Alan Ball

Occupations: screenwriter, actor, writer, producer. Industry credits:

Television:

- ✔ *Oh Grow Up (Executive producer, writer)*
- ✔ *Cybill (Executive producer, writer)*

> ✔ *Grace Under Fire*
>
> ✔ *Six Feet Under*

Film:

> ✔ *American Beauty* (1999)
>
> ✔ *Nothing Is Private* (2007)

Alan Ball may be one of the few writers on his way to becoming a household name. His film, ***American Beauty,*** swept the Oscars in 1999, earning him the award for Best Original Screenplay, after which many critics called him the new rising talent in Hollywood. Yet, truth be told, Ball is anything but new to the world of writing. He began his career as a noted New York playwright, a profession that helped sharpen his craft but ill-prepared him for the actor-driven world of television. His four years as a sitcom writer and producer were frustrating. As a playwright, he was encouraged to maintain a firm enthusiasm and connection to his work. As a sitcom writer, the opposite seemed true. Most of what he wrote was altered or rewritten entirely before being taped, and Ball discovered that he had to detach himself from the writing more often than not — a difficult task for a writer with such grand vision.

Ultimately, though, that frustration became the foundation for ***American Beauty.*** The film, which follows a man struggling to change his mundane life, is a piercing look at what it means to be spiritually awake. Its tenor, at once nihilistic, romantic, and exceedingly funny, seems to pervade much of Ball's writing, including his HBO series, ***Six Feet Under,*** which is about a family that runs a funeral home. Although he does extensive research prior to writing each project, Ball calls himself an instinctive writer, rarely mapping projects out in advance. He trusts his instincts to get him to the next event.

Nora Ephron

Occupations: screenwriter, director, producer, novelist. Industry credits:

> ✔ *Silkwood* (1983)
>
> ✔ *Heartburn* (1986)
>
> ✔ *When Harry Met Sally* (1989)
>
> ✔ *This Is My Life* (1992)
>
> ✔ *Sleepless in Seattle* (1993)
>
> ✔ *Michael* (1997)
>
> ✔ *You've Got Mail* (1998)

- ✔ *Hanging Up* (2000)
- ✔ *Bewitched* (2005)
- ✔ And many more . . .

Nora Ephron's professional resume scrolls well past the page that most screenwriters are encouraged to maintain. Film credits aside, Ephron is also a successful novelist and essay writer, who penned *Heartburn, Crazy Salad,* and *Scribble Scribble* prior to becoming a successful screenwriter. Her prolific bent makes sense, however, when you consider her upbringing. Ephron is the child of screenwriting team Phoebe and Henry Ephron, noted for scripts like **There's No Business Like Show Business** and **Desk Set.** Her childhood included many bouts of verbal repartee, and one of her sisters has compared family dinners to "the Algonquin Round Table."

Ephron quickly decided to become a writer, though she originally sought work as a reporter. After graduating from Wellesley with a journalism degree, she went on to write for the *New York Post, Esquire,* and the *New York Times Magazine.* So when did the screenwriting bug kick in? Her first movie assignment was **Silkwood.** It was nominated for an Oscar, and the rest, as they say, is history — or herstory as the case may be. Twenty years later, Ephron is one of the few women *always* working in Hollywood. In several interviews, she speaks very candidly about the industry. She notes that good books are generally published, but much of what is written in Hollywood goes unproduced. Her advice? Keep writing. Don't worry about the final product or if there's even going to be one. Just keep writing.

John Logan

Occupations: screenwriter, playwright, executive producer, teacher. Industry credits:

- ✔ *Tornado* (1996)
- ✔ *RKO 281* (1999)
- ✔ *Bats* (1999)
- ✔ *Any Given Sunday* (2000)
- ✔ *Gladiator* (2001)
- ✔ *Time Machine* (2002)
- ✔ *Star Trek: Nemesis* (2002)
- ✔ *The Last Samurai* (2003)
- ✔ *The Aviator* (2004)
- ✔ *Sweeney Todd* (2007)

John Logan didn't always live in Hollywood; he spent much of his early career in Chicago. Although he entered Northwestern University to pursue acting, he left school very much a writer. While at NU, his play *Never the Sinner* won the Agnes Nixon Playwriting Festival and later received a production in Chicago. He stuck with that script, rewriting and removing characters between other projects, and 13 years later, it went on to win the New York Outer Critics Circle award for an off-Broadway play. That same dogged determination won him an Oscar nomination for the HBO film **RKO 281,** the story of the making of **Citizen Kane.** Its release was the result of seven years of research on Logan's part. He received his second Oscar nod for **Gladiator,** a film that he wrote with David Franzoni and William Nicholson, and his third Oscar nod for *The Aviator*, which he wrote by himself.

One of John Logan's most inspiring qualities is his unwavering passion for his craft. He advocates a fierce regimen of reading, writing, and being "multi-tentacled" (as he puts it), or knowing something about as many subjects as possible. His writing routine includes rising at 6 a.m. and working well through the day, stopping only to eat, sleep, and to walk the dogs. When crafting a first draft, Logan commits to "total immersion." He researches the era, reads literature, and listens to music of the time; he looks at the story from every angle. He tends to juggle several projects at once, although each one is in a different stage of development, and without fail, he finds something to celebrate in each one. It's difficult, if not impossible, to speak with John Logan and leave uninspired. He's the perfect salesman for the screenwriting craft — because he means what he says.

Sofia Coppola

Occupations: screenwriter, actress, director. Industry credits:

- ✔ *New York Stories (segment Life without Zoe)* (1989)
- ✔ *The Virgin Suicides* (1999)
- ✔ *Lost in Translation* (2003)
- ✔ *Marie Antoinette* (2006)

Though Sofia Coppola is relatively new to the world of screenwriting, she's certainly no newcomer to Hollywood. Sofia is the daughter of director Francis Ford Coppola and the cousin of actors Jason Schwartzman and Nicolas Cage. She's worked as an actress for many years and, in fact, made her film debut in **The Godfather.** (She played a baby boy.) She's also the first American woman to be nominated for Best Director, for the movie **Lost in Translation,** which earned her the Oscar for best original screenplay instead.

As a writer, Coppola is known for creating characters who share a sense of disconnection from their environments. Characters in her screenplays share intimate information with strangers because it's easier than sharing it with friends. In *The Virgin Suicides,* a group of men become obsessed with five sisters who have been sequestered away from society by their parents. In *Lost in Translation,* Bill Murray plays a faltering actor who comes to New York on business and strikes up an intimate friendship with an unsatisfied housewife, played by Scarlett Johansson.

Coppola has said it's those relationships that interest her the most — the people you've just met who feel as if their longtime friends, the small, surprising connections between strangers that remind us we're not alone. She admits she initially feared that *Lost in Translation* would seem self-indulgent, but it's immediate success proved otherwise. Her advice to new screenwriters, therefore, is that if a subject compels you, it will probably compel somebody else. Coppola's scripts are also poetically spare. Actors say she provides just enough visual information to allow them to comfortably improvise. They also say she is a fervent believer of trying to write something before you know what that something really is. It's a risky formula that seems to be paying off in full.

Wes Anderson

Occupations: screenwriter, director, producer. Industry credits:

- *Bottle Rocket* (1996)
- *Rushmore* (1998)
- *The Royal Tenenbaums* (2001)
- *The Life Aquatic with Steve Zissou* (2004)
- *The Darjeeling Limited* (2007)

Wes Anderson's known for experiencing his stories prior to writing them. *Rushmore,* a movie about an elite private school was filmed at his alma mater. Anjelica Huston wore his mother's glasses in *The Royal Tenenbaums,* and while scripting *The Darjeeling Limited,* a film about a train ride through India, Anderson and his cowriters took a train ride through India. However, Anderson's films also come equipped with their own jargon, their own color scheme, their own distinct landscapes, and a cast of characters that seem unable to inhabit any world but the one created for them, which is very different from yours or mine. Perhaps this attention to detail combined with an obviously personal connection to the subject matter is what has made Anderson's films so easy to recognize.

Anderson often collaborates with other writers. His last few endeavors were written with the actors Owen Wilson or with Jason Schwartzman. Descriptions of their writing process sound more like theater rehearsals than anything else. The cohorts generally agree to allow any conflicts that arise to become part of the script, if possible, and most of the dialogue is agreed upon by trying it out loud.

Anderson distinguishes the screenwriting process from that of writing fiction. He believes writing a film is more akin to preparing a project, you have to consider production while considering plot. In other words, you're writing the what of the story, but you're also thinking about the how of it all. Anderson also tends to overwrite his scripts and then cut away details in revision. In this way, his characters felt fully-rendered, but they retain a certain degree of mystery as well.

Charlie Kaufman

Occupations: writer, director, producer. Industry credits:

- ✔ *Being John Malkovich* (1999)
- ✔ *Human Nature* (2001)
- ✔ *Adaptation* (2002)
- ✔ *Confessions of a Dangerous Mind* (2002)
- ✔ *Eternal Sunshine of the Spotless Mind* (2004)

Charlie Kaufman is one of the best-known screenwriters in Hollywood today, perhaps because his films are simultaneously funny and upsetting. His popularity also may be because his subplots rival the main plot in complexity, and his stories demand that audiences question their definition of reality. It may also be because he tends to write himself into his screenplays — directly as in *Adaptation,* or indirectly as in *Being John Malkovich* or *Eternal Sunshine of the Spotless Mind.* The quirky main characters in these films are both self-deprecating and self-involved, and all seem to exist in a constant state of emotional crisis. Most of these characters also narrate their experience as they have it. As a result, audiences walk away feeling like they know the characters in the story, but also the writer behind them.

While Kaufman admits he's not a highly disciplined writer, he does tend to concentrate on the characters first and allow them to lead him to a story. His final step is to flesh out the dynamics between characters, their logic for behaving as they do, and so on, and this stage of the process requires the most time.

His advice for young screenwriters is both practical and thematic. First, he says, find a good agent. Kaufman was without one for the first ten years of his career, and he says hiring a good agent made all the difference. Also, write stories that seem true to you. If they cease to feel true as you're writing, scrap what you've done and go back to the beginning. Finally, when you're stuck, try writing your personal anxieties into the film. After all, he says, you can only use that anxiety once, as it happens, so it tends to result in an authentic voice.

While Kaufman is very private about his career, he has said that he rarely worries about critical acclaim or reviews. Making movies is about collaboration, and that collaboration is what matters at the end of the day.

Christopher Nolan

Occupations: screenwriter, director, producer. Industry credits:

- ✔ *Following* (1998)
- ✔ *Memento* (2001)
- ✔ *Insomnia* (2002)
- ✔ *Batman Begins* (2005)
- ✔ *The Prestige* (2006)
- ✔ *The Dark Knight* (2008)

Christopher Nolan began his career at age 7 when he picked up his father's Super 8 camera. He went on to make 16mm films while he was a student of English Literature at University College in London. He divided his time between reading books and working at the college film society, though it was hardly an equal division of labor. The result of this training was a black-and-white film noir of sorts titled *Following.* Like most film noirs, *Following* relies heavily on shadow, suspense, and a pervading mood to hold it together. The title stems from the protagonist's primary action in the film — following strangers on the street. The film was highly acclaimed in several festivals, but it never reached the mainstream audiences. His second film, however, did.

Memento is another film noir that's told entirely in reverse. It's based on a short story written by Christopher's brother, Jonathan Nolan, and it earned a nomination for Best Screenwriting at the 2001 Academy Awards. As if this sophomore effort weren't exciting enough, Nolan's third film, *Insomnia,* roped him a celebrity cast. The film stars Robin Williams, Al Pacino, and Hillary Swank and is a remake of the 1997 Norwegian effort. It's an understatement to say that the past few years have been exciting ones for Mr. Nolan, and he seems in no hurry to slow down.

Diablo Cody

Occupations: screenwriter, producer. Industry credits: *Juno* (2007)

Diablo Cody has one of the most colorful names in show business, and her journey to screenwriting is equally dynamic. Diablo, formerly known as Brooke Busey, relocated from Chicago to Minnesota after college to be with the love of her life whom she met over the Internet. She promptly found a job at an ad agency, but soon thereafter began supplementing her income as a stripper. She eventually quit her ad job to strip full-time and run a phone sex operation, which led her to pen a popular sex blog, take a job as movie critic for City Pages, and write a book, *Candy Girl: A Year in the Life of an Unlikely Stripper.* How's that for a compelling backstory?

As you may imagine, those writing gigs led her to write *Juno,* a film about a teenager who becomes pregnant and decides to give the baby to a young couple. This film earned her an Oscar for best original screenplay of 2007–08 at the age of 29, and her career is on a fast track to more where that came from. She is already fast at work on an original television series for Showtime.

Cody claims to enjoy poking fun at controversial topics and reveling in awkward behavior. *Juno* was crafted around the image of a teenage girl auditioning 30-something-year-old couples for the role of parents to her unborn child. She also believes Hollywood still has a hard time accepting women who write subversive material, which may also explain her success. She's fast becoming an icon to actresses and writers who strive to create full and complex roles for women. Her advice for writers is to keep at it, despite the cruelty that is often part of the film industry. In one of my favorite quotes to date, Cody says stripping made her tough, but reveling herself as a writer has been brutal. Nevertheless, judging the projects on her metaphoric plate, she seems to have survived it all with spirit and sense of humor intact.

Chapter 22

Ten Screenwriting Myths

In This Chapter

▶ Debunking common myths

▶ Making it in the business

Any profession that's been around long enough, or as my grandfather would say "any profession worth its salt," is riddled with myths. As you may imagine, screenwriting is no exception. This chapter challenges ten of those myths — the top offenders, if you will. I encourage you to begin trouncing them now so that they don't hinder your progress later.

1 Have to Live in Los Angeles to Write Screenplays

"No, you don't" is the fastest and most complete response for this myth, especially for anybody writing a first screenplay. Producers and agents don't care where you live. If you can write a strong story and e-mail them a draft, they're satisfied. If your screenplays are produced, you'll probably spend time in California or other parts of the country. The more films you sell, the more traveling you will do, but with the advent of electronic communication, fax machines, and priority mail, you should be able to write from virtually anywhere. Remember also that film companies are cropping up all over the country. New York and Chicago are adding their names to the list of cinematically thriving cities, and smaller production companies are launching new work all the time.

"Do I *want* to live in Los Angeles?" is really the question to ask. How immediately connected would you like to be with the Hollywood scene? If you thrive on hustle and bustle, if you're an inherent salesman and your own best agent, you might love L.A. life. However, don't think that you'll miss out if you live in the opposite direction. Many writers feel that life outside L.A. keeps them grounded and focused on the work instead of the image. M. Night Shyamalan, writer of **The Sixth Sense** and **Signs,** lives and works in Philadelphia. Your story is the key. Write a good story, and the world will come to you.

You Have to Go to School to Learn How to Write

If this myth were true, half of today's screenwriters wouldn't be writing. If your aim is to teach screenwriting, then yes, a degree in writing or film will probably help. If your aim is purely artistic, your career depends on your ability to tell a story. If the script is exciting, innovative, and marketable, it's going to generate interest. If the story is flat or cliché-ridden, a degree from the best film school on the planet can't help you.

A writer should be curious, passionate, alert, and determined. In many ways, determination gets you farther than raw talent can. You may dream up the next *Casablanca* or *American Beauty,* but if you don't sit down every day and pound it out, who will know? Screenwriting is a difficult job. It requires hours of writing, a capacity to meet deadlines, a mind that can juggle many tasks at once, and constant collaboration. Getting through all that is more than half the battle.

Will a film school or a creative-writing program help you? It depends on what you're looking for. Educational settings offer perks that may be worth investigating:

- ✔ **A network:** The students, mentors, and visiting artists you meet may turn out to be invaluable when you're trying to sell your work later.

- ✔ **A workshop:** Film schools and writing departments generally provide a critical forum for your work. You'll have to bounce your work between readers later on — why not do it here?

- ✔ **Deadlines:** Schools require you to write at least one screenplay during your stint, sometimes three or four. You may generate an entire portfolio by the time you leave.

- ✔ **Classes, classes, classes:** Everything that you learn strengthens your writing. Universities provide an array of subjects for you to explore.

If you want some of these perks but would rather not commit to an entire program, see whether the educational institutions near you offer writing courses or seminars. Colleges, libraries, and community centers tend to schedule creative-writing classes or workshops after school hours, at night, and in the summer. Also, screenwriting expos are held all over the country, but in Los Angeles in particular. I encourage you to consider the educational route, but don't place undue importance on it. In order to write, you must have a story and a will to write. If you have those things, a diploma's just icing.

Screenwriting Is Entertainment; It's Not a Real Profession

I would argue that storytelling is one of the few professions that has stood the test of time. Throughout the ages, cultures of all kinds have crafted stories to preserve their heritage, chronicle historical events to explore what it means to be human, and make sense of a nonsensical world. Why do people continue to flock to theaters? Some people may say as a means of escape, and that may be true. But I argue that, more often, people go in search of something. Is it inspiration? Hope? An education? A better understanding of themselves or some part of their world? If they go for even one of these reasons, screenwriting's a noble profession.

If the question you're trying to answer is "But does it save lives?", stop trying. It probably doesn't, but then how would you ever know? At its best, screenwriting asks questions, challenges tradition, inspires action, sparks debate, and makes people think and feel on a potentially grand level. Now, how many professions do all that?

If You've Never Written Before, It's Too Late to Start Now

It's never too late to start writing. The older you are, the more stories you've encountered, the more wisdom you can impart, and (hopefully) the more questions you have to ask. Margaret Mitchell completed her first and only novel when she was 36. It won the Pulitzer. Perhaps you've heard of it — it's called *Gone with the Wind,* and it was adapted into a screenplay by Sidney Howard. Frank McCourt wrote his first novel, *Angela's Ashes,* when he was 66. It was a bestseller and also won a Pulitzer. Ray Krok founded McDonalds in his 50s, Grandma Moses began painting at 78; the list goes on and on. If you don't start writing now, the only regret you'll have in five years is that you didn't start writing five years ago. As a student of mine once said, "You're going to be 72 anyway. Why not be 72 and a writer?"

Writing Is a Lonely Profession

I'm not going to lie to you: Writing involves a lot of time alone. When crafting a first draft, you will (hopefully) spend three or four hours a day, four to five times a week, in a room with your computer, your characters, and your plot, which is really just another way of saying "by yourself."

On the flip side, screenwriting is a highly social profession. A screenplay, like a stage play, isn't really complete until you've handed it to a production team. You craft the story, and they transform it into a three-dimensional piece. Want a metaphor for that relationship? You build the boat and the sails, and the production team provides the wind. Research for each project will undoubtedly require interaction of all sorts, as will revisions. Frankly, you can't do this job without collaborating at least 60 percent of the time. You may become *more* social as a result of the craft.

Screenwriting also differs from many professions in that the kind of work you do varies in form. Working means spending time alone, but it also means taking long walks, conversing with friends, or cooking dinner for six. Writers work everywhere. So keep writing or start writing. When cabin fever sets in, and it will set in, go work somewhere else.

Hollywood Has No Ethics; It'll Ruin the Integrity of My Script

I think that the underlining question here is "Can I work in Hollywood and remain an artist?" The answer is yes, you can. Commercial success doesn't negate artistry. As in any profession, you have to know what you're getting into, and you have to be savvy. Do your research. Know the answers to the following questions:

- What movies are current box-office hits?
- What are the major production companies, and what kind of work are they producing? (See Chapter 19.)
- What are the smaller production companies, and what kind of work are they producing? (See Chapter 19.)
- Who's writing scripts you enjoy? Who represents them?
- What are the artistic strengths of your piece? The commercial strengths? (See Chapter 20.)
- What parts of your piece are you the most interested in protecting? What parts of your piece are you flexible on? (See Chapter 12.)
- How can you sell someone on *your* story? (See Chapter 20.)

Answering these questions in advance enables you to plan an appropriate marketing campaign. You'll know which studios and executives are more likely to champion your story and keep it intact. If you prioritize the elements of your story prior to meeting with those executives, you'll also know how to respond should they propose changes. You'll know what elements you want to safeguard at all costs, and you can entertain suggestions on the rest. This strategy allows you to be both protective and flexible.

Hollywood has a lot of money and, like any business, it has a lot of people interested in that money. Hollywood also has many champions of strong work. Finding them may take a while, but they're there. If you go into the profession with your eyes open, if you know your story backwards and forwards, if you know the market in advance — those supporters will eventually find you.

It's Not What You Know; It's Who You Know That Matters

I'm going to address this myth in two parts. First, does it help to know someone in Hollywood? Probably. Approaching the business isn't unlike going to a new school or your first day on a job; if you know people in advance, the transition is usually less frightening. A Hollywood contact can do the following:

✔ Introduce you to agents, producers, directors, actors, and so on

✔ Help you find temporary work that may further your career

✔ Show you the town

✔ Pass your work onto readers

✔ Fill you in on what kind of work various companies are doing

Knowing someone in L.A. also considerably cuts down on the fear factor and, if you're moving to the West Coast, on the loneliness.

However, is it who you know that really matters? No, the story is what matters. If your story is compelling, it will make the introductions for you. If you're passionate about what you know, someone will respond. So, to the beginning screenwriter I say, get out there. It's a social profession, so meet as many people as you can. But worry about your script first. In the end, everything comes back to the story.

I Have Too Many Obligations to Be a Writer

The first thing to do when you encounter this myth is to list those obligations — all of them. That list might start with any or all of the following: a family to support, a job (or two or three), classes to take, social functions to run, and a household to maintain.

Think about it for a while. Jot down anything that takes time out of your day. If you're responsible for walking the dog or looking after the neighbor's flowers, include those tasks on the list, and when you're through, add one more item. At the bottom of the page, write "Work on screenplay." Now, it's on the list of obligations.

If you want to write a screenplay, you need concentrated chunks of time, at least an hour for each session, and any schedule can be managed. Anton Chekhov wrote his short stories between seeing medical patients and supporting a family. J. K. Rowling was a single mother trying to make ends meet when she wrote *Harry Potter*. You have time if you *make* time. Face it, any one of the top items on the obligation list can take up your whole week, if you allow that to happen. You simply can't allow that to happen.

You're Only as Successful as the Last Screenplay You Sold

What if you've never sold a screenplay? Does that mean that you're not successful? What if your screenplay was purchased but never produced? Or if it was produced, it bombed at the box office? Or if it was commercially successful and critically panned? Or if it was critically successful and socially panned? Are you successful then?

The real questions to ask are "Why am I writing?" and "How do I define success?" If you're writing to make money, you're writing for the wrong reasons. You may never make money. If you're writing to seek critical acclaim, you're writing for the wrong reasons. Think of all the artists who died prior to achieving that goal. In order to write continually, you have to love the process, writer's block and all. You have to love finding an idea and developing it into a story. You have to love pounding away at a computer all day, even when you hate it. You have to love words and images and action.

More importantly, you have to redefine success. Know what you're trying to achieve in each script and push yourself to accomplish that task. If your purpose is to write a piece that sells, so be it. Do the research, watch the market, and sell the script. If your purpose is to ask a question, ask it in every scene. If you write because you love the process, you'll be far better off when you approach the West Coast. Your scripts aren't always going to sell; those that sell won't always make money. If you love the process more than the product, you'll write regardless of how your last script fared.

I'm Not Talented Enough to Be a Writer

This myth is so common that it borders on an affliction. Every writer harbors an internal critic, otherwise known as the "little voice," and "I'm not talented enough to be a writer" is the voice's favorite quip. It is, of course, a false notion. You have talent. Anyone who's made it through adolescence has a story to tell and the experience with which to tell it. The real issue here is whether you have something to say. Do you have a question that you want to explore on the page? Has something made you angry, confused, exhilarated, or curious? If you answer yes to these questions, you should be writing.

Fear is a funny thing. It can be your best friend; it can force you to do research and prepare for a project in ways that you wouldn't have attempted in a more relaxed state. It can also completely shut you down. If you're worried about your own talent, remember this: If you choose to honor the fear, it will weaken your work. If you choose to honor the work, it will weaken your fear.

Index

BUSINESS, CAREERS & PERSONAL FINANCE

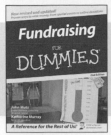

0-7645-9847-3

0-7645-2431-3

Also available:
- Business Plans Kit For Dummies
  0-7645-9794-9
- Economics For Dummies
  0-7645-5726-2
- Grant Writing For Dummies
  0-7645-8416-2
- Home Buying For Dummies
  0-7645-5331-3
- Managing For Dummies
  0-7645-1771-6
- Marketing For Dummies
  0-7645-5600-2

- Personal Finance For Dummies
  0-7645-2590-5*
- Resumes For Dummies
  0-7645-5471-9
- Selling For Dummies
  0-7645-5363-1
- Six Sigma For Dummies
  0-7645-6798-5
- Small Business Kit For Dummies
  0-7645-5984-2
- Starting an eBay Business For Dummies
  0-7645-6924-4
- Your Dream Career For Dummies
  0-7645-9795-7

HOME & BUSINESS COMPUTER BASICS

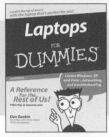

0-470-05432-8

0-471-75421-8

Also available:
- Cleaning Windows Vista For Dummies
  0-471-78293-9
- Excel 2007 For Dummies
  0-470-03737-7
- Mac OS X Tiger For Dummies
  0-7645-7675-5
- MacBook For Dummies
  0-470-04859-X
- Macs For Dummies
  0-470-04849-2
- Office 2007 For Dummies
  0-470-00923-3

- Outlook 2007 For Dummies
  0-470-03830-6
- PCs For Dummies
  0-7645-8958-X
- Salesforce.com For Dummies
  0-470-04893-X
- Upgrading & Fixing Laptops For Dummies
  0-7645-8959-8
- Word 2007 For Dummies
  0-470-03658-3
- Quicken 2007 For Dummies
  0-470-04600-7

FOOD, HOME, GARDEN, HOBBIES, MUSIC & PETS

0-7645-8404-9

0-7645-9904-6

Also available:
- Candy Making For Dummies
  0-7645-9734-5
- Card Games For Dummies
  0-7645-9910-0
- Crocheting For Dummies
  0-7645-4151-X
- Dog Training For Dummies
  0-7645-8418-9
- Healthy Carb Cookbook For Dummies
  0-7645-8476-6
- Home Maintenance For Dummies
  0-7645-5215-5

- Horses For Dummies
  0-7645-9797-3
- Jewelry Making & Beading For Dummies
  0-7645-2571-9
- Orchids For Dummies
  0-7645-6759-4
- Puppies For Dummies
  0-7645-5255-4
- Rock Guitar For Dummies
  0-7645-5356-9
- Sewing For Dummies
  0-7645-6847-7
- Singing For Dummies
  0-7645-2475-5

INTERNET & DIGITAL MEDIA

0-470-04529-9

0-470-04894-8

Also available:
- Blogging For Dummies
  0-471-77084-1
- Digital Photography For Dummies
  0-7645-9802-3
- Digital Photography All-in-One Desk Reference For Dummies
  0-470-03743-1
- Digital SLR Cameras and Photography For Dummies
  0-7645-9803-1
- eBay Business All-in-One Desk Reference For Dummies
  0-7645-8438-3
- HDTV For Dummies
  0-470-09673-X

- Home Entertainment PCs For Dummies
  0-470-05523-5
- MySpace For Dummies
  0-470-09529-6
- Search Engine Optimization For Dummies
  0-471-97998-8
- Skype For Dummies
  0-470-04891-3
- The Internet For Dummies
  0-7645-8996-2
- Wiring Your Digital Home For Dummies
  0-471-91830-X

* Separate Canadian edition also available
† Separate U.K. edition also available

Available wherever books are sold. For more information or to order direct: U.S. customers visit www.dummies.com or call 1-877-762-2974.
U.K. customers visit www.wileyeurope.com or call 0800 243407. Canadian customers visit www.wiley.ca or call 1-800-567-4797.

 WILEY

SPORTS, FITNESS, PARENTING, RELIGION & SPIRITUALITY

0-471-76871-5

0-7645-7841-3

Also available:
- Catholicism For Dummies
  0-7645-5391-7
- Exercise Balls For Dummies
  0-7645-5623-1
- Fitness For Dummies
  0-7645-7851-0
- Football For Dummies
  0-7645-3936-1
- Judaism For Dummies
  0-7645-5299-6
- Potty Training For Dummies
  0-7645-5417-4
- Buddhism For Dummies
  0-7645-5359-3

- Pregnancy For Dummies
  0-7645-4483-7 †
- Ten Minute Tone-Ups For Dummies
  0-7645-7207-5
- NASCAR For Dummies
  0-7645-7681-X
- Religion For Dummies
  0-7645-5264-3
- Soccer For Dummies
  0-7645-5229-5
- Women in the Bible For Dummies
  0-7645-8475-8

TRAVEL

0-7645-7749-2

0-7645-6945-7

Also available:
- Alaska For Dummies
  0-7645-7746-8
- Cruise Vacations For Dummies
  0-7645-6941-4
- England For Dummies
  0-7645-4276-1
- Europe For Dummies
  0-7645-7529-5
- Germany For Dummies
  0-7645-7823-5
- Hawaii For Dummies
  0-7645-7402-7

- Italy For Dummies
  0-7645-7386-1
- Las Vegas For Dummies
  0-7645-7382-9
- London For Dummies
  0-7645-4277-X
- Paris For Dummies
  0-7645-7630-5
- RV Vacations For Dummies
  0-7645-4442-X
- Walt Disney World & Orlando
  For Dummies
  0-7645-9660-8

GRAPHICS, DESIGN & WEB DEVELOPMENT

0-7645-8815-X

0-7645-9571-7

Also available:
- 3D Game Animation For Dummies
  0-7645-8789-7
- AutoCAD 2006 For Dummies
  0-7645-8925-3
- Building a Web Site For Dummies
  0-7645-7144-3
- Creating Web Pages For Dummies
  0-470-08030-2
- Creating Web Pages All-in-One Desk
  Reference For Dummies
  0-7645-4345-8
- Dreamweaver 8 For Dummies
  0-7645-9649-7

- InDesign CS2 For Dummies
  0-7645-9572-5
- Macromedia Flash 8 For Dummies
  0-7645-9691-8
- Photoshop CS2 and Digital
  Photography For Dummies
  0-7645-9580-6
- Photoshop Elements 4 For Dummies
  0-471-77483-9
- Syndicating Web Sites with RSS Feeds
  For Dummies
  0-7645-8848-6
- Yahoo! SiteBuilder For Dummies
  0-7645-9800-7

NETWORKING, SECURITY, PROGRAMMING & DATABASES

0-7645-7728-X

0-471-74940-0

Also available:
- Access 2007 For Dummies
  0-470-04612-0
- ASP.NET 2 For Dummies
  0-7645-7907-X
- C# 2005 For Dummies
  0-7645-9704-3
- Hacking For Dummies
  0-470-05235-X
- Hacking Wireless Networks
  For Dummies
  0-7645-9730-2
- Java For Dummies
  0-470-08716-1

- Microsoft SQL Server 2005 For Dummies
  0-7645-7755-7
- Networking All-in-One Desk Reference
  For Dummies
  0-7645-9939-9
- Preventing Identity Theft For Dummies
  0-7645-7336-5
- Telecom For Dummies
  0-471-77085-X
- Visual Studio 2005 All-in-One Desk
  Reference For Dummies
  0-7645-9775-2
- XML For Dummies
  0-7645-8845-1